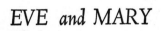

EVE *and* MARY

EVE and MARY

By Peter Thomas Dehau, O.P.

*

Translated by the Dominican Nuns

of the Perpetual Rosary

LA CROSSE, WISCONSIN

B. HERDER BOOK CO.

15 & 17 South Broadway, St. Louis 2, Mo.

AND *33 Queen Square, London, W.C.*

This book is a translation of *Ève et Marie*, by Pierre-Thomas Dehau, O.P., published by Monastère du Coeur Immaculé de Marie, Bouvines, Par Cysoing, France, 1950.

Imprimatur: ✠ Joseph E. Ritter, S.T.D.
Archbishop of St. Louis

December 27, 1957

Translator's Preface

No ONE holds more interest for a child than his mother, the center of his little world. As children of God, we not only have one mother to interest us, but two; one who estranged us from Him, the other who restored us to Him: Eve and Mary, both of whom exercise a dominant influence on us. A most profound application of the comparison of this motherly influence on us has been culled by Father Dehau from the theological doctrine of St. Thomas Aquinas and other saints and scholars as well as from Holy Scripture, for which we are deeply grateful.

We are also grateful to the Very Reverend Father J. L. Callahan, O.P., for the opportunity and pleasure of translating this French work and to Father Jordan Aumann, O.P., for the invaluable assistance he rendered both during and after the actual translating. To Sister Mary Camille Bowe, O.S.F., of the College of Saint Teresa in Winona, Minnesota, we also wish to extend our deepest sentiments of appreciation for the time she so generously spent in critically reading the translation and for the advice she so kindly gave. Nor must the prayers and encouragement which they and others have so benevolently proffered throughout the entire work be overlooked. May the blessed peace promised to those of good will descend in its fullness upon them.

May Mary, the Mother of God and our Mother, teach us her children how to use her antidote for the venom which has flowed through the veins of Eve to us so that the banner of Jesus Christ may wave victoriously in the kingdom of our hearts.

Dominican Nuns of the Perpetual Rosary
La Crosse, Wisconsin

Preface

THE supernatural life is peopled with divine annunciations. Like so many other graces which St. Teresa saw so easily lost, they risk escaping our attention and we let them pass without profiting from them. It is this attention that we want to arouse. Now, to arouse attention, says St. Thomas, nothing is more successful than astonishment. It seems to us that the first pages of Genesis contain annunciations particularly suited to accord us the benefit of astonishment.

Our first parents' state of original justice created in them and around them a world very different from ours. Aside from the similarities and identities founded on their natures and which, therefore, cannot change, extreme diversities separated and estranged this state from our actual state. These diversities will contribute to the astonishment which can be so useful to us. The deep-rooted identity of certain laws will provide fruitful applications to the practical cases which can be presented for us. We shall analyze Eve's sin, about which we shall have much to say, both in itself and in contrast with Mary's graces and virtues, and we shall analyze it little by little by drawing near and by successive touches and retouches. The evolution of the ideas and facts will invite us to this analysis and will facilitate it for us.

We can distinguish three principal annunciations in Eden. The first is the mystery of pure joy, for it is concerned only with superabundant life and the transmission of life. The third reveals to us a mystery of sorrow and death. Why this terrible contrast, this violent chiaroscuro? Because between these two mysteries is insinuated the second annunciation, the mystery of iniquity which interrupts the one and flows into the other. Sin entered, and through sin, death likewise entered.

Contents

PART ONE

THE GARDEN OF EDEN

1

First Divine Annunciation:

MYSTERY OF JOY

This now is . . . flesh of my flesh . . . and they shall be two in one flesh.

The Place and Characters

WE are in Eden. This garden of delights was planted by God Himself, and there He exercised all His art. But the art of God always leaves room for the art of man, which must be consecrated to cultivate and to preserve Eden. The nobility of these two tasks requires a very great art but it is a pleasant work, a blessed work, in contrast to the extremely hard labor imposed after the Fall by the accursed earth. To be cultivated by its children and guarded and defended against the enemy, this land will necessitate the development of great human arts which will cause inferior beings and other men to be conquered and dominated. Such are the arts of peace, to which must be added the cruel art of war.

We read in Genesis that God placed man, whom he had formed, in the paradise of pleasure. But the only terrestrial paradise possible for us in our fallen state is the paradise of prayer, and God places us there, also. He must take and even snatch us from many things to place us there. Moreover, let us not forget that here, as in Eden, man must cultivate and preserve the paradise of prayer. God's gift deteriorates and diminishes for want of assiduous work.

"Cursed is the earth in thy work." The curse of sin still echoes over this land of the living and even, at least indirectly, over the work of prayer. This land produces thorns and thistles for us and this work requires efforts and struggles. But it is our proper place, as the ancients used to say, and the place which eminently corresponds to the nature God gave us and the graces He bestows on us. However, many centrifugal forces tend to turn us away and make us deviate from it. When God puts us back on the road, and we must begin bravely to walk there again, His liberty and ours must constantly intervene, heaven must help us and we must help ourselves. At one and the same time we must have humble docility and energetic initiative. We must repeat the cry of the prodigal son, "I will arise and will go," and the cry of Moses, "I will go and see." The Psalmist asks: "Who will give me wings?" God must give them to us, but we must learn not only to fly but to come to rest. The latter is often more difficult to our volatile nature, which is more quickly fatigued from rest than from activity.

Among the problems which the practice of prayer poses is that of "composition of place." This term designates a sort of preparation for prayer by which we place ourselves in the atmosphere of prayer. Since the rest of our life is adapted to regions which are far removed from this atmosphere, the effort will obviously be all the more difficult, painful, and even violent. To facilitate this effort it is helpful to fix our attention now on one landscape, now on another, in this beautiful land of prayer. We are like the traveler who sets up his tent at a new site every day, choosing according to the conveniences of the moment and the suitability of the place.

This labor, with its intellectual and imaginative elements, will be accomplished even more by the sweat of our brow because to return to the one thing necessary we, like Martha, must turn away from everything that ordinarily occupies and troubles us. Mary is as completely repatriated as the conditions of our exile permit. She is established, or habituated as St. Augustine says, at the Lord's feet. It is the place which she chose, the place He wills for her and assures to her by defending her against Martha's objections and recriminations; the place which shall not be taken from her and which she will never leave. It is the resting place where she will dwell forever. This place was made for her and she was made for it. She does not have to compose it; she has only to abide in it.

Poets such as Milton or even Dante, whether he speaks directly of the terrestrial paradise at the summit of the mountain of purgatory or by the reflected beauty of all that he has said in the *Paradiso*, have been more or less successful in describing Eden. Moreover, all the mirages of splendor which we could be tempted to attribute to Eden, everything that is addressed to our senses, and all that is capable of exciting flesh and blood is infinitely surpassed there by the riches of the intellectual and moral order of original justice.

We have seen human art manifest itself under its most delicate and most perfect form, under its ideal form, in the cultivation and preservation of Eden. We see human science appear in the name given by Adam to the animals, a sign profoundly and fully expressive of their nature and characteristics, which our meager science gropes for and recomposes with halting speech.

Eden is the place where harmonious operations of the highest activities are freely developed. For the first human contemplative it is also a place of rest, of wonderful sleep visited by ecstasy. The fruitfulness of this rest under the hand of God resulted in a second character of the great human drama, in that other self so similar to himself and yet so different. She had to be complimentary to be able to become a fully and completely efficacious helper. Similarity and difference are elements of proportion and equilibrium which certain stupid forms of feminism misjudge.

The Unity of Husband and Wife

According to Holy Scripture, woman was formed from man, from the rib of man. Why that origin so much beyond and above all that the animal world presents to us? Let us meditate attentively on the reasons given by St. Thomas.[1] The first reason appeals to the dignity of man. He is created to the image of God. He is the source of his species, of the human world, as God is the source of the whole universe. He is the origin in the strong sense of the word, that is to say, the universal beginning, the basis of the wife and mother as well as of the child. His dignity is that of an agent, and an agent's dignity is always greater because it has more unity in the action, more unity in the principle of the action.

Duality of sexes is necessary for propagation, but precisely because it is duality and in the measure that it remains duality, it is an obstacle to the unity of the action and diminishes this unity. Adam avoids this obstacle from the very fact that not only do his children come from him but his

[1] *Summa theol.*, Ia, q. 92, a. 2.

6

wife as well. She is not his daughter because she does not proceed from him by way of generation,[2] but Adam's love for Eve participates in parents' love for their children so far as the children are something of themselves. The underlying reason is the love of the whole for its part. From this point of view Eve is like a daughter to Adam and very different from all other wives.

According to St. Paul, God brought forth the entire human race from one single man; He has made the human race from one. Let us preserve all the force of this last word. Every agent's ideal is to assimilate his work completely, making it his own in every respect and from every point of view. This is the husband's ideal, an ideal, however, which is capable of realization by the divine Bridegroom alone: the assimilation of the spouse (here again it is the *simile sibi*), to make her His own, and let us say even more emphatically: "to form her." St. Paul says this in speaking of Christ, who desires to form His Church (*ut faceret sibi sponsam*). On this single condition His human spouse will no longer have any stain or flaw in His eyes.

The essential jealousy of every husband consists in this: what does not emanate from him in one way or another is never purified enough, never rejuvenated enough. It is to this extent that he wishes to make his spouse his own. Exigencies and gentle or violent tyrannies are the consequence, the sign, and the proof of true love. Hence the wife loves to submit to them even though she must sometimes suffer from them.

The husband attains this ideal as nearly as possible in the moral nature. He cannot do so in the physical nature precisely because his wife does not emanate from him, but comes from somewhere else. That is why the father as an agent is not able to make his children his own in the meas-

[2] *Ibid.*, ad 3um.

7

ure desired, that is to say, completely, to the point of assimilation which would reach to the least individual details. From this we derive the explanation of a multitude of strange facts and difficulties of the marriage state and of family life.

The father is unable to make his family "his own" in the fullest measure. He encounters abrupt limits and insurmountable frontiers. The reason is that his co-principle does not proceed from him corporeally, not to mention all the hereditary factors which both the father and mother transmit and are manifested in the most unexpected and most defeating manner, sometimes a long time after the early years of life.

None of this existed for the first human procreator who alone had, so to speak, full play with all the compelling freedom of his action. As the centuries pass and accumulate, all kinds of necessities and limitations weigh more and more heavily upon his successors. Thus, the tendency is to endeavor to obtain somewhere other than in their ordinary milieu of life, especially perhaps in artistic creation, that glorious liberty which is the ideal of all agents.

Certain fathers are able to love the child all the more who shows a greater resemblance to his wife whom he deeply loves. But here we are no longer considering him simply as an agent, but also as a patient. From this point of view, he who loves is passive, drawn and swept toward the one he loves. St. Thomas, opposing the word, *amor*, to the word, *dilectio*, calls attention to the greater passivity in the former whereas *dilectio* possesses something more active; it implies more knowledge and choice and, therefore, more liberty.

Spouses other than the first (of Eden) are chosen from thousands of concrete personalities, very real ones, but the danger of making a mistake increases in proportion to the numbers. This is the law of every choice. That is why a choice is often easier and more certain when it is more limited in its object. The single means is imposed without any conceivable error, and this was true in Adam's case. God chose for him from an infinity of possible spouses. The choice was infallible and, for Adam, was free of anxiety.

Certain people flaunt their liberty and even their fickleness in the choice of a spouse. Others have the grateful impression that God chose for them. They have only to accept. By this acceptance their liberty intervenes, an intervention necessary for a contract. Such was the case of the first conjugal love in Eden, the prototype and model of all love. Adam loved Eve more than all other spouses will ever be loved, says St. Thomas. Let us except only the one who was at the same time Mother of God and a true earthly wife.

The first human wife was not preferred to others. In virtue of his free acceptance Adam made God's choice his own. He freely accepted fatherhood by uniting his body with his wife's as Mary would freely accept motherhood by an ineffable union with her Son's Spirit. In this way, with his wife and through her, Adam accomplished his work as head of all humanity. Nothing egoistic, nothing of the purely individual, existed in the ends of that union. The entire human race was present in his moral intention as in its fullness it has descended from him in its physical being. The first man's choice of his spouse was made with all the more strength and efficacy since she was the means directly proposed by God for the procreation of sons and, through them, of all generations to come. Adam's choice participates in all the perfection of the choice of God.

In conjunction with the husband's dignity—the dignity of the agent—we have already had occasion to allude to the lovableness of the wife. It was a kind of link between the first reason given by St. Thomas and the second reason, which is stated as follows: "That man might love woman the more and cleave to her more inseparably, since she was fashioned from him." [3]

All things taken equally, we love more what we give birth to, because in it we find ourselves again and it is more ours. We always measure purely human love in terms of what is not ourselves. In the divine love of charity, whose supreme measure is none other than God, the love of self still imposes a certain mode of exercise. Thus we say: to love one's neighbor as one's self.

All this is admirably expressed in the Sacred Text: "She was taken out of man. Wherefore a man shall leave father and mother and shall cleave to his wife." This adherence must necessarily be so much the more firm and secure since, unlike the animals, the husband and wife are to remain together for the rest of their lives. Therefore, a bond which demands indissolubility must be made as strong as possible in every respect.

Here unity is produced and maintained more easily because it proceeds from unity, because the "two in one flesh" comes from the one flesh. The attraction between husband and wife can be all the stronger when the wife differs more from the husband in mind and even more so in body, but eventually the preservation of unity is threatened. It becomes necessary to watch and pray in order not to enter into certain temptations of the enemy. Let us not forget that it is essentially the schismatical mind, always jealous of unity, which is constantly seeking to destroy this unity or at least to diminish it.

In order to combat these centrifugal forces it would be well to recall or to become acquainted as thoroughly as possible with all the factors of unity, not only those after

[3] *Ibid.*, a. 2.

marriage but also, and sometimes even more so, those previous to marriage which are more firmly established by time. In woman should be found as many things as possible over which man may be the principle.

The ideal, realized in Eden, is that man be the principle of woman herself, of the complete woman. Eve comes wholly from Adam as the Church comes wholly from Christ.

This precious unity alone can assure the future and should plunge into the past as much as possible. Furthermore, unity is necessary—and this is St. Thomas' third reason—for all domestic life, which is characteristic of the rational animal and is the secondary end of the marriage state. In other words, man and woman are not only united, like animals, for generation but also for the fullness of that domestic life which among the animals, and then only among certain ones, knows only vague attempts and imperfect plans. Domestic life is dominated by two great truths which must be maintained at any cost and which often tend to be obscured or diminished by the clash of practical or speculative illusions or under the impact of passions or temperaments.

The first of these truths is: in marital cooperation there is a part proper to the male and a part proper to the female. The one must not encroach on the other nor more or less consciously restrain the other. A certain liberty must be maintained between the two and therefore a certain equality. Let us remark, moreover, that equality is necessarily present between the husband and wife if the word is understood in its most formal sense. Every contract requires the equality of the contractants as such; furthermore, a special equality is involved in the marriage contract, not only in its cause, which is free consent, but also in its effect, the right over each other's body (*jus petendi debitum*).

The second truth is this: in spite of the equality between husband and wife, a certain deep-seated inequality is present between man and woman and determines that man is the head. Let us never forget these two paramount affirmations: that of the Philosopher, *alia opera viri et feminae*; that of the Apostle, *caput mulieris vir*.

From another point of view let us unite God's first two great proclamations on man. These are two annunciations which open and sum up the whole future: "Let Us make man to Our image and likeness." O incomparable dignity of man which separates him and elevates him above all that is not human!

The second announcement reveals man's limits even in the human domain: "It is not good for man to be alone; let Us make him a help like unto himself." This is the first form and proclamation of the *vae soli* which summons so many distinctions and is clothed with so many shades of meaning. It is also the profound revelation of woman's role, her habitual role, even and especially in the midst of the splendors of original justice, in God's first gaze upon her. Eve is formed from man for the purpose of belonging to him; she is before all else man's helper, his wife. She is a virgin (certain Doctors of the Church have insisted on this point), but she is a virgin only for a time. She is not like Christian virgins, or rather, she is not like those who by vocation choose to remain virgins always.

After the sin and because of the sin, virginity became the necessary means of certain marvels, of the increase of all life, especially by the contemplation of divine things. Let us thank God for having widely proclaimed from the beginning of the Church's life so holy a truth which was to prove so fruitful. By virginity, unity of life is assured because there is no longer any division between what pleases the divine Spouse and what pleases the human spouse and there is a minimum of that fragmentation and destruction of the harmony of the state of innocence which is a consequence and punishment of sin.

It was simply and fully through the earthly husband that Eve went to the heavenly Spouse. To please both spouses was her calling and her perfection. She was everything to Adam, body and soul, in order to be everything to God, and Adam did not impede God in the least. She was completely ordained for Adam, and her only duty was to seek ways to please him, confident that the orientation to God and the pleasure God derived from her soul were only the better safeguarded because of it.

The husband is at the same time priest and prophet. That is why we hear only his word in that nuptial announcement which supersedes and absorbs all else. He is the sole mediator between his wife and God. That is also why woman's temptation and fall hinges on this precise point: by not resorting to man in the capital act of judgment and, therefore, by reason of a kind of apostasy from him, she separated herself from God. Woman's initiative, as soon as she isolated herself from man in such a grave act, necessarily became disastrous and, let us venture to say, was condemned beforehand.

At the same time that woman is subjected to man, she is the one who completes him, for she alone is able to permit him to become the principle of the transmission of human life. St. Thomas remarks that she is necessary to man only for the work of generation. For any other works considered in themselves, woman is not absolutely necessary to man. Another man would be a more perfect helper and therefore would advantageously replace her. This doctrine can be marvelously efficacious on condition that it is carefully limited.

We have said that the above statements are true as regards the other works taken in themselves, because we are here considering in an abstract manner these works and woman's opposition with man. If, on the contrary, we regard certain works in a concrete manner, placing them in their proper surroundings and particular circumstances, and if we plunge woman herself into a family or religious group or in some special circumstance, she will accommodate herself better than man in respect to a certain formation, habit, or psychology. She will assimilate more easily or more perfectly than man. These distinctions should be helpful in clarifying certain discussions on feminism.

Woman cannot compete with man on man's own territory in an efficacious and victorious way, but the possibility is there, and sometimes easily so, by remaining on her own terrain and profiting from the ways in which she differs from him and cannot be imitated by him. Two occupations, sewing and cooking, should be ignored by the husband in the domestic community, but outside the family, not as a husband but as a man, he may have to follow these trades (let us only mention tailors and chefs), and become more appreciated than the woman and also make his services more costly. We must never forget that these observations garnered by Cajetan were made a long time ago. Their vestige or germ can be found in certain words of Aristotle. Ecclesiasticus had already said: "Where there is no wife, he mourneth that is in want." We only have to recall the self-sacrifice of so many mothers, religious, and nurses; a self-sacrifice that nothing can replace. Man learns to do with great difficulty what almost every woman accomplishes so easily and almost instinctively.

St. Thomas' doctrine on the work of education, which continues that of generation and is one with it, must also be brought to mind. Here again the wife, the mother, is irreplaceable. If she happens to die before her time, all the most marvelous ingenuities of paternal love will not quite succeed in filling the void created by her absence.

In that incomparable contemplative life that they lead together in one mind, a place remains for certain operations proper to the woman, depending on the definitive judgment reserved to the man. A certain freedom must be allowed these operations so that the totality of their utility and harmony may be retained. Thus, even in Eden the words of Aristotle and St. Thomas are justified, for the words touch the essence of immutable natures. From certain points of view they applied less in Eden than now, because man was more perfect and had less need of being completed. From other points of view they applied more than now, because life was more perfect and held more marvelous possibilities.

Let us see how the words of Scripture, words pronounced by man himself under divine inspiration, emphasize and clarify these first and vital truths. "Man shall leave father and mother," from whom he has received so many necessary benefits, in order to attach himself to the one with whom and by whom he will in turn assure the same benefits to others. Thus the stream of human life will gradually progress, extend, conquer, and fructify the earth.

In passing, let us admire the balance maintained between the two parties of the matrimonial contract. In certain deformations to which human weakness has subjected this contract in the course of centuries—in polygamy for example—the woman leaves her father and mother only to become the slave of the spouse, nothing more than his plaything. Here man is the one who leaves them, for with the spouse he is to create a new unity, two in one and the same flesh but also two in one and the same heart and one and the same spirit, *cor unum et anima una*. This, the law of the primitive Church as well as of primitive marriage, is already great because it is already in Christ and the Church, *magnum sacramentum.* We find these analogies between the Church and marriage everywhere.

Nostalgia for Eden

Thanks to the state of innocence, this primitive marriage from certain points of view surpasses all others, even Christian marriage which, despite its sanctity, cannot quite eliminate certain characteristics of the fallen state, especially that dispersion of powers to which we referred. In Eden man was God's representative for woman in all ways and from all aspects. He could not now become a representative in quite the same way without ursurpation and tyranny. And yet, in his relationships with his wife, he always has a certain tendency to claim all that Adam was for Eve.

That he can no longer be. He has become an "earthly man"; he no longer transmits grace to his sons; he no longer is their "priest." No longer is he God's unique representative for his spouse because he has lost his title of contemplative, of God's intimate friend, of prophet, and of priest. The "New Adam" must impart this title, but in a wholly new way, to those whom He choses, to a small number. Not to all, but to His apostles is reserved the privilege of being His representatives in this purely spiritual domain infinitely above flesh and blood.

Certain reminiscences tinged with vague or obscure analogies, obsessed with mirages and dreams of a distant and abolished past, can revive for man the temptation of that nostalgia for Eden. The history of Jansenism is there to recall what misery his grandeur can become for him, like a fallen god who remembers heaven, and especially the heaven on earth that was Eden. It was a reality but now it can be nothing but a dream, illusionary, false, and therefore bad.

Nostalgia for Eden cannot be truly beneficial because Eden is no longer our native land and because the idea of true nostalgia is necessarily linked to the idea of a true native land. We are no longer able to be in paradise except with the Crucified and through the Crucified.

The thief who was penitent and was finally saved is each one of us. What he asked, we also ask. No longer can we stand near the tree of life except with her who is the Mother of the Crucified, crucified herself in heart. The new Eve must stand erect in order to show each one of us, particularly women, how suffering can be for her a divine means of attaining a new nobility more beautiful than the first, and to teach silence in the midst of sorrows.

And yet woman will also always seek enjoyment, rejecting suffering and the yoke of man and weakening his protectorship. She will claim her equality. Undoubtedly, woman has many powers equal to man's in what directly and precisely regards the work of marriage, but in domestic society she should be subject to man.

In our present state of fallen nature and of laborious and difficult reparation, the divine sword must often begin to operate again, always taking care to maintain a certain division between what St. Paul calls the soul and the spirit. (We understand by "soul" that which seeks to elevate itself higher.) Any other sword, any other word would not fit. Our spirit can command the body only if it is separated from it.

This universal law so dear to the ancients is renewed here and finds some applications as yet unknown. The spirit which is separated from God by sin must separate itself from the body by a total and rigorous mortification. Only in this way do we truly live according to the warnings and promises of St. Paul. The spirit can live only by mortifying the body and in the measure that it has the courage to do so. Whoever wishes to devote himself completely to spiritual things must totally disencumber himself from the cares of temporal things. These integrations and separations, simultaneously painful and liberating, are both the effect and the remedy of sin.

Instead of these dispersions under the action of centrifugal forces, everything in Eden was united in a union and a concentration of power. It sufficed for the woman to adhere to the husband in one spirit as the man adhered to his wife in one flesh. This was a perfect union, not only in the flesh but also in the spirit, not only between the flesh and spirit of each but between them both in their whole flesh and in their whole spirit. There was no concupiscence of the flesh set against the spirit nor vengeful concupiscence of the spirit against the flesh. Heart and flesh were united to leap with one single bound toward the living God.

Now that is no longer possible. Sin has come to separate. Another has also said that He came to separate, and it is Jesus Himself. He added that if these necessary separations do not occur, man will encounter his worst enemies in his own house. If in our present redeemed state we hope to re-establish a unity as complete and perfect as Eden's, only an artificial unity born of misunderstandings and unfortunate struggles will be produced.

Furthermore, what sufficed in Eden was rigorously required. The attack was sustained on this vital point: adhesion to the head, because only in that way can a woman be elevated to live the fullness of the spiritual life. One could almost say that all proceeds from man's spirit as all proceeds from his flesh. Woman's spirit was not able to leap with essential joy except in the one who saved her beforehand by attaching her to God. To leave him, were it only for an instant, when it was a question of a definite act, an act which involved questions of salvation, meant leaving God or the risk of leaving Him. Both formed a society, the most perfect and therefore the most concentrated, exacting the maximum of immanence. The branch can give its fruit of spiritual life only by remaining on the vine; the string can give its vital vibration only when fastened to the lyre.

Heraldic Principles

Every principle as such is perfect. That is why beings, to become perfect, have only to return to their principle. That is also why all principles announce all that should emanate from them. They do this in diverse manners which are more or less obscure but potent and fruitful. We insist on this messenger-like virtue of principles, for it can emphasize and illuminate the entire course of the present meditations.

Great things always begin with a prolific, and therefore a full and perfect principle; all the more perfect because it is more "first," in the full significance of this word. There is no superabundance without fullness and fullness is equivalent to perfection. So it is, for example, that in the Church everything begins with true preaching, that is, preaching which superabounds in that which is most lofty: contemplation. Success may be more or less immediate and easily established but everything will descend from that preaching. Crusades of all kinds, if they are to be fruitful, begin with preaching. A Peter the Hermit or a St. Bernard rises and leads others. Contemplation preceded and all that follows descends from its summits. Therefore the various crusades must not be represented as simply prepared for by preaching, which would then be merely a material provision; on the contrary, the preaching is something formal and perfect from which the rest is derived.

Undoubtedly all this is opposed to the evolutionist point of view, which subordinates everything to movement, to its measure which is time, and to history. But principles are outside of time and becoming; they are in being, somewhat like God who, as the first Principle of all, is in the immobile instant of His eternity which coincides with all the successive instants of time.

In the first creation God produces all natures in the state of a principle overflowing with vitality and fecundity. Human nature will not be excepted. Adam, the principle of the woman and of the entire species, comes forth from the Creator's hand in all perfection, in all the actuality of multiple human potencies, full of wisdom and knowledge. Every angel possesses this quality by nature, thanks to the immediate actualization the same nature requires. The first man has it, we may say, not by reason of being man, but by reason of being the first, the principle of all the others.

However, let us note that his nature considered in its essential elements would require the extremely slow passage from potency to act which is evident in us and around us. There is an antinomy between the priority of the imperfection of human nature as such and the priority of the perfection of the principle. In Adam, it is the latter priority which prevails.

Therefore, the angel and Adam are perfect from the first instant, but for different reasons. Adam had to be able to instruct, govern, and preside over all that concerned man in all his activities, whether individual or social and political. Adam is thus the principle and head of the whole order of nature and, before sin, of the entire supernatural order whether in relation to his spouse or his posterity.

Eden's Society

We had to immerse ourselves in the atmosphere of these great doctrines in order to understand something of Eden's society, a society so different from all societies after the first sin, even that of the Holy Family. The latter, while having a supernatural fullness greater than that of Eden, remains nevertheless a family ordained to the city, as are all human families in this *cursus communis* which the Son of man has designed to respect for Himself and for His own.

Eden's perfect society, corresponding to and satisfying all human tendencies, had to put the contemplative life in its proper place, at the summit of all human activity, though this has been so often and in so many ways misconstrued in the course of past centuries and even more, perhaps, in the present century. All rectitude of practice depends on rectitude of speculation. The least deviation from the higher level is translated into some dreadful confusion in the lower level.

From this point of view it can be said that everything human is an overflow from contemplation, irrespective of who it is that contemplates, the more or less felicitous manner in which he contemplates, or the way in which the contemplation prepares for that which in the last analysis will emanate from it. We so rarely grant contemplation its proper place! Yet it cannot overflow if it does not have this place. Nevertheless, everything derives from its fullness, but this fullness was found only in Adam. To him as to all the angels is applied the wonderful phrase: *plenus sapientia ab initio* (full of wisdom from the beginning).

In the poem, *Sacre de la femme*, there is an admirable line which describes, seated side by side, "Eve who looked and Adam who contemplated." She was like the child whom the same poet depicted, "allowing her astonished and delighted gaze to wander, and fully offering her young soul to life."

Eve could do this, thanks to the special powers of her state of original justice. She could turn her gaze on all the creatures that presented themselves to her sight, even on the serpent, and listen without any imprudence on her part. Such imprudence would have been a first sin and no sin could be found in her as long as pride had not passed and shown the way; as long as it had not attempted to make a judgment, that is, to exercise the definitive intellectual act. To make that act she had to appeal to authority and place herself under the protection of the head.

It is the same everywhere and always. The glances which science and art cast on things are true and secure only when they are guaranteed in some way or other by the intervention of wisdom. Wisdom alone contemplates in the full meaning of the word because it does so in virtue of the highest causes. Thus every contemplative who is in any way inferior needs to take refuge in contemplations superior to his own when he must pass a definitive judgment on something which involves his whole responsibility and his whole future. Let us recall our invocation to her who is pre-eminently the Seat of Wisdom: "we fly to thy patronage."

One now understands that Eve's complete liberty was good as long as it was united to Adam, the authority, but that the least break with his authority immediately abolished all her liberty. Adam was the master who was obliged to dispense to her and to their children every light and every instruction, the priest from whom all natural and supernatural life had to emanate, for in the state of innocence their two lives were closely aligned to each other.

Let us try to grasp these delicate principles which apply in every instant and regulate the exercise of all authority. Definitive acts demand that one be closely united to authority, and every preparatory action ordained to these definitive acts requires the spontaneous and free performance of inferior causes. The head must perform and at times impose its influence, but it must not presume to absorb the other members. In the family, in society it must be careful not to hinder or thwart the activity proper to the mother and the wife. Not only would it militate against the interest of all, but also against her personal interest, and she could no longer fulfill the role reserved to her. One of the greatest marvels of the state of original justice was precisely that the mean between insufficient and excessive subordination was perfectly guaranteed and assured and the disorder produced by sin could never have occurred as long as a grave fault of pride had not intervened.

Let us add that the principles of wisdom directly command the entire human order, even the purely intellectual. The arts, and especially the sciences, must submit themselves to the influence of wisdom. In our times they scarcely do so; at all events, they do not do so sufficiently. But neither must wisdom absorb them as she has sometimes tended to do in other ages. Particularly in what is called "the way of invention" or induction, which in our day invades almost the entire scientific domain, some hardy pioneers must strive by a lively initiative to attain those truths which are partially seen. But when the moment of synthesis arrives, when the science is integrated, it will also be necessary that the conquered truth be able to descend from the summits and fructify all forms of human activity.

The Wife Springs from the Husband's Heart

Eve comes from Adam as from her principle, in the same way that the Church comes from Christ. What is the precise point from which she springs? From the half-opened side, from the depths of the heart itself. Why? St. Thomas gives two reasons.[4] The first reason is derived from the truly social character of the couple's union. They must form a society in the full sense of the word, a society in which each

[4] *Summa theol.*, Ia, q. 92, a. 3.

one must respect the rights of the other so that all oppressive domination, whether from the man or the woman, may be avoided.

What an admirable balance is established by these simple words: woman is taken from man's heart. She is not taken from his head, because she must not dominate him as the head dominates the body. She is not taken from his feet, because she is not his slave. She is not subjected to him in servility, and hence man is not to deride her. Woman is not dominated tyrannically, but she must not take advantage of the gentleness of this regime to usurp a tyranny which would be worse because it would be less reasonable.

In order to comprehend this doctrine, let us recall an objection which St. Thomas raises. Only after sin, he says, was woman condemned to be under man's power, for all inequality proceeds from sin, according to a famous quotation from St. Gregory: "Where there is no sin, there is no inequality." But by her very nature woman possesses less strength and less dignity than man. Therefore she should not have been produced before the sin.

St. Thomas' answer introduces a vital distinction between two kinds of subjection: one which is servile and a consequence and punishment of sin; the other which is economic and civil, a consequence of human nature which will be manifest in every possible state that human nature can assume. In other words, "the supreme good of proper order would have been lacking to the human race if certain ones were not governed by others wiser than themselves." Nature herself destines woman to be subordinate to man from the fact that she causes the *discretio rationis* to abound in him. Inequality is not always an evil, a consequence of sin. It is a condition for order and by that same token for goodness and beauty also. Inequality is therefore natural and was found, as was nature itself, in the state of innocence.

It is especially important in the practical order to distinguish carefully and separate these two kinds of subjection. One is the fruit of original sin and has been aggravated by all the sins and vices of men. It must be curtailed as much as possible, even to the point of striving to make it disappear completely. The other subjection is essential to conjugal life. Not only must its delicate exigencies be respected but they must be permitted to produce all their benefits and be aided to do so.

If we wish to advance further and investigate more deeply, we encounter a profound and delicate problem: the problem of two opposed finalities, of two acts of intention which are hidden and difficult to reveal. When we make use of things it can only be for a good which in the last analysis is never the good of those things but the good of persons. When we make use of persons, it can be for our good or for theirs. If it is for their good, we are treating them as free and loved beings, as friends.

Here is the important consideration, for underlying that which we have just said is the whole question of the two kinds of love: an interested love, in which we love ourselves alone and refer things and persons to ourselves, and a disinterested love, the love of benevolence or friendship, in which everything is referred to the persons loved because we love them as ourselves, according to the beautiful language of charity.

But St. Thomas teaches that conjugal love, especially since it has become a sacramental love among Christians, ought to be a supreme type of friendship. Moreover, it is important to bear in mind that true friendship is not easy or frequent, for our hearts are greatly inclined to egoism and self-love. Friendship can only be virtue or accompanied by a virtue, said Aristotle.

Egoism is a kind of cramp that prevents our arms from

stretching forth and our hand from opening. After many efforts and some success it still has the tendency to withdraw and close in upon itself. The egoist goes out from himself—goes out perhaps too far and too long—but he emerges with empty hands so that he can return within himself with filled hands. We should go out of ourselves with full hands and return with empty hands, after having given everything to others, for it is more blessed to give than to receive (except when it is from God that one receives). The egoist sees and desires nothing around himself but slaves, but he who truly loves makes himself the slave of those he loves.

It is hard to see clearly into our intentions because they often conceal many illusions. Let us try to be enlightened by deeds and by effects, to know others and especially ourselves by our fruits. We endeavor to hide the secret of our egoism from everyone, and from ourselves more than anyone else.

The second reason given by St. Thomas is a sacramental reason. To say sacrament is equivalent to saying sign. Therefore, here one deals with symbols and annunciations which have unlimited perspectives and are contained in the mysteries of the Sacred Heart. The saints alone, and only the greatest among them, are permitted to lift the veil which hides such secrets and they alone dare to make themselves heard.

Let us listen to St. Augustine as he compares the origin of the first spouse in Eden with the origin of the Church on Calvary. In Eden, God acts all by Himself without intermediary and without instrument. With His infinitely delicate, paternal, and maternal hands, He opens the side of Adam, lulled into an ecstatic sleep.

In the case of the Church, the second Adam is sleeping a sleep still more profound. It is the greatest ecstasy of death. By a violent and bloody death the soul is released from the poor, tortured body. It is put to sleep, not in the garden of pleasure but on wood, both sterile and fertile, the wood of the tree of death and life. Men have nailed Him there to hold Him forever in a gesture of justice and mercy. At this time God opens the side of the new Adam, but the divine hands have put off the fragrance of Eden. They are equipped with force alone and, I would almost dare to say, they have taken on the rigor of steel, the penetrating keenness of the lance.

For this work of works God seized upon the hand of a man and the iron of a lance as instruments. It must be pointed out that the Gospel speaks here of a man of war and of an arm of war. It is very strange that this heart was not opened by a priest but by a soldier, and not by a particular soldier, but just any soldier—as if just any soldier could do that! What springs from the side opened by the lance? The new Eve, the new spouse, Holy Church. She bursts forth with the water and the blood, with the supreme efficacy which always continues to gush forth in baptism and the Eucharist. The Church issues from this side, returns there unceasingly, and lives in this ebb and flow. Unceasingly the husband leads the wife back to the lips of that Sacred Wound and it is the Church, this new spouse, who through the first spouse, Eve, was greeted by Adam as "bone of my bones and flesh of my flesh."

"This is why I, the Spouse, I, Jesus, renounced all glory and joy and left the bosom of My Father as I left the bosom of My Mother Mary, the nests of My eternal adolescence and My earthly infancy. Because of Me her maternal heart was broken, rent by the sword. When twelve years old, I left her for several days to be about the business of My Father. This act and My words rewakened in the Temple the echo of Simeon's words and began to raise the Cross before her. Later, in complete departure, I abandoned her to go to souls. As much as she was My Mother, I preferred souls to her and I impressed this fact on her in a cruel manner. Finally, at the foot of the Cross, I left her behind while I led My companion in anguish away to the kingdom of Paradise. Of My Mother I asked the renunciation of her only-begotten Son in order to adopt that humanity of executioners which at the same moment was crucifying her Beloved Son. I left all. I left My Father and My Mother in order to attach Myself to My spouse and We are two in one flesh, the unique flesh of My Eucharist eaten by My Church in each of your Communions. Yes, the result of all this is the Eucharist in which each soul, each member of the Church, becomes one with Me in this Flesh and Blood present under the species of bread and wine. It is the supreme flowering of all the mysteries at the same time that it is the summary of the marvels of the All-Powerful. In it I can incarnate Myself in each of the members of My Church for in truth he who eats My Flesh and drinks My Blood becomes flesh of My flesh and bone of My bone."

"Bone of my bone and flesh of my flesh." Everything is contained in these first lines of our Sacred Books. With the eyes and heart of the Church let us read every single detail of the Sacred Text. We see that in this the first of all prophecies everything was told, even what had not yet been accomplished, even what is yet hidden from us in the limbo of the future. We find ourselves before a universal law: all being proceeds from a principle and must re-enter that principle. Beings are perfect only when they return to their principle and plunge themselves into it again. Everyone who speaks or sings in the name of the Church can do so only for the purpose of announcing or explaining something of these supreme truths. The devotion to the Sacred Heart which is developing more and more is only the awareness of that marvelous reality of the re-entry of the Church into the Heart of the Spouse.

Holy Scripture confides only two words to us. It speaks of the lance and of the side. It does not even mention the Heart, but only the half-opened side. St. John speaks of the side of Jesus as he speaks of the Mother of Jesus. He names neither Mary nor the Heart. We are to name them. At the Last Supper he rested on this adorable Heart and at the Cross he was present at the moment of the lance's stroke, and "he that saw it hath given testimony." He had rested his head against the rock of Israel, like Jacob, exhausted with fatigue, on the stone which was Christ. It was not yet the hollow of the rock, the ultimate shelter of the tomb, where the contemplative dove makes its nest in order to live and die there.

Behind the intact wall of Jesus' breast the beloved disciple could hear the murmur of the spring which aroused thirst but could not quench it. Now, on Calvary, he sees it gush forth. As soon as the lance struck, like the rod of Moses on the rock, all was opened before him with the opening of the divine side. The spring will continue to gush forth and will not stop flowing until the Crucified's words are repeated by the Judge when all is ended: *Consummatum est.*

Behold the open Heart of the Lord. Still it is not open wide enough. The lance was only able to half-open it. This fissure will be enlarged more and more, and first by the finger of an incredulous apostle. These last two words are almost contradictory. "Be faithful, you who ought to spread fidelity. You, Thomas, going forth from this doubt, will perhaps carry farther than all the others the triumph and martyrdom of your faith. As the fingers of the All-Powerful opened Adam's side to draw the first spouse from it, so your feeble, incredulous finger, none the less apostolic, completes the crude work of the lance, enlarging the divine Wound so that the Church may be able to contemplate the Heart of her Spouse more and more."

After that, Scripture says no more. The great light is extinguished. Almost gropingly we must divine what could be called the progressive stages of the widening of the Sacred Wound. The Fathers and Doctors have succeeded. The great contemplatives have scrutinized this mystery and have conquered some of it. As at dawn on the high mountains the tips of the peaks become illuminated and the summits become enlightened—St. Bernard, St. Gertrude, St. Catherine of Siena. More and more the side is opened and the Heart appears, and the whitening light descends into the valley and a great joy is for all the people. The angel who announced the great joy is St. Margaret Mary. Her role is very beautiful, but one must not imagine that she began all. She was the publicity agent, if I dare to say so, and may Our Lord be ever blessed for it! But like all the instruments in the course of the centuries, she has begun nothing nor has she ended anything. Everything remains open, and more and more so, just as this side and this Heart remain open.

It must be this way. As the centuries pass, everything must grow and be developed in the Church and at the same time must return and re-enter more and more into the Spouse's Heart. When everything re-enters there, when everything disappears there, everything being accomplished, then the world will no longer have any reason for existing and it shall be finished under the hand of justice and in the arms of mercy.

Let us not forget that contemplatives (those who are found in religious communities as well as those who are spread across the secular world) are the inhabitants of the only Eden which survives sin's destruction. They are, on the lips and in the heart, the aftertaste of the paradise of the past, the earthly paradise, and the foretaste of the paradise of the future, the paradise of heaven.

Adam knew how to cultivate the garden but he did not know how to preserve it. May the contemplatives, they above all, continue not only to cultivate but also to preserve it by defending its dear possession for everyone and for themselves. It does not necessarily follow that because everyone quenches his thirst at its source that they should be the ones to desert it. They ought to maintain relations of intimate and ineffable tenderness with the Heart of the divine Master. They ought to be precursors always and everywhere, especially at this central and royal post. They are the nearest and the farthest, the farthest from the world and the nearest to God, hidden behind all, placed before all at the feet of the Lord.

Their most essential movement elevates them unceasingly from His feet to His Heart. It is through them especially that the Church drinks from that source of its whole life. The Church thirsts. Let them drink! The Lord thirsts that someone thirst for Him.

Only Latin satisfactorily expresses those very strong words of St. Gregory Nazianzen: *Sitit sitiri.* The spring thirsts to be drunk.

Eden's inhabitants must take cognizance of this thirst. They must also realize, by experiencing more than anyone else, the immense need we all have to drink at this spring. They must drink not only for themselves but for every soul, for every soul that relies on the ardor of their desire and even more on the fervor of their prayer. They must drink at this river which "went out of the place of pleasure" so that they can water all the garden of the Church. No one else can profit from it if they do not know how to profit from it first. This is indeed the "irrigation of the Catholic garden" of which Dante speaks. This irrigation depends on contemplation on the summits before it depends on the apostolic torrents of preaching which promote the fruitfulness in the plains.

2

False Annunciation:

MYSTERY OF INIQUITY

You shall be as gods, knowing good and evil.

LIKE the mystery of joy which we have just treated, it is in Eden's joyous setting that the mystery of iniquity will insinuate itself. Without it, the mystery of joy would never have replaced the mystery of suffering and death. The scene therefore remains the same but a new actor will appear.

Human Temptation

Why is not the drama of sin enacted exclusively within the human world, as it had been enacted in the angelic world by the angels alone? An angel had sufficed to tempt an angel, but we shall see that everything contributed to the temptation of man.

In order to understand the reason for this we must recall one of the most characteristic differences between the angelic and human natures. The angelic nature is sufficient to itself, in the sense that from the first instant of its existence it possesses its fullness and happiness in the natural order. We could compare it to one of those feudal estates of the Middle Ages which contained everything necessary for the life of its inhabitants. There was no need to leave it. But man is democratically confined to a small house in a big city. If he goes out, he will find everything he needs in the neighboring shops, but he must go out for everything. He cannot procure anything for himself except outside of his home. His intellect depends on his senses; his senses, on exterior things. The effects of sin augment his dependence.

Adam alone, in an infused manner, possessed from the very beginning all knowledge of the natural order, which permitted him to be master and doctor immediately. All other men have to acquire this knowledge. Even with Christ there was an acquired natural knowledge. Everything must be acquired by us and, since the first sin of man, by the sweat of our brow.

Man is also a microcosm, that is, a miniature world, a reduced "totality." But this totality exists only in potency. It must be actualized by a dependence on everything that already actually exists around him. Hence, the words of St. Thomas, which are so simple and definitive: "It is a condition of human nature that one creature can be helped or impeded by another." [1] Any creature can, without a moment's warning and often in the most unforeseen manner, come to the aid of a human being or lay a trap for him.

It was inherent in man's nature and was therefore fitting even in the state of innocence that God, at the same time that He caused the good angels to help man, also permitted the bad angel and the other creatures serving him to tempt man. In the first instance God causes an action, but in the second instance He merely permits it, though both are conformable to man's nature, which respects the smooth mo-

[1] *Summa theol.*, IIa IIae, q. 165, a. 1.

tion of providence. That is why every man can and, let us dare to say, should be tempted, even the Man-God.

The man who has not been tempted, what will he know or of what value is his knowledge? Those who strive at any price to avoid every kind of temptation, however light, fall into this extreme without wishing to do so and often without knowing it, no matter how great their benevolence or their gentleness might be. Here the confines of prudence and charity are delicate and difficult to specify.

The Temptation in Eden

So much for human nature, which is the same in all states. Now for the state of innocence. By a special gift of grace it was accorded to man that no creature, even those who were capable of tempting him, could harm him against his own will. He could easily resist every temptation sent by the devil. St. Thomas raises the objection that since temptation is a penalty of sin, it could not exist in the state of innocence.[2]

He responds to this objection by a distinction. Temptation which is difficult to resist is a penalty of sin. That is why the more we sin, the more temptation increases, oppresses, and takes on the appearance of fatality. But as long as the state of innocence lasted, man could resist temptation without any difficulty. To man's facility in resisting temptation there corresponded a minimum of influence exercised by the devil on the human faculties. He could not tempt by interior suggestion, which at first sight might have been more in harmony with the spirituality of the state of our first parents. He could not affect the imagination directly as he so easily does with us. That is why he was forced to use material instruments and hence the necessity of the serpent.

[2] *Ibid.*, ad 3um.

Something similar happens with certain saints; the enemy is forced back little by little and reduced to means that are increasingly obvious as these saints become more spiritualized and, by virtue of this fact, more approximate Eden's condition. As for us, who are so far from Eden, the devil seeks to lead us astray in the labyrinth and subtleties of vainglory. Thus he profits by the difficulties peculiar to the spiritual domain from which we have not yet banished him and in which we ourselves have great difficulty in orientating ourselves because it is so far removed from our senses, which are the principles of all our knowledge. It is easier for us to see clearly and to distrust ourselves when we are tempted in regard to material things, without which no human can live here below, for example, the question of our daily bread. We shall speak more about this later.

The Tempter's Instruments

We must not be astonished that in man's first temptation the superior powers of evil mobilized against him and in a certain way all beings inferior to him: woman, from her species; the serpent, from the genus to which it belongs; the tree and the fruit, from the vegetable order. Each of the kingdoms of living nature delegated its representative in that assault against the king of the visible world.

Woman was simultaneously the most efficacious instrument of active deception and the easiest object of passive deception. She could deceive man more easily, St. Thomas tells us, because of her social union with him. It was the sole union which existed before the sin, in contrast with the dominative union, the consequence and punishment of sin, which alienated the woman from the head and heart of man and put her at his feet. This dominative union separates more than it unites the two spouses and diminishes the power of the woman's seduction by making her a slave if

36

the man disdains her, unless she herself, striving to dominate him, succeeds in disdaining him even more. This power of deception was in direct proportion to the perfection and intensity of their union, a power which could be turned toward evil but which had its source in what was best in the conjugal union.

Let us not forget that the tempter had himself been tempted and deceived by his own excellence. Everywhere and always he tries to avail himself of what is most excellent and his ruses and artfulness increase in proportion to the degree of excellence which he perceives. Never was the excellence of marriage more splendid or more radiant than in Adam and Eve. Never was the love of friendship which merges the spouses into total union sweeter or stronger, save in the Holy Family.

Scotus denounced Adam's first sin as an excess of that love of friendship, but that is impossible, since his first sin, like Eve's, could only be a sin of pride. Suffice it to say that because of the movement of pride which was aroused in him and to which he submitted, he could not resist the spouse who tempted him. But let us not indict their marvelous love. If it could have been an indirect cause or an occasion of sin, the love itself remains sinless.[3] Undoubtedly Adam should have resisted and in doing so he would have proved his love all the more, but he had already given in to pride. Sin had intervened and had begun to trouble everything.

Why was the woman more capable of deceiving and also easier to deceive? This greater facility evidently springs from a certain inferiority of the woman in comparison with man.[4] But are not these points of view contradictory? If she is inferior to man, how can she triumph over him? As an instru-

[3] *Summa theol.*, IIa IIae, q. 163, a. 4.
[4] *Ibid.*, q. 165, a. 2, ad 1um.

ment of some power superior to man. Woman, more easily than man, becomes an instrument because she more readily surrenders and thus allows herself to be deceived. If she surrenders to God, she will often advance more quickly and soar higher, possessing a more perfect devotion in the theological sense of the word. But if she lets the enemy deceive her, it will be for everyone's ruin. In these two contrary instances she as an instrument arrests the power of the principal cause which moves her. But when woman arrests this power it is often in an unconscious manner, much more unconscious than in man. No one knows, nor does she herself know, who or what impels her to speak or to act. Sometimes it is herself, for she remains a free agent; sometimes it is another, who does not suppress her liberty, but diminishes it. And who might that be?

As for the serpent, everything is very simple and clear, for it can be only an instrument. Its prudence is only fundamentally the cunning of the devil. The devil deludes us through the serpent, as St. Augustine remarked. The serpent did not understand the sounds which went from him to the woman any more than the possessed understand the strange words which burst from their mouth. That is why God did not say to the serpent as He said to the woman: "Why did you do that?," because it was the devil who had acted through the serpent.

Our Imprudence

Everything that took place in and around Eve is full of lessons for us. We no longer possess any of the marvelous powers of harmony and balance which the state of original justice bestowed on her. Things that were not imprudent for her would be imprudent for us, and the first of these fatal imprudences would be to isolate ourselves, especially to isolate ourselves from the authority which the enemy does not dare to attack. To isolate ourselves from authority means the loss of our head, and since we cannot get along without a head, we take it wherever we find it.

This is what Eve did in her first sin, which was a sin of pride, whereby she subjected herself to the him who is king over all the sons of pride. She placed herself under the power of the serpent by letting him deceive her. To exercise her universal act of judgment in full security she should have remained subordinated to Adam, and since Adam was not near her, she should have searched for him or awaited his return. In any case, she should have postponed the act of judgment which could prove fatal.

The suspension of judgment is a difficult act of prudence, especially for a woman. The fear of judging too quickly or rashly is one of those fears which are the beginning of wisdom. Did not He who is infinite wisdom say: "Judge not, that you may not be judged"?

Eve had not received the grace to exercise the act of judgment by herself, but to be subordinate to God's representative. Together they formed a whole and of this whole, under pain of death, Eve could only be a part in the definitive act she was to perform. Eden's social organism was the most perfect of all, for the more a person is elevated, the less possibility there is of division. This is a supreme and indisputable law. Any division immediately causes death, either for the separated part or for the whole.

Our second imprudence would be to listen to temptation and still more to respond. In cases of this kind not only every judgment must be suspended, but even the least answer to the tempter. We should not permit ourselves to engage in conversation with him. If we consent to listen, he will interrogate us and corner us into answering. "Why hath God commanded you, that you should not eat of every tree of paradise?" His question could not be more insidious.

On the surface it appears completely normal, conformable to God's law, and even in the interest of God's law. Let us beware of conditionals. We may even be led to answer as Eve did, and then we are caught in a trap.

Who is this new character who questions her and who is so interested in her, in her fate? The answer she gave him was in itself just and true. "Of the fruit of the trees that are in paradise we do eat," and then, recalling the divine precept, "but of the fruit of the tree which is in the midst of paradise, God hath commanded us that we should not eat and that we should not even touch it, lest perhaps we die."

On our lips that answer would be imprudent. We should hold our tongues, distrust ourselves, and not expose ourselves to a betrayal of what is God's secret. The precept was a positive law and depended on God's will. It was perhaps unknown to Satan, but seeing the respect Adam and Eve had for that mysterious tree, he was able to surmise that there was something extraordinary about it. So also when we are tempted, in case he does not know but desires to know, we run the risk of delivering one of God's secrets to him if we answer him.

Eve's case is not without analogy with the life of Jesus, who answered the tempter in the sacred words of Scripture. So Eve answered: "God said we should not eat; and that we should not touch it." Her retort is less trenchant than Christ's and sharpens the sword of the divine words with less force. In response to "If you be the Son of God," Jesus gives the sword's edge its maximum keenness. The divine word attains its maximum intransigence. As for us, we should not answer the tempter at all and when, for some reason or another, we are forced to answer, we must do as Jesus did.

We are not surprised at so many shades of meaning. It

often happens that a thing is imprudent in a general manner, taken in the abstract, but is not imprudent for certain individuals placed in a particular situation. These persons are armed, preserved, or protected in some manner or another. Exorcists, for example, sometimes go so far as to interrogate the devil who speaks through the mouth of one possessed. At any rate, it is certain that Eve had not sinned before the serpent told her she would be like God, although we ourselves would have already committed grave sins of imprudence if we were to do what she did.

The mother and wife of a family can and should exercise certain initiatives which man ought not oppose. Undoubtedly Eve's case was the same. But the last word, the definitive judgment, was the duty of the man, husband, and priest, as it continues to be the duty of the man, husband, father, or priest. If woman usurps this function of the definitive judgment in certain grave matters, everything will necessarily be awkward, unpleasant, and destructive of the order which submits her to man.

The woman's first words cited for us by Scripture are addressed to the serpent before the sin. The second are addressed to God on the subject of the serpent after the sin: "He deceived me." In deceiving her, the serpent had usurped the place of the head, which man alone should be, says St. Paul. It is precisely this head that is to be crushed and, by a stupendous reversal, Eve will crush it through Mary.

Because the promise proceeds from the mouth of God, the first sinner is converted in a single stroke; the despairing one will be reborn in living hope and will strain with all her energy toward Mary and the Cross. These words of mercy will permit the woman to accept the words of justice which will soon follow: the condemnation to her own cross, to her maternal sorrow and cruel pain, and to her dependence as a wife, which can become so crushing! She accepts her cross, and like every true cross it resembles somewhat the cross of Jesus. In a sense she is already standing with Mary, because we are with Mary as soon as we are near the cross.

The serpent, that is to say Satan, quickly answers the command cited by Eve, whereas he will answer nothing to the strong language of Jesus. He denies what God affirmed: "No, you shall not die." He implies that God had a hidden intention of preventing man from becoming like God; hence, to become God, it will suffice to disobey: "God doth know that in what day soever you shall eat thereof, your eyes shall be opened, and you shall be as gods, knowing good and evil."

Through the woman, the serpent assumed the role of the announcer of all the perverse destinies of humanity, just as Adam, by his first words, was the announcer of all the joyous destinies, including the mystery of the Incarnation, which was not yet envisioned as redemptive. Satan wanted to make our first parents believe that he was revealing the secrets of God; therefore he speaks in the name of God, although against the intention of God.

This false annunciation ought to be meditated upon attentively by the sons of the true light, for it contains some precious lessons. Every man is a liar. Consciously or not, the past or the present is always explained more or less in the wrong way, and the future is likewise announced falsely. Human information almost always misleads, at least a little. These things should be scrutinized under the light of God. Indeed, it is only under this light that they can be scrutinized without danger.

The First Sin

From all that has been said, we see the importance of St. Thomas' precise statement: Eve's first sin, as well as Adam's, could only have been a sin of pride. But it is in Eve, more perhaps than in Adam, that it is interesting to consider it. Genesis describes it more fully than it does the sin of Adam, of whom it merely states that he ate of the fruit. In Eve the cursed flower of sin blossoms and spreads out more widely than in Adam, as we shall see.

In any case, because of the perfection of the state of our first parents, no other malice could have preceded the sin of pride. It is impossible to conceive, for example, a wickedness attaching itself to one of the forms of intemperance, which presupposes a rebellion of the flesh against the spirit, since that rebellion would in turn presuppose a first sin. The Sacred Text says that the woman saw that the fruit was good and beautiful, and this seems to be Eve's first reaction to words of the tempter. But the goodness and beauty of the fruit was the primary motive of her sin, and the mere act of looking at the fruit would have been without danger if the movement of pride had not already preceded and envenomed it.[5]

Neither could Adam and Eve sin at the outset by curiosity, which is an intellectual intemperance. Certainly they desired knowledge and such a desire was appropriately human, but the desire proceeded from a deeper desire of being like God, a desire common to sinful man and the bad angel.

The human being in the splendor of his state of integrity could no more sin against the theological virtues than the bad angel could. Every disorder in him had to be preceded by pride, for pride is the beginning of every sin. It is

[5] *Summa theol.*, IIa IIae, q. 163, a. 1, ad 2um.

therefore universally true that man, like the bad angel, begins to turn away from God by reason of the special aversion of pride, for he does not want to be subjected to God and the divine rule.[6] Such an attitude always involves, necessarily, a certain contempt for God, at least implicitly. Disobedience was caused in man by pride, and it is but a logical consequence. Everything is contained in St. Augustine's solemn affirmation: "Yielding to pride and following the serpent's persuasion, man scorns God's precept."

Our first parents' sin of pride had for its motive the serpent's promise: "you shall be as gods." You, that is to say, you, Eve, your husband, and your children. Maternal pride is a terrible temptation in itself for any woman. It would be so for all our poor mothers and it would seem that it should have been so for Eve, if we did not remember with St. Thomas that by reason of her state of original justice every temptation was easy for her to conquer. And let us not say that Eve's imagination must have been dazzled for, again according to St. Thomas, the tempter could not then act on her imagination. Eve's action was therefore inexcusable!

It is a question of a sort of seizure of the divinity, as St. Augustine says: *Adam et Eva rapere voluerunt divinitatem.* St. Thomas states that in willing a spiritual good beyond the measure fixed for them by God, they desired to become like God in an inordinate manner.

They who were made to the image of God certainly possessed a likeness to God which they could and should love. But this is not the question. We are concerned rather with a perverse imitation of God, according to another celebrated passage of St. Augustine, and not with the legitimate imitation that their nature and their grace permitted.

[6] *Ibid.*, q. 162, a. 4.

Let us state again that their first sin was the desire of likeness to God in regard to the knowledge of good and evil and not the knowledge of truth. The tempter knew that this would be the vulnerable point, the most sensible to their pride, on which he would succeed in making them fall.

An angel cannot desire to know more than he knows because he is full of wisdom from the beginning. Adam also personally possessed this fullness, not by virtue of his nature but by virtue of his privilege and his office as head of the other members of humanity. An angel possesses all knowledge immediately, even supernatural knowledge, because his whole destiny was decided in an instant. Man's way, however, implies a certain slowness and a certain multiplicity. Throughout his entire earthly life Adam was always capable of perfecting himself in the order of supernatural knowledge, especially in regard to its multiple practical applications. But thanks to his privileges as chief of humanity, he was perfect and unimpeachable on the terrain of the speculative sciences. Neither the serpent nor Eve could prevail against him. Other men, his descendants, are always capable of growing in all the orders of the sciences, supernatural as well as natural, speculative as well as practical.

Every appetite for knowledge is natural to man. Although it is difficult for him to depend on another in the acquisition of knowledge, he accepts a master more easily in speculation than in practice, and for that reason in practical matters it is most difficult for him to attain a truly consistent science.

To possess; that is the important word. That is what man would wish especially. He succeeds in possessing, in making his own in the full sense of the word, those speculative sciences which are perfectly proportionate to him, such as mathematics. But wisdom far surpasses him because of the sublimity of its object which, the ancients say, can be conceded to him only if the gods bestow it on him. Practical knowledge also, because of the infinite multiplicity of the concrete, surpasses and escapes an intellect which is geared to the processes of abstraction. The Holy Ghost alone, through the gift of counsel (so St. Thomas remarks), can reduce the infinity of contingencies in which our actions are engulfed. But that is precisely what man always dreams of effecting himself, by himself alone. His first sin, therefore, consisted in wanting to determine by himself what in the practical order was good and better for him, what he had to do and how he had to act.

Prudence, unlike art, proceeds by ways which are un-determined but determinable, and man always wishes to make up his own mind according to his initiative and his preferences. Let us clearly understand that on this point God will be very exacting, if only by reaction against this first sin which continues to operate in all others. The more man is urged by his temperament or by circumstances to make up his own mind, the more that divine reaction tends to make itself felt. This is what happened to St. Peter: "Another shall gird thee and lead thee whither thou wouldst not"; and to St. Paul: "There it shall be told thee what thou must do."

Other texts from Scripture show us at what point it pleases God to restrain or to hide from us the ways by which He intends to lead us. All these restrictions must be accepted, for they will lead us to life even though our poor nature may be astonished, may groan and cry out sorrow-fully: "How narrow is that gate!"

The delicacy of the divine plans is often irritating to our short-sighted eyes. They are cobwebs in which we must know how to let ourselves be enmeshed without stirring, for fear of tearing them. Many times, in the most unexpected and baffling fashion, God will allow to slip into nothingness, plans which were dear to us, which had cost us much time and labor, and which even seemed approved by Him, in order to replace them with His own.

Autonomy, to be one's own rule of action, to be self-sufficient in the moral order, all these expressions arouse many modern echoes round us. We are flattered to seem to know, to discover, and to conclude by ourselves what is good or bad for us. But God asks His own, those who want only to be His, to renounce these perspectives, these foresights, in order to plunge themselves into the maternity of His providence. Let us establish firmly in our minds and especially in our hearts these great words of St. Thomas: "The first man sinned chiefly by coveting to be like God in regard to the knowledge of good and evil, at the instigation of the serpent, so that by his own natural power he could decide what was good and what was evil for him to do." [7]

We must always return to this point if we wish to combat the fatal consequences of that first sin. We must make more and more of an effort to understand completely what it was in itself, particularly by comparing the sin of man with the sin of the angel, and the sin of Adam with the sin of Eve. This second comparison will occupy us for a longer time. As for the first, let us limit ourselves to a completion of the sketch whose most salient features we have already emphasized.

That which characterized the first human sin was the desire for knowledge; the desire for power characterized the angel's sin. According to St. Augustine, he wanted to enjoy his power more than God's. He wanted to act by himself. But St. Thomas remarks that the two sins, angelic and

[7] *Ibid.*, q. 163, a. 2.

human, had a common goal: the angel and the man willed in some way to equal themselves to God in their mode of action, by the fact that they relied on themselves against the divine rule which they scorned. That is why St. Augustine could say of Eve that her spirit had been captivated by the love of her own power, for this is common to every sin of pride.

Since the definitive judgment on anything is based on that which is proper to that thing, it is useful for us to note carefully what is and always will be proper to human sin: it comes from the direction of knowledge. Not by this was the devil tempted, but it is by this that he tempts men.

Let us sum up the entire doctrine as it appears plainly and distinctly in the two parts of the devil's sentence. "You shall be as gods": this is common to the two temptations, angelic and human; "knowing good and evil": this is proper to the human temptation alone.

Eve's Sin

Let us now compare woman's sin with man's. According to St. Thomas,[8] Adam's sin seems graver than Eve's because the woman was deceived and the man was not. It seems that Eve sinned through ignorance, while Adam acted with full knowledge, which is always graver. St. Thomas answers his own objection by saying that Eve's deception followed her pride, and therefore it cannot be a question of antecedent ignorance excusing sin, but of consequent ignorance, which makes it still more grave by intensifying the movement of pride. Let us add that the character of deception is proper to Eve's sin, since Adam was not deceived.

A second objection is derived from the role and duty of man as the head of woman. As a result, he was obliged to give her example, to precede her in good, and not to follow

[8] *Summa theol.*, IIa IIae, q. 163, a. 4.

her into evil. If he sins who is responsible for acting more wisely, he sins more gravely.

Let us answer with St. Thomas: If we consider the circumstance of the condition of the sinful persons, a circumstance which is not merely accidental to the species of the sin, it must be said that Adam's sin was graver that Eve's because Adam was more perfect than Eve. He was the head, the chief, and the sin of one who is first is always graver from this point of view, although it may be less from other points of view more essential to the sin itself. It can, moreover, have many more consequences.

If Adam had not sinned, there would not have been "original sin," the sin of nature. In that terrible moment when humanity was cut in two, Adam could have perhaps saved Eve if he had not given in, if he had resisted her as he should have. How many things are saved merely by resisting! What makes the gravity of the fault is the capitulation of authority, which is always disastrous.

This circumstance of persons, despite the extreme gravity of the consequences, is nevertheless extrinsic and accidental to the sin itself. Eve's sin is graver in itself because of the conditions and elements which are essential to it. The sins of Adam and Eve are of the same species, but Eve's sin was more grave *simpliciter*. St. Thomas gives three reasons and we shall invert their order, starting with the second and third and then returning to the first.

Eve became Satan's accomplice, for not only did she herself sin, but she suggested sin to her husband. She sinned against God and against her neighbor, against the one who was one with her in the flesh and, until that fatal instant, in the spirit. She sinned against him who was God's representative for her in every respect, who with her was the principle of all humanity. The mother of life thus becomes the mother of death for souls and for bodies. "She is full of sin, the serpent is with her, and she is cursed among women." One day she will be converted, touched by a ray from the Morning Star who will receive Gabriel's salutation, but until then she remains crushed under the weight of her crime.

The third reason given by St. Thomas is derived from the fact that the unique motive of Eve's sin had been pride, whereas Adam had allowed himself to be led by his love for Eve. This is what "diminished" his fault. St. Augustine says that Adam consented to sin in virtue of that benevolence of friendship which too often impels us to offend God rather than turn men into our enemies. This complacency was culpable in Adam as it is in ourselves and it merited the rigor of the divine sentence: "Because thou hast hearkened to the voice of thy wife . . . cursed is the earth in thy work."

Let us insist on opposing Scotus' opinion which we already mentioned: not only is Adam's love for his wife not excessive and sinful, but it is the excuse and the dimunition of his sin. In any case, we find only one motive in Eve's sin: pride, and it can only be bad. In Adam's act, we find two motives: pride, which is indeed a sin, and love, which is good in itself.

Let us come finally to the first reason stated by St. Thomas. We must endeavor to state very precisely in what way Eve's pride was greater than Adam's. "The woman," says St. Thomas, "believed in the serpent's persuasive words, namely, that God had forbidden them to eat the fruit of the tree lest they become like Him. Hence, in desiring to attain to God's likeness by eating the forbidden fruit, her pride reached the point of desiring to obtain something against the will of God. But the man did not believe the truth of the serpent's words and he therefore did not desire to attain to God's likeness against God's will. His pride consisted in desiring to attain it by his own power." [9] He willed or would have willed to acquire it by himself if it had been possible. Adam's sin was therefore much more similar to the angel's than was Eve's.

Because of the suggestion of the serpent and Eve's credulity, there was in her sin a greater contempt for God. The text of St. Augustine, cited by St. Thomas, admirably explains it: [10] "The Apostle rightly calls this seduction, for Eve was persuaded to accept a falsehood as being true, namely, that God had forbidden them to touch that tree because He knew that if they touched it, they would be like gods, as if He who made them men, begrudged them the divinity."

But then it seems that, in all logical necessity, we are forced to say that Eve's sin was a sin of infidelity and therefore of another species than Adam's. St. Thomas responds by referring to another text from St. Augustine: "The woman would not have believed the serpent's statement that God wished to deprive them of something good and useful had her mind not already been filled with a love of her own power and a certain proud presumption." This does not mean that her pride preceded the serpent's persuasion, but that immediately after the serpent's words, pride invaded her spirit. Her belief in the serpent's words was a result of her pride.

When moved by vanity or self-love, how easily we believe commendations and compliments, which would otherwise seem absurd and ridiculous to us. We admit as perfectly true and a solid reality that which is but a miserable and fleeting illusion which, by flattering us, finds a way of insinuating itself in us. What must be remembered is that Eve's first sin was a sin of pride and was of the same species

[9] *Summa theol.*, IIa IIae, q. 163, a. 4.
[10] *Ibid.*, IIa IIae, a. 163, a. 1, obj. 4.

as Adam's, regardless of the infidelity which this sin caused in Eve and not in Adam.

It seems evident that Eve's deception consisted in her belief in the serpent's promises. It also seems that for St. Thomas the difference between Eve's and Adam's pride comes back to two essential points. In the first place a definite opinion resulted from the movement of pride in the woman, which did not result in the man. In the second place there was a certain belief in the serpent, about which we will speak later.

In regard to the first point, we have seen that man's sin differs from the angel's because man adds to the desire for power, which is common to both, the desire for the knowledge of good and evil. Similarly, the woman's sin adds an intellectual element to the desire for knowledge which she shared with man, namely, a definite opinion which we do not find in the man. It is not clear how this definite opinion could be compatible with the virtue of faith, but we can say that the virtue of faith can be opposed only by an opinion that is deprived of all objective certitude. Hence the celebrated and precise saying of Bossuet: "A heretic is one who has an opinion." He has and can only have an opinion and not the objective certitude of faith. It is impossible for him to have more because his object does not have firmness in itself. If he appears to be or thinks that he is sure of himself, it is only in virtue of subjective elements which are not of a purely intellectual order, irrespective of what they may be in themselves. In Eve a very particular and characteristic pride gave her opinion all its strength.

Let us come now to the second point which we have referred to briefly. At the outset it is necessary, following Scripture, to attribute to Eve a certain belief in the serpent. Her pride was formally opposed to the will of God in order to follow the will of Satan. She obeyed Satan and therefore, practically speaking, she believed in him.

We can then ask ourselves what became of the virtues of faith and hope in her. In place of a minimum of belief in the serpent which we have attributed to her, we find the maximum. In this sense it could be said that her movement of pride ended in infidelity. She became Satan's slave, and even his intellectual slave. Everything collapsed in her, every part of her spiritual edifice fell into ruin, even the foundations of faith.

Adam's Indefectible Faith

For Adam, there had been no deception. Sin could not penetrate as far in him as in Eve. Adam's love for his wife prompted him to sin and at the same time partially excused him. His love was not excessive in itself, as it would undoubtedly be for us, any more than the diverse circumstances which led to Eve's sin were culpable in her, though they would have been culpable in us. Adam did not speak to Satan and he did not listen to him, but he received the forbidden fruit from the hands of his wife.

Let us quote the curious words of St. Augustine: "Through a movement of pride, man was desirous of the experience, seeing that the woman did not die after eating the forbidden fruit." How many experiences are fancied by our poor pride when divine justice seems not to strike or not to strike quickly enough! A little humility would prevent these fancies from forming or would immediately disperse them.

"As for the man," says St. Thomas, "the love of his own excellence was not sufficiently developed to pervert his judgment and make him believe that the serpent's promise would be fulfilled. He would have desired this only if he had considered it possible." We are dealing here with a whim, a conditioned appetite. The speculative judgment was not affected. There was no speculative error in Adam's sin, just as there had been none in the angel's sin. From the beginning the angel was "full of wisdom" by right of nature. The first man, as head of the human race, was also full of wisdom.

There was, however, practical error, and that is the meaning of the words of Genesis: "knowing good and evil," rather than "knowing truth." As long as error does not affect the speculative domain, one is not deceived; therefore, Adam was not deceived. His sin was confined to the point of view of good and evil and did not attack, as did Eve's sin, the point of view of truth. In this sense speculative error was impossible to Adam because it would have constituted an error in faith, which was incompatible with his role as head. Every man is the head of woman but Adam was furthermore the head of the Church. Being first in humanity, he united the two roles in a necessary and unique title.

With Adam as with the angel error, at least initial error, could only be practical. Practical error does not directly oppose faith because faith is a speculative virtue, as St. Thomas teaches and the Vatican Council seems to insist. It can only be practical in an eminent sense.

This whole doctrine would lose part of its strength or even its meaning if faith were made a formally practical virtue. Adam's sin does not engage questions of faith. He is stopped by the barrier of infallibility which prevents him from becoming engaged in this domain of faith. The gates of hell cannot prevail against the inviolable privilege of one who is head of the Church.

The two sinners, Adam and Peter (the latter in all the infirmity of our present state), are called to strengthen their brethren and everything ordains them to this mission, even their sin. There are two fundamental virtues in the

Christian life: humility and faith. Adam and Peter will strengthen their brethren because they themselves needed conversion, and therefore humiliation, and both are indefectible in the faith.

In the book of Job, God says to the ocean: "Hitherto thou shalt come, and shalt go no further. And here thou shalt break thy swelling waves." The movement of Adam's pride is broken on the immobile rock which protects and defends the sacred domain of faith. This domain cannot be attacked and invaded in Adam as it was in Eve to a certain degree. Eve's sin is the only one whose poisonous flower can blossom in full liberty and can spread out in every direction. Adam's sin is limited by the imperious and glorious necessities of faith. Our personal sins are, on the other hand, weakened in every respect by the miserable impotencies of our fallen state. If all are not sins of infirmity, all or nearly all contain a great share of infirmity which lessens, so to speak, the notion of sin. Adam's sin is hampered by his role as head; our sins are the prisoners of all our limitations.

Eve's sin alone is free from these diverse servitudes and limitations. It benefits from—and misuses—all the splendors which the state of integrity could accumulate within her, a state which it destroyed after having borrowed or stolen from her something of its fullness and grandeur. Woman, more radically than man, surrenders immediately and entirely to sin just as she would surrender to good. That is why it is so useful for us to study it thoroughly and to meditate on its diverse aspects, especially for us moderns, more seduced than our ancestors by the desire for knowledge and more exposed to the weaknesses of faith. This is also why Scripture, when it describes Eve's sin, is so lavish with explanations and details although it is so sparing in regard to Adam's sin.

As for Adam's sin, Cajetan cautions us that we cannot

attain perfect clarity on all points. Actually, it is a question of a particular fact which cannot properly become an object of knowledge and on which we would have to be able to project the light of precise indications and descriptions which are lacking to us.

Adam therefore preserved his faith full and entire without any mitigation or diminution. The Church in Eden is already the Church. Faith cannot disappear from the Church and that is why it remains in Adam. In the course of centuries there will be parts of the Church which will detach themselves, but something indefectible—faith—always remains in the head. St. Augustine, speaking of the consequences of Eve's sin, says that if woman must always be taught and directed and cannot have a teaching role in the Church, it is because of her sin.

We must understand woman's role in sin in order to understand her role in redemption. Eve explains Mary.

Adam became Satan's slave by sin but not in regard to his intellect as such. In him, all have sinned. If he did not go as far as infidelity, Eve is more or less sunken in it.

After this first degree, the descent is more and more rapid in the twisting spiral which sweeps toward hell. The sins of humanity become more grave as regards their species, for the sin of the first parents was not the gravest of all, under the aspect of specification. It was grave only as regards the circumstances of the condition of persons. Being more perfect than all their descendants by reason of their state of innocence, they sinned more gravely from this point of view and from this point of view only.

Adam sinned more gravely than Eve because he was more perfect than she. Their first child was guilty of fratricide and was cursed by God and by the earth. Their children's children went as far as idolatry, and later to atheism. According to the serpent's promise, which their mother had believed, they would be as gods. From fall to fall, from abyss to abyss, they have fallen down even to adoring devils. They have adored them as idols of stone, wood, or metal, fabricated by their hands. They loved them as idols of flesh to which their depraved hearts became attached and, according to the prophet's sentence, they became as abominable as the things they loved.

Divine and Diabolical Deception

The "assumption" of Peter, James, and John by the divine Master took place on a high mountain. This mountain was set apart and it was there and there alone that He was transfigured before them. He leads the soul into solitude and there alone speaks to the heart. It was therefore a deception *par excellence*, a divine deception, according to the terrible saying of Jeremias: "Thou hast deceived me, O Lord, and I am deceived." [11] He exercises this divine deception on certain members of our poor fallen humanity to raise them up and separate them, to lead them apart to the mountain of contemplation, which is the only Eden now possible for us. Undoubtedly, the grace which comes to us from Christ is in itself superior to all the others, but the blessings of prayer are a reflection of the splendors of the primitive Eden.

In the terrestrial paradise entire humanity had been established on the summits, above everything that pertained to the condition of its pure nature. The light and truth of God had led it to His holy mountain. God had conducted it into a sacred solitude and there He spoke to its heart. Thanks to these incomparable revelations of the mind and heart, everything was transfigured in and around humanity.

Contrary to that divine deception is the deception exer-

[11] Jer. 20:7.

cised by God's enemy. He found Eve in a blessed solitude and led her into the disastrous isolation of the intellect which tries to judge by itself and there he spoke to a heart which was too docile to diabolical suggestions because it was already proud.

Such was the "assumption" of holy Eve at the moment when she was about to cease to be holy. She was led apart, apart from God and from her husband. She was exalted on a mountain whose false sublimity dazzled and blinded her. She ascended to the top, while Adam remained half-way up, stopped by the insurmountable barrier of his faith. There the wave of his pride was broken.

This assumption to the summit and solitude through temptation has been experienced by all the saints at some moment of their earthly sojourn. The Saint of saints was Himself led to this high mountain where all the kingdoms of the earth were shown to Him. He cast a look on them which would be dangerous for anyone else but Him. He heard the audacious words, so easily seductive for any hearer who is only human: "If Thou therefore wilt adore me, all shall be Thine." It is a proposed pact; give and take. I will give you everything if You give me this one thing: adoration.

Let us now consider what the tempter proposed to the dazzled eyes of our first mother: "The day you shall eat thereof, your eyes shall be opened, and you shall be as gods." Whether the kingdoms of earth be offered to us in return for our prostration before Satan, as they were to Christ, or whether with Eve we are promised the divinization which is attached to the forbidden fruit, we are faced with the same alternative and the same promise: "If you eat the fruit, you will be as gods, and if you fall down before me and adore me, you will be the true kings of the earth."

We should convince ourselves of the profound connection between temptation and sin, as seen in the serpent's words in Eden and those of Satan at the summit of the mountain, and in the first sin of pride of the mother and in the definitive fall of her children into idolatry. Everything is linked by the most implacable logic. Eve has fallen. She believed the serpent, but she did not adore him. Her sinful children, entangled by the weight of sin, will descend to the depths of idolaters.

Eve, while still holy, was led by the enemy to the terrible mountain on which her doom was consummated. Like her and after her, the holiest of her sons are also led to a mountain. Their temptation is placed between the temptations of Eve and those of Jesus. May they deviate as much as possible from the deathly example of Eden and follow the divine Model of resistance and victory.

In and through her holy children Eve resists throughout the course of centuries, in spite of the weakness of fallen nature, as she should have done in Eden; in and through her sinful sons she accepts and follows the deathly proposal offered to the Saint of saints on the mountain and will thus know the most humiliating consequences of her fatal pride. Thus the great law will be accomplished: He who exalts himself shall be humbled. In her holy and therefore humble sons and in them alone Eve will be able to rise up again and know the divine exaltation of redemptive grace, but her sinful sons, by the inevitable consequences of their pride, will grow more and more like the devils whom they adore and love. Her sanctified sons, by a strange and marvelous reversal, will realize the only acceptable meaning of the fallacious promise: "You shall be as gods, knowing good and evil," for the only authentic assimilation to divinity is that which grace confers on us. Moreover, grace alone initiates us into the knowledge of good and evil.

3

Second Divine Annunciation:

MYSTERY OF SORROW

I will put enmities between thee and the woman. . . . She shall crush thy head.

The Scene and Characters

ALL that has happened thus far has remained enclosed in the splendors of Eden. We are still in Eden, or rather at the gate of Eden, which is about to be closed forever. The cherubim is already approaching, armed with his flaming sword to defend the entrance. Before an angry and avenging God stand three beings: the serpent who tempted the woman; Adam, bent under the weight of his sin; and Eve, bowed down even more than Adam because she is more guilty. Fear and shame seize upon them the moment God approaches and they hide themselves in the midst of the trees of the garden. All their familiarity as contemplatives and friends of God has disappeared. They are guilty and they can no longer look at the face of God nor speak to Him heart to heart.

Now it is God and God alone who is the prophet. The man, who just now prophesied before his spouse, is stripped of this honor. By sin he lost something of his dignity as a prophet. He remains infallible in his faith but that faith remains more or less enveloped in silence.

There will still be men who will be prophets, but only after having been prepared for a long time by the Spirit of God and sanctified by trial and suffering. They must re-ascend the mountain and reconquer the summit. Then they can partially regain the gift of prophecy, but a prophecy which springs from the splendors of the state of innocence is ended, completely finished. Satan, the prophet of misery and malediction, has usurped both man's place and God's before woman. He wanted woman to usurp the word over man or, if not the word, at least the gesture which imposes and commands, and thus make him fall.

Eve lost everything. She was injured even in her faith, which is why woman's role in the Church will always be so different from man's. Even consecrated virgins do not preach, do not teach, although they officially chant the divine praises. A certain participation in the prophetic charism always remains possible to woman, but this does not determine the place she should occupy in the Church.

Who is now going to prophesy? The prophetic charism, which the first human couple have let fall by making themselves unworthy of it and which the serpent has polluted with his venom, must be picked up from the dust of the garden by God and returned all its former sanctity and purity by His using it Himself. Above Eden, whose splendors are paling, the sky darkens and thunder rolls. God speaks to pass sentence. Justice is done and it is both infinitely adorable and lovable because it is an attribute of

God; indeed, it is God. But it is not, it cannot be, the last word of God.

Justice is a relative attribute, that is, it supposes the existence of creatures. If God had not created, justice would not have existed formally, even if God had not created, His love would still be infinite. But the love that God showers on His creatures can bring nothing to God comparable to the love with which He loves Himself. Thus we understand why love everywhere surpasses justice; why, when terrible love appears, the terror of justice is effaced; why it was love especially which rent the Sacred Heart. That is also why the justice which is about to be expressed on God's lips is not the last word. It will meet mercy, be effaced before her, and almost disappear and melt away in her kiss.

If mercy did not shine forth brilliantly, God would not be fully revealed. He would only have been manifested to us superficially, so to speak. According to the powerful words of the *Benedictus*, if our God had not visited us because of the kindness of His mercy, the divine Orient would not be raised up for us.

Regenerated man lives by the prophetic words which are about to proceed from the mouth of God. Jesus is going to be revealed in Mary. God's ultimate revenge on the serpent through the woman is going to be proclaimed. The standard of the great King is advancing toward us and its victorious fanfare resounds and fills our ears and our hearts.

Unlike the serpent, God first addresses Himself to the man and not to the woman. In spite of his fault, man remains the chief, the head. God questions him so that he might confess his fault and repent. But man does not have the courage to confess and recognize himself as culpable. His sin prevents him from looking at God and turns him toward Eve, as sin will turn Eve toward the serpent.

Adam excuses himself. He renounces his privilege as

God's representative over woman by throwing the fault back on her. He obliges God to speak directly to Eve without passing through him. She in turn being no more than Satan's accomplice, throws the fault back on the serpent and thus obliges God to punish it before any other.

God therefore addresses Himself to Satan, the first and irreconcilable enemy hidden in the serpent. He says, "Because thou hast done this thing, thou art cursed. . . . I will put enmities between thee and the woman."

God's cause has just been conquered, but this defeat by the woman was itself preceded by another battle between angels, in which God's enemy was overwhelmed. To take his revenge, the devil used all his cunning and all his guile: he tempted man through woman. If he had addressed himself directly to man, let us dare to doubt that he would have succeeded. The devil is always broken against authority because authority fundamentally is God. Therefore he maneuvers obliquely, he does not attack from the front. He performs his work of pride and illusion and he succeeds in isolating the woman's mind in the act of her judgment and thus assures himself of victory.

The Woman and the Serpent

War had already existed in the angelic world, which it had ravaged and partly depopulated, and from there it came to win the earth. It was not God's doing but He is in the struggle. "I now will this war and I turn it against you, vile enemy and momentary conqueror. I establish it forever between you and woman. Woman served you as an instrument to conquer Me, the Lord! Now, out of this human being, injured in her very faith and nearly fallen to the depths of her nothingness, I shall fashion the arm of My omnipotence and through her I will triumph over you. It is she who shall crush your head."

Mary, daughter of Eve—and therefore Eve in Mary—will crush the head of pride by the miracle of her humility. Because she is immaculate, Mary need not make any effort: she crushes the cursed head without even seeming to perceive it. Look at the statues of Our Lady of Victory, which are always so beautiful even when they are not artistic, because they explain the Church's thought so well. The holy Virgin, hands joined, looks up to heaven and with her foot crushes the enemy's head without even looking at him. She is looking toward God. Mary is the only one who crushes the serpent's head and when we crush the serpent's head, it is in and through Mary. It would be too difficult for us to do by ourselves; she must come to our aid with all the strength of a mother.

We have mentioned the meeting of justice and mercy and have stated that the strength of justice kissed the gentleness of mercy. Something similar is evident here. Without purity, something is always lacking to strength. Other mothers are not pure enough; other virgins are not strong enough. Mary alone can give us everything in limitless measure, thanks to the privileges identified with her immaculate conception and her divine maternity. Only this Mother can act thus because she is immaculate and this immaculate one can act thus because she is a mother.

But we must not, by our inconsistencies and cowardice, prevent her from doing what she can and wishes to do for us; what, in the impulse of our fervor, we beg her to do in us. We must entrust ourselves completely to her. She wished that her children live more and more, that they be more and more her children and not the serpent's, for the war continues unceasingly between the woman's race and the serpent's race.

This is the struggle of life against death, of good against evil, of the Church against her enemies. But that is not all.

It is also a war against ourselves. The most deep-seated and dangerous character of this struggle would be misunderstood by considering it to be completely exterior to ourselves. It is also in us; indeed, it is principally in us.

We are the woman's race and the children of God but we are also in great measure the serpent's race and the children of pride. We ourselves are the most exposed and the most disputed section on the field of battle. The line of battle passes through the center of our hearts and each day, each hour, brings its deeds of war: advances, retreats, sometimes to the benefit of one race, sometimes to the other.

This holy war, which has gone on since the beginning of the world and will go on until its end, this war is still more terrible and more intense in the depths of hearts. At each instant, in the midst of the events which baffle us, we can see the head of the serpent rise up and hear its hiss. It is a war, a hand-to-hand combat between the race of the serpent, which is pride, and the race of Mary, which is humility.

It is not for us to make definitive judgments on others, to divide humanity into two distinct camps, to say "This is the serpent's son and that is Mary's son." No, the battle is much more complex than we think, and more intimate too. Mary's child is undoubtedly in us, but the venom of the serpent is also in us. In the measure that we retain the vestiges of original sin, the serpent's race survives in us. The saints complain, even until death, about being encumbered with these vestiges of sin. It is a source of great sorrow to them and it should also be for us to feel that we are not exclusively the children of Mary and our Lord but that we are too often the sons of pride whose king is Satan. The great Paschal duty, according to St. Paul, is to purify ourselves of the old leaven and become the unleavened bread of sincerity and truth.

What took place in Eden unceasingly continues to invade the immense theater of the world with alternating triumphs of sin and grace, of the serpent and the woman. Whenever self-love gains the upper hand in our actions, that self-love which always insinuates itself everywhere, it is a new victory for the serpent, added to so many others. Moreover, like the serpent itself, self-love becomes more dangerous in the measure that it is more hidden; rather, it is truly dangerous only in the measure in which it is hidden. What must we do as soon as we take cognizance of it? We must recall the divine word, a word of menace for the adversary and a word of comfort and promise for us: "She shall crush thy head." Contemplate the ray of hope which springs from the morning star and invoke the aid of Mary. *"Respice stellam, voca Mariam!"*

Refuge of Sinners and Help of Christians

Too many good Christians do not give to the devotion to Mary all its nobility, all its grandeur, nor even, I would say, all its seriousness. They do not understand sufficiently the role of Mary as refuge of sinners and help of Christians. Practically speaking, if we would let her intervene more in our education as soldiers of God, if we would let her form us according to her own methods, we would make greater and more rapid progress. But because we are afraid of the struggle, a necessary and indispensable condition for victory, we fear the strength of our Mother who wants to conquer us, and we fear her because we do not yet love her enough.

Our love must grow and, like perfect charity, must put that fear to flight. Let us rid ourselves of the fear of belonging to Mary and of the cowardice of our self-love, which senses that it must die and hence instinctively flees the crushing and merciful pressure of her virginal foot. Our ego is a sort of mask behind which our self-love tries to hide. We do not abandon ourselves completely to the divine Mother, and yet that is the very definition of true devotion toward her.

We love her and undoubtedly we want to love her more, but our love has not yet reached the point where we place everything in Mary's hands and at her feet. Yet there can be salvation only in the complete abandonment to her who is all wisdom and all love. That is why we need so many purifications and sufferings, so many very hard "purgatories," which we would so easily avoid by allowing the holy Virgin to accomplish in us all that she wishes.

As for the other purgatories which it is impossible or harmful for us to avoid, they are good since they are necessary and she will teach us how to accept them and how to profit from them. Let us call to mind what St. Louis Montfort dared to say: "When we belong to the Blessed Virgin in so completely exceptional a manner that we are absorbed and lost in Mary, to the point that we become, so to speak, immaculate, it can happen that some of the most terrible trials of the spiritual life may be softened and we may even be dispensed from them." This is a strange and marvelous privilege that nothing can prevent us from ardently pursuing and from soliciting with love and humility.

If we let Mary act, we do not need those formidable interior wounds to detach ourselves from self-love since, very gently, her hands will reach out to us and she will take us to her heart. Looking toward heaven and holding us pressed against her, she will crush the serpent's head with her foot. The divine Mother has the habit of these liberating operations which are so gentle and yet so strong. We shall acquire this habit ourselves in contact with her and we will no longer desire nor need any other ramparts or any other refuges.

This doctrine is so extremely simple. We know in advance what the Blessed Virgin wills. If we let her do what she wills, she will do it immediately. It is the fault of our negligence if things drag on for a long time. She wants to do things quickly and well. We are the ones to make it long and mediocre. But in order that everything be accomplished and quickly, we must be her little children to the extent that we are absorbed in her and belong to none other but the race of the woman to whom victory was promised. As Mother of each of us, the true Eve crushes the serpent's head in each one of us. This office is totally maternal since it consists in giving life to us again by giving death to our enemy, and this death of the enemy liberates and vivifies us.

We are now fully informed, and we have found an incomparable arm. It is a question of being little children of the Blessed Virgin, as the great saints have been known to be. These giants of sanctity, who crush us by their stature, these men so powerful because they were lost in her, were of the race of the woman who crushed the serpent's head. Like them we have but to give ourselves completely to Mary. The serpent's great ruse will always be to diminish this gift and this abandonment and, if he can manage it, to separate us from her.

This is the maneuver which has succeeded with so many heretics. They are far from the Church in the measure that they are far from Mary. The degree of their error in heresy is commensurate with the degree of their misunderstanding of the mysteries and privileges of Mary. And yet, without a clear and intact notion of these mysteries and privileges, the history of the world becomes unintelligible, since it is but the history of the great war of enmities imposed by God.

Imagine, if you can, God standing in all the formidable apparel of His anger and justice before these three beings:

the serpent, the instrument of the temptation, now crawl-
ing in the dust, and his two victims. Eve, head lowered, is
crushed under the weight of her fault. Who will give back
to her the joyous attitude of her innocence totally surrendered to the perspectives of Heaven? The *Stabat* of Calvary
will be Eve's definitive reparation in Mary. Of the two
guilty spouses, God henceforth seizes upon the more guilty
and the more humbled for the struggle and the victory.

Through Adam this victory would have been less beautiful. God chose the one who descended the lowest. This is
one if the laws of His government, proclaimed by St. Paul.
It is the woman who will crush the serpent's head. If man
intervenes in the struggle (and certainly he will intervene),
it will be as a member of the race of the woman.

I insist on these points. They are of primary importance
if one wants to understand the economy of the Redemption
and woman's role and fate in the battle. With the perfect
Christian, with the saints of the Church, note the militant
(I was about to say military) conduct: Always forward!

Queen of the Angels

The angel intervenes in this war by attaching himself to
the race of the woman as an instrument of the Redeemer
who, as regards His human origin, is of the human race only
through the woman. To clarify this, let us say a word on the
hierarchical relations which are established between Mary
and Michael during the struggle. Michael is a warrior archangel, armored with steel from head to foot, as our ancestors
loved to represent him. Now he must place himself under
the orders of the one appointed by God to be the great
Commander-in-chief and Queen.

In the first battle among the angels, with heaven as a
battleground, Michael, prince of the celestial armies, was
commander-in-chief. Mary intervened only in a somewhat

objective fashion, by reason of the mystery of the Incarnation which was proposed to the faith of the angels, according to the doctrine of St. Augustine. It is Michael who, in that first encounter, crushed the dragon's head. However, note carefully that in all his pictures you will see him using much more effort than Mary will use. In his stroke of the lance he seems to display all his strength; his gesture is less facile than that of the virginal foot. But the fact remains that he also combats, dominates, crushes.

The first battle, totally celestial, totally spiritual, is continued in the second, the terrestrial battle, in which flesh and blood have their great part. These two battles are mingled and inextricably entangled. But will there be competition here? What will the ultimate hierarchy be? How will the angelic authority and the virginal authority be subordinated to each other?

In human affairs it is not easy to bring leaders into accord. In war, more than anywhere else, the greatest disasters often have no other cause than the lack of agreement between leaders. One does not want to be placed below the other or one does so only with great difficulty. In the choirs of angels, Michael prevailed. To his conquering cry—which is none other than his own name—rallied, as around a standard, all those who did not yield to the tempter's voice.

But now the enmities are between the race of the woman and the race of the serpent. God has willed it thus according to the words of Scripture. In the midst of these enmities the angels are called upon as marvelous allies. With great joy they fly to that appeal and they exhaust in our service all the strength of their devotion and all the sweetness of their tenderness. They are great kings in the order of nature and of grace, but they reign even more truly when they accept the sweet domination and sovereignty of Mary by acclaiming her Queen.

Angels are the eldest members of the spiritual family of the Father who is in heaven. In every family the greatest happiness of the older ones consists in devoting themselves to the little ones. They must even be given charge of them, otherwise there would be no way of giving proof of loving one another. The angels are therefore at our service. At their head goes Michael, cutting and thrusting, under Mary's orders, under her gentle but firm command.

Indeed she does crush the head of the serpent in us all and through us all, this immense "us" of the angelic and human communion. This reality must be clearly seen, in order to understand the divine will, to grasp in all its fullness and precision the plan which it imposes and the means chosen by God to bring about the triumph of His reign. The fact which dominates everything is that neither man nor angel nor archangel can conquer the serpent except in Mary and through Mary.

That there is devotion and a marvelous submission of Michael and his angels toward their Queen is proclaimed by many private revelations. With an incomparable fervor Michael, the celestial conqueror, abandons himself completely and humbly to the one who now commands and directs the vicissitudes of the struggle unfolded here below through the centuries until the end of the world.

God Speaks

In Eden, after addressing the serpent, God speaks to the conquered woman. Sin abounded in her and her sufferings will be multiplied relative to the beings to whom she is ordained: her children and husband. As regards her children, physical sufferings will accompany her maternity. "Thou shalt bring forth children." This should be in joy, since she was made for that, a joy which nature so lavishly dispenses everywhere when things follow a natural course.

But Eve will bring forth in sorrow. Deceived by the mirage of glory, she dreamed that she would bring forth her children joyously into a divine life, but she will bring them forth sorrowfully into a life of fallen humanity from which they will be raised only with difficulty and by the grace of Christ.

As regards her husband, her sufferings will be principally moral. Instead of the sweet yoke to which we have referred, without domination on the part of either, instead of that social union in which everything was so perfectly harmonized, there will be a penal domination which easily becomes egotistical and brutal. This domination is hard when the husband makes it weigh on the wife but it is worse yet when the wife usurps the husband's place; when she wants to dominate and actually succeeds in dominating him.

Deceived by the serpent, woman wanted to deceive man but she will be deceived by him. "Thou shalt be under thy husband's power and he shall have dominion over thee." Accomplice and slave of the serpent, she will become man's slave and sometimes his accomplice in sin. She will be used, she will be abused, without thought of her good, for mere utility or pleasure. Her head will be crushed, like the serpent's, but by man's contemptuous heel.

If she accepts this heavy subjection with repentance and the love of God, she will be able to profit from it and disengage herself little by little from Satan's slavery. Her strength will be in her humble silence and her ardent hope in God. Silence is at one and the same time the punishment and the refuge of her who allows herself to be deceived.

After speaking to Eve, God addresses Himself to Adam. He does not want to curse man nor does He want to curse the earth itself, but note that He curses the earth in the work of man. In other words, in this work, by this work, an indefinable curse will rise up from the bowels of the earth.

In the measure that science advances, and God knows with what staggering rapidity it does advance, the repercussion of this curse weighs more and more heavily on the earth. The very progress of science more and more crushes all things in man and around him. The earth is cursed in man's work as the woman is punished in the work of the flesh. The more humanity extends and multiplies, the more the consequences of this punishment of woman will extend and multiply. The more man's work on earth is intensified and perfected, the more the curse of the earth in man's work will be developed.

This last prophecy is much more universal than the prophecy addressed to Eve, although it is connected with it and even results from it in a certain way, just as man's sin comes from woman's. But Adam is the head of the physical universe as well as of the human race. Also, it is clearly specified that it is not only in his work but because of him that the earth is cursed. The earth, this sweet mother which has become such a hard stepmother, will no longer produce what is necessary for man's subsistence without work. "With labor and toil shalt thou eat thereof all the days of thy life. Thorns and thistles shall it bring forth to thee; and thou shalt eat the herbs of the earth. In the sweat of thy face shalt thou eat bread till thou return to the earth, out of which thou wast taken; for dust thou art and to dust thou shalt return." Coming forth, you will return there after having stripped its entrails by means of stubborn work, entrails which are so fruitful when they shower upon you what is not useful to you, and so miserly in apportioning the bread necessary for your everyday life. This will be the struggle for life with the earth and all earthly things. The earth will have the last word and will devour everything, work and workers. The furrow receives the grain but it awaits the sower.

Earth-Bound Man

The Creator had turned the face of Adam, the contemplative, toward heaven and He commanded him to keep his eyes and his face lifted up. But now Adam no longer turns toward heaven like the angels, but toward the earth like the animals.

The anguishes and cares of the active life henceforth become man's master and tend to usurp all. What efforts there are in him and around him to find again the primacy of the contemplative life. It will be like a discovery which always must be re-made. Man's heart and head always give way too easily to the fatal weight which brings his operation down to the earth, which is cursed in that same operation. But the rediscovery of the *sursum corda et ora* will not be too much for the initiatives of divine grace which come to the aid of the weaknesses of human sense and mind.

The exile of the sons of Eve thus begins, full of moans and tears, but filled with marvelous consolations. The way to the tree of life is barred by the cherubim's flaming sword but recourse to the true Mother of the living to whom we call with all the cries of our misery is accessible to all. Mary alone can bring us to see the flower and the blessed fruit which rise from the root of Jesse to replace those of the tree of life after this exile.

The history of woman and the vicissitudes of this history are explained by the triple ordination which sums up this first part of our work. First, by virtue of the institution of her nature, woman in the state of innocence is completely ordained to the husband. Then, by sin, she obeys the command of the serpent as his accomplice and his instrument. Finally, she is punished by God's justice and ordained by His mercy to become the instrument of the victories of redemption.

PART TWO

THE NEW ALLIANCE

4

First Divine Annunciation:

MYSTERY OF JOY

Behold thou shalt conceive in thy womb and shalt bring forth a son. . . . He shall be great and shall be called the Son of the Most High.

HERE again, as in Eden, we begin with a mystery of pure joy, the pure joy of the first two mysteries of the Rosary, which comprise the Annunciation *par excellence* and the *Magnificat.* Similarly, Simeon's words "announce" the mystery of sorrow and death, which will be realized on Calvary. But between these mysteries of joy and sorrow is again inserted the mystery of iniquity. The developments of these mysteries in and through human destinies are "announced" in the deeds and words of Jesus' temptation.

The Annunciation to Mary

St. Thomas gives four reasons why it was necessary that what was to be accomplished in Mary should be announced to her.[1] "Necessary" does not mean that without the Annunciation the Incarnation would have been impossible, but that certain laws or dispositions arranged by divine wisdom would not have been respected or would not have been sufficiently respected. By employing the term "necessary," St. Thomas invites us to meditate on these four reasons with great care. We shall endeavor to do so both in their particular application to the first joyful mystery and in their general import as they clarify the meaning of our present work on the various annunciations.

The first reason indicates the two modes of union between Jesus and His Mother, their reciprocal agreement, and the manner in which a hierachy is established between them. To maintain perfect order it was necessary that Mary's mind be instructed before she conceived in her body. According to the admirable words of St. Augustine: "The blessedness of the Mother of God is greater by perceiving the faith than by conceiving flesh."

This antithesis brings out the antithesis that the Gospel itself had proposed between the blessedness of the womb which had borne Christ, a blessedness later proclaimed by a woman in the midst of the crowd, and the still greater blessedness of those who hear and keep the word of God, which Mary always did more than anyone.

Long before this crowd and this woman, Elizabeth's voice was raised, in the intimate scene of the Visitation, to magnify the blessedness of Mary's faith. This *magnificat* of Elizabeth was like a prelude to Mary's *Magnificat*. In Mary, all the happy consequences of what the Lord had said to her overflow from her faith in these words of the Lord. Beatitudes flow from the beatitude of her faith. This faith is therefore not only blessed but more blessed. We just noted the same word in St. Augustine. The holy Doctor goes so

[1] *Summa theol.*, IIIa, q. 30, a. 1.

78

far as to add that the nearness of Mary's maternity would have been of no avail, had she not carried Christ in her heart, a greater happiness than carrying Him in her body.

During our entire spiritual life let us be penetrated by this teaching. We have such a great need of knowing that this beatitude of faith, so often unconscious, is greater than all the other beatitudes! We so need to learn that only charity is preferred to it. Let us dare to say of it what we say of the very objects of faith: it is not apparent.

Faith alone can introduce us into the mysteries of divine works, into the abyss of eternal secrets. God does nothing without first announcing it to his prophets, as one of them has proclaimed. But what God thus unveils to His instruments He later imposes, at least in part, on the faith of other men. Everything that is viable and fruitful must spend an obscure period in the womb of faith, just as the child is born to light only after a long stay in the night of the maternal womb. The *fiat lux* of birth bursts forth from these oppressive accumulations of darkness. *Ex tenebris lumen.*

To the child hidden in his mother's womb, certain revelations are made, often more excellent and more universal than many others, as the revelation made to John the Baptist, which determined his austere and glorious destiny. Let us see in it the symbol of what takes place for the happy prisoners of faith. It is the supreme application of the great law posed by the Gospel: You have revealed it to the little ones. Perhaps we could thus extend St. Paul's *non apparentium* from the objects of faith to its subjects themselves.

The third reason given by St. Thomas is that the Annunciation was necessary so that Mary could present to God the voluntary offering of her fidelity and obedience. The *Ecce ancilla Domini* explains all the enthusiasm and promptness of that offering. This ought also to be the promptness of our own spirit as Mary's sons and daughters. In spite of the infirmities of a flesh which is not immaculate, God awaits that impulse in order to intervene and arrive unexpectedly within us with all the powerful promptness of the Holy Spirit.

God could scarcely obtain this promptness of our spirit in the service of His own Spirit without the burst of an annunciation.

To this third reason a fourth can be added: The consent of the Blessed Virgin represented the consent of the entire human nature at the Incarnation, which was almost a kind of spiritual marriage between this nature and the Son of God. The annunciation by the angel came to solicit this consent.

Divine annunciations are often the prelude and the preface of new unions with the Lord; they are the light which shines in the eyes of our intellect and prepares for infusions of grace into our heart. So Cajetan remarks that the gentle dispositions of divine providence intervene here, for it is proper to our double nature that what reaches to the flesh should be preceded by what takes place in the spirit. Even purely natural conceptions presuppose acts of the spiritual faculties by which one agrees to proceed to the act of generation.

Mary also had to be informed of this ineffable conception through the operation of the Holy Spirit, by an annunciation which permitted her to conceive the mystery spiritually before it was accomplished in her virginal flesh. It was imperative that the great law which requires that a kind of conception by the heart and in the heart precede the other should be realized more wonderfully for this unparalleled Mother than for all others.

The Economy of the Divine Annunciations

The second reason given by St. Thomas introduces us to a circle of ideas that must be examined apart. That is why we have taken the liberty to invert the order of these reasons.

Mary, instructed by that annunciation on the ineffable mystery which was accomplished in her, becomes by that fact its most certain and most assured witness. Here again let us listen to Cajetan. "This annunciation, coming first, before everything else, caused in Mary a certitude of the mystery much greater than if she had not been instructed or had been instructed at a later time. The annunciation made her attentive to the initial realization or *actum primum* of this mystery. She would not have been attentive or at least not to such a degree if it had not previously been announced to her. Greater attention and greater elevation of spirit augment certitude." What has not been announced surprises us too much or not enough, and in both cases there is danger that our reactions and responses may be insufficient or clumsy.

But the mysterious interventions are much too spiritual not to escape us, at least in part. Therefore, except in cases where for some reason or another, God prefers to reserve for Himself alone the secret of His operations, it is good for us that everything should be preceded by an announcement made through our senses, especially our external senses on which human certitude is founded. That is why it is desirable that the most important annunciations rely not on imaginative visions or dreams, as St. John Chrysostom has noted, but the testimony of the external senses. That is also why St. Thomas teaches that the vision of Gabriel was corporeal.[2] Let us note carefully his third

[2] *Summa theol.*, IIIa, q. 30, a. 3.

reason: The certitude of that which was announced was increased by it. What is placed before our eyes is perceived in a more certain manner that what we merely imagine. Besides, Mary not only saw the bodily vision but at the same time was favored with a totally spiritual illumination.[3] This is the perfect case. There is imperfection as soon as one of these elements is lacking.

The basis of the entire doctrine appears in the response to the second objection: The principle of human knowledge is the external senses; in them therefore we find the maximum certitude. In other words, the beginnings of knowledge must always be more certain than all the rest. Joseph, to whom the angel appeared in a dream, was favored with an apparition less excellent than the apparition of Gabriel to Mary by the very fact that it occurred in a dream. This must be noted with the greatest care if we wish to appreciate the authentic hierarchy of these divine annunciations.

Typical Cases of Annunciations

A few words may be said about the hierarchies to which we have alluded. In Mary's case—the perfect case, we have said—human knowledge finds its amplitude and normal development. It attains the two extremities of its domain, the external senses at the base and intellectual splendor at the summit, a splendor which, some would say, is a reflection of the beatific vision.

In direct contrast, God sometimes shrouds His action in the darkness of the midnight of faith. Actually there is no annunciation. Little by little a certain epiphany of the divine work will emerge from this purifying and meritorious darkness. To make us worthy or to increase merit in us, God permits the sorrowful captivity of this obscure night.

[3] *Ibid.*, ad 1um.

But at first there is a kind of ignorance and sometimes even a misunderstanding of the beginnings of the mystery that God wishes to effect in the soul. During this period the fundamental virtues of faith and humility are practiced but in a manner very different from that which Mary offers us as a model in the Annunciation.

St. Joseph's case is mixed. He, too, had an annunciation but it did not precede, as did Mary's, the accomplishment of the mystery of the Incarnation. It allowed him the merit of the anguish which tortured his heart before the liberating words were spoken: "Joseph, son of David, fear not to take unto thee Mary thy wife."

The Annunciation and Mary's Faith

Let us now consider one of the objections which St. Thomas raises against the necessity of the Annunciation.[4] He says that when one possesses certitude concerning certain truths of faith, there is no need for further instruction. This formula would bring us to the *Sola fides sufficit* of the *Pange Lingua:* Faith alone suffices. But, the objection continues, Mary did possess faith in the mystery of the Incarnation. Certainly she possessed it, since this faith is necessary to all and the state of salvation cannot be attained without it, according to the Apostle's words: God's justice is found only through faith in Jesus Christ. Therefore, Mary did not need to be instructed in it and above all not by an angel. For her, proclaimed blessed in faith by Elizabeth, faith alone sufficed.

Let us consider this syllogism as it has just been presented. Much could be said of its major premise. To confine ourselves to theological precisions which have been made explicit during the course of centuries, let us merely note that if they are contained in the principles of faith,

[4] *Summa theol.,* IIIa., q. 30, a. 1.

it is only virtually, and faith alone does not suffice to free them. Instruction is necessary in this case.

Without entering into these considerations or similar ones, St. Thomas confines himself to answering the objection which touches the case of the Blessed Virgin. She believed explicitly, he tells us, in the mystery of the Incarnation. Her faith was full and overflowing, but her humility was as great as her faith. This humility did not permit her to be raised to such lofty thoughts concerning her own person. It was therefore necessary that she be instructed on this point. Faith and humility are the two fundamental virtues. We see them oppose each other here and then become perfectly harmonized and marvelously completed. Faith lavishes its revelations on those who have become children through humility.

According to Cajetan, we must distinguish between faith in the mystery of the future Incarnation, absolutely speaking, and faith in this mystery as it was to be accomplished in Mary and through Mary. The Blessed Virgin had explicit faith in the Incarnation but she did not have explicit faith in the Incarnation as it was to be accomplished through herself.

There are two reasons for this. The first was common to all before the mystery was accomplished in Mary. It had not yet been promulgated in a clear fashion that the Incarnation would be effected through Mary. The second reason is peculiar to Mary and is derived from her incomparable humility, which prevented such thoughts. As St. Luke says: *Cogitabat qualis esset ista salutatio.* Because of her humble thoughts, Mary wondered what the angelic salutation could be, since it corresponded so little with the opinion she had formed of herself or, rather, was so contradictory to it.

In like manner, in their humility certain cherished souls who received instructions and divine announcements were able to cry out with Mary: "He that is mighty hath done great things to me." The grandeur of these things has its explanation solely in the omnipotence of Him who made them and certainly not in the omnipotence of those who received them.

Divine announcements often take us at our word. David was indignant against a crime similar to his own forgotten crime, and the prophet recalled it to him by saying: "You are this man." Mary believed with all her heart in the annunciation of another prophet: "Behold a virgin shall conceive and bring forth a son." She believes now with all her heart in the angel's annunciation, complimentary to that of the prophet: "You are this virgin." The angel Gabriel had been sent to the Virgin to tell her this word of infinite sweetness as the prophet Nathan had been sent to David the sinner to speak the word of anger to him.

Let us now consider the third objection raised by St. Thomas. Just as Mary conceived Christ corporeally, so every sanctified soul conceives Him spiritually. This analogy is quite in line with the Apostle's doctrine: "My little children, of whom I am in labor again, until Christ be formed in you." If Christ is formed little by little in souls it means that He has begun to be conceived in them. But this spiritual conception is not announced to souls. Therefore, neither was it necessary that Christ's physical conception be announced to Mary.

The answer given by St. Thomas enlightens the entire spiritual world, and particularly the major role that preaching plays. It is not true, says St. Thomas, that spiritual conception is not announced to souls. This conception is made by faith and is announced by the preaching of faith which precedes it, presupposing that the word of God is heard. *Fides ex auditu, auditus autem per verbum Christi.*

The preacher is like the mediator, the angel, and the

priest, about whom we shall speak. Instruments that we are, and more or less unconscious ones, we must give the most docile attention to the least indications that may be revealed to us under various forms of the mystery and sacrament of preaching which is confided to us. It is not unusual that we are tempted to disregard or we do not sufficiently appreciate the benefit of a sermon because of defects in the instrument, without realizing that these very defects can test and greatly augment our faith.

Let us note with St. Thomas upon what certitude depends. It does not depend, as certain Protestants would hold, on a more or less conscious subjective state, but on the objects of faith revealed by God and proposed by the Church. Man does not know with certitude, at least not with absolute certitude, that he possesses grace, but he does know that the faith that he receives is truth itself.

In somewhat the same way Mary's faith depended on the mystery of the Incarnation. Furthermore, it was by means of the Annunciation that she had to receive the knowledge that she would be the privileged one and the Mother. From that time it was a matter of faith for her and for us.

It is not without interest to point out this analogy with the economy of our own faith. It depends on objective realities which have been revealed and not on the subjective faith that we are actually privileged to be in the state of grace, unless we receive personal revelation to give us subjective certitude. Calvin's error consisted in placing this exception, which is foreign to common faith, in the essential object of every act of the virtue of faith. But there is an immense difference between Mary's case and ours: Belief in her divine maternity is an article of faith for all, whereas a private revelation as such is an article of faith only to the one who receives it.

The Order of Divine Annunciations

The Annunciation *par excellence* puts all other annunciations in a clear light. St. Thomas says that divine annunciations normally come to men by means of angels, who are mediators between God and men. This is the simplest and most elementary of all the orderings of divine providence, since it depends on the hierarchy of natures which is itself the most fundamental.

Likewise, divine annunciations will come to woman through man, who is the head of woman. At least, man is the one who holds the authority as to judgment. We may add that other annunciations will come to souls through the priest, the mediator between God and souls by virtue of his priesthood.

Let us attentively consider these three mediations. We have seen how and why, in Eden's first prophecy—"This . . . is . . . flesh of my flesh"—the prophet is Adam himself, the first spouse. In the prophecy of malediction, addressed to the serpent, the prophet is none other than the God of anger and justice, crushing the serpent into the dust and raising up the guilty woman in order to fashion from her the instrument of future mercy. Having listened to the rebellious angel who was hidden in the serpent, the woman was unworthy of the good angel's mediation and even of all mediation. Angelic mediation is re-established in Mary, thanks to the merit of her faith and her humility.

Here again we are confronted with great laws which we must note and ponder with great care. Restorative interventions of a moral order and sometimes even of a physical order re-establish the currents of grace which have been interrupted by grave faults. They cause the supernatural sap, held back by winters which ravaged and seemed to destroy everything, to flow forth again and even to unfold in flower. These are the springtimes, the renascences, the resurrections, the joyous Easters, warm and blooming after the glacial rigors of justice.

To Eve, the sinner, fallen and separated from God, comes the message through Mary, the friend, the spouse, the mother: "Rise and come. You, Eve, made the serpent's slave, will through Mary be crowned queen of the world."

Thus we have a kind of a triptych formed by the announcers. In Eden, man alone and then God alone; in the Eden of Nazareth, the angel, the mediator between the divine and the human. The angel comes to fill the void formed by sin, which separates God from woman. Man, a sinner himself, remains apart. Thanks to an immaculate woman, everything is now complete and harmonious, and the Man-God can come. All this is fitting in a supreme degree of fitness. It was fitting in any event that the announcer of the definitive mystery should be neither the man of the nuptials of Eden, so quickly interrupted by sin, nor God aroused for an instant to the severity of anger and then quickly disarmed by mercy. It was fitting that the sweet order of divine providence should resume its course in and through Mary.

The first reason for the annunciation to Mary by the angel, will therefore be that ordering by virtue of which divine things come to men though the mediation of the angels. Mary, like Jesus, here follows the common order for which both will be taken as models. It is the great law which explains the whole economy of the Gospel and the whole genre of life.

Spouse of the Holy Spirit and of Joseph

Angelic mediation is common to all human beings, but there is one which is more proper to virgins because of a marvelous and intimate affinity, a kind of kinship between the life of the pure spirit and the life led in the flesh as if the flesh did not exist. "That life," says St. Jerome, "is no longer terrestrial; it is entirely celestial." Therefore it is fitting that the angel be sent to the Virgin.

But if the common order ordains that divine things be revealed to men by angels, it also ordains that they be communicated to woman by man. In this connection St. Paul invokes the practice and tradition of the Church: "As also I teach in all the churches of the saints. Let women keep silence in the churches. . . . But if they would learn anything, let them ask their husbands at home."

Therefore, Mary should have been instructed in the mystery of the Incarnation, not by an angel but by a man, especially since, according to St. Matthew, an annunciation of this mystery by an angel would be accorded to Joseph, her spouse. The normal order would have been that the annunciation come from the angel to man, then from the man to the woman, or at any rate that the annunciation made to the wife be subordinated to the annunciation made to the husband. Mary was the wife and therefore everything should have come to her through the husband, as everything came to Eve through Adam. Man is the head of the woman and everything ought to come from the head to whatever is placed under its influence and its domination. We reproach Eve for being detached and separated from Adam for the capital act of judgment. (We say *capital* with a purpose, meaning what originates very specially from the head.)

Let it not be said that this is a question of an economy reserved to the state of innocence. Woman's dependence on man is based on nature and therefore will be found in all the states that nature can assume. The fallen state merely increased this dependence. Moreover, to emphasize this increased dependence it was among the penalties which weigh on woman from the commission of the first sin: "You will be under the power of man." Careful attention must be given to the response made by St. Thomas, who follows the teaching of St. Augustine.

Let us not forget that Mary is first of all a mother and a virgin, and that in the order of dignity she is so before being Joseph's spouse. She is the spouse of the Holy Spirit, through whose operation she received Christ in her most pure womb. Not only is Mary the Mother of God before being Joseph's spouse, she is also Mother of all humanity, whose head is Christ. From these points of view, Joseph can be considered the head of his spouse only so far as she is a member of the Holy Family and Mother of another member, the Divine Infant. It is only by reason of membership in a family that both of them depend on the one who, as in all families, is the chief and the head.

This whole order is marvelously respected by the angels themselves. Authority resides in Joseph according to the common order of human families. We could perhaps say that temporal matters are placed under his power and left to his ordering. This domain is confided to him. But beyond this the exception begins, in virtue of which Mary, by reason of her divine maternity, is immediately attached to the Holy Spirit, depends only on Him, and is henceforth under His power and the shadow of the virtue of the Most High.

Here the consequences and evils of sin disappear before the privilege of the Immaculate One, the unique Mother, the Mother of the Unique. Her maternities and her conceptions have not been multiplied. She is not under man's power. Words of anger and justice are not for her. That is why she should not be instructed in the mystery of the Incarnation through man's mediation but through the mediation of an angel. That is also why she was instructed in it earlier than Joseph, for she was to conceive beforehand. Joseph was informed after his wife's virginal conception.

On the contrary, whatever concerns the goings and comings of the Holy Family is announced to Joseph first, and sometimes to Joseph alone. Mary is, as it were, subordinate to him in this temporal order. But when it is a question of spiritual things, of things of the Holy Spirit—Mary's divine Spouse—the Spirit comes and overshadows her first of all and alone. Whatever spiritual marvels superabound in Joseph originate and overflow from Mary's fullness and are therefore subordinate to that fullness.

Mary is Mother of a Son who is God and man. She is the spouse of a divine Person, the Holy Spirit. She also has a human spouse, Joseph. Placed as it were between these two spouses, she exercises her role as mediatrix between one and the other in a very special way. We must not be surprised to note here a sort of reversal of the common order according to which St. Thomas told us that divine things are communicated to woman by man. Through Mary, the things of the Holy Spirit are communicated or deferred to Joseph. Therefore it was not necessary that the common order be conserved in its entirety.

Let us note to what extent Joseph was Mary's first spiritual child, if it is correct to define "spiritual child" as one who receives from someone else the things of the Holy Spirit. At any rate, we see to what extent the annunciation to Joseph was subordinate to the annunciation made to Mary.

Mary and the Common Law

The common order is followed and respected wherever it should be followed and respected. Let us clearly distinguish here what pertains to Joseph and what pertains to Mary. There is Joseph's portion; what goes to Joseph, what comes from Joseph, what we should receive from him. That is why we say: "Go to Joseph." Then there is Mary's portion; the wholly spiritual part where she is in immediate contact with the Spirit, her Spouse, and can alone teach us the wonders which had been announced only to her. In these things we must go to Mary and only to her. Here we can only repeat St. Bernard's words: *Respice stellam, voca Mariam*. In the temporal order, beginning with the members of the Holy Family, obedience and submission are due to Joseph, who alone is to receive from the angel the directives which save the life of Jesus and permit the divine work to be accomplished according to eternal designs. We could almost dare to say that in the Holy Family, so far as it is holy, everything depends on Mary; so far as it is a family, an earthly family, everything depends on Joseph.

Certain analogies are helpful here. By examining the words "spiritual" and "temporal" we are reminded of difficult questions concerning the relationship between Church and State. We could speak of the obedience of the children of the Church and of the obedience of the Church itself to the decisions of temporal power in its proper domain, and of the obedience that the Church has the right to exact from all in spiritual matters.

Let us be wary of other analogies which are difficult to handle and could lead to dangerous sophisms. This caution has been advised in regard to any analogy between the relations of Adam and Eve in Eden and those of spouses of the present time, a situation created by the sin of our first parents and made more serious by our own sins. This analogy could lead us to all kinds of usurpations in the spiritual domain on the part of the husband. Mary is perfectly subject to the human spouse for temporal things, perfectly subject to the divine Spouse for all things, and immediately for the things of the Spirit. She appears to us as the incomparable model of the Christian wife, docilely submitting to her husband in all that regards the temporal and, for the things of above, to the Holy Spirit Himself and to those who represent Him.

For other reasons the analogy between the spouses of Eden and those of Nazareth could be deceptive in certain respects. Here it is no longer a question of sin but of sanctity; the sanctity of the state of innocence and, much greater still, the sanctity of Mary and Joseph. But these two sanctities are as widely different as are the two divine vocations of which they are the response and the development.

Above all, Mary is a mother and a virgin before being Joseph's wife because she is the virginal Mother of God. Her virginity is ordained to her divine maternity. Her virginity is not, like Eve's, ordained purely and simply to the human spouse in the same way that Eve's maternity depends entirely on the human spouse. There is therefore a supreme reason for dispensing Mary from the common order of earthly espousals. Her dignity, to use the term St. Thomas used, dispenses her from the *ordo per virum* but it is not seen how it should dispense her from the *ordo per angelum.*[5] The status of the present life, which she shares fully with us, maintains for her the subordination of human nature to angelic nature. That is why in the present case God makes use of the intervention of His celestial messenger.

It is fitting that other wives seek direction from their husbands, as St. Paul said. Certain lights shall thus come to them but not all lights as in Eden. We have seen that the role of priest, instrument of the Holy Spirit, must be reserved for the direction of souls. For the direction of the family as such, the husband has the grace of his state. This

[5] *Summa theol.,* IIIa, q. 30, a. 2, ad 1um.

is the reason why some annunciations were made directly and immediately to Joseph in spite of the supereminent character of the annunciation made to Mary.

The three annunciations described at the beginning of the New Testament (to Zachary, to Mary, and to Joseph) respect the order of angelic mediation. Gabriel is named in connection with the first two annunciations, Zachary's and Mary's, but in Joseph's case only an angel is mentioned. Is it Gabriel again? St. Thomas, following St. Augustine, affirms it in his *Commentary* on St. Matthew: "Any other angel could not have defended the virginity of Mary as well as he who had been so intimate a witness." [6] As the prophet's words had carried pardon to the repentant David, so Mary, daughter of David, was delivered by Gabriel, "the angel of the Savior," who intervenes in her favor. We can see in Gabriel, remarks St. Thomas, that angel described in the Psalm, sent to "envelop" those who fear the Lord and to deliver Mary from infamy and not to abandon Joseph in his trouble.

Joseph is silent with a great perpetual silence. Mary and Joseph are silent with one another, awaiting the divine decisions and consolations. The revelation made by the angel to Joseph is independent of any that Mary could have made to him. Mary, Mother of the Word, speaks to Gabriel as she will sing before Elizabeth.

For the purpose of clarifying all Mariology, let us keep this Augustinian and Thomistic principle in mind: Mary was exempt from certain general laws: tedious multiplication of maternities, domination by a tyrannical husband, and the order which imposes women to be instructed by men. But she is more subject to certain other laws, for example, those on the instruction of human beings by angels. "Great prudence is therefore imposed on doctors," says

[6] St. Augustine, *In sermon. de Nativ.*, XIV.

Cajetan, "to distinguish carefully the various reasons given and to know in what matters Mary shares our subjections and dependence and in what matters she is exempt."

But even when she is exempt and dispensed from certain common laws, Mary still finds the means of being a model for those who, for some reason or another, enjoy exemption or dispensation. For they must always carefully distinguish the limits of this exemption, the cases where it is valid and those where it is expedient to return to common rules. This return must be dear to virtuous hearts whose true country is obedience and who, though close to its strict frontiers, always feel somewhat exiled and out of their element.

Joseph's Anguish and Mary's Faith

We have just cited St. Thomas' *Commentary* on the Gospel according to St. Matthew. There we find, in the first chapter, a comparison between the annunciation made to Mary and the one made to Joseph. This comparison is rather different from those suggested by the text of the *Summa*, and perhaps it will be of some value to observe certain features drawn from the *Commentary*. St. Thomas asks why the revelation had not been made to Joseph at the outset, before he was so cruelly troubled.

He answers, and we cannot insist enough on all that follows: "If God acts in this way toward Joseph, it is that his testimony may be still more worthy of faith. The Lord permitted Thomas to doubt His resurrection so that his doubt would cause him to touch Him, so that his touch would make him believe, and that his faith would cure the wounds of infidelity in us."

It would be well for us to recall two major truths in Thomism: All human knowledge is based on the experience of the external senses and all the other senses are based on the sense of touch. Moreover, the sense of touch is the least subject to illusions. The sense of sight is undoubtedly the most noble, but one does not see quite as well if one has not first touched. *Palpate et videte.* Likewise, when it is a question of mysticism, one can only see well if one has first tasted. *Gustate et videte.* In the most literal acceptance of the word, the hand must be placed in the work of knowledge, sometimes the finger must be inserted here or there, and then one can no longer be incredulous. Never will sensible inquiry be sufficiently pursued. Never will the things of above become tangible enough nor sufficiently examined.

But a person who does not doubt at all may neglect the verifications. Doubt is a sleepy state of the mind. The eyes of a person who doubts are closed, but if his hands are very active, if he examines by feeling, his eyes will be opened and he will be convinced that he is not confronted with phantoms but with flesh and bone. Let us remember the *palpate et videte.* We could add with St. Thomas not only *ut palpans crederet* but also *ut palpans videret.*

God permitted Joseph to doubt with a doubt which did not imply any imperfection and for which he was in no way reproached. In Zachary's and Thomas' doubt an imperfection or fault is present which the angel of our Lord Himself points out with severity. But in Joseph's doubt, the term "divine permission" should not even be used in its theological rigor, since the least trace of evil could not be found in this doubt. If Joseph doubted, it is that this doubt would attract the angelic revelation and that this revelation would increase his faith and ours.

According to St. Thomas there are, from the point of view of faith, two useful purposes for this doubt of Joseph: the increase of the value of his testimony and the increase of his personal faith. This double usefulness is often discovered for us also when we are obliged to pass through certain trials of faith more or less analogous to his.

This doubt, so fruitful in Joseph, was to find no place in Mary. In the first place, as regards her being informed before conceiving the Son of God, there was the supreme reason that God wanted to subordinate to her acceptance the realization of the mystery of the Incarnation. But we can also say with St. John Chrysostom: "The angelic annunciation took place before the conception to spare Mary the anguish she would have felt if that annunciation had not been made until after the conception. Of necessity, the Mother who received into her womb the Creator of all things had to be spared this anxiety. . . . Every state of fear had to be dispelled so that only joy be there." This is truly the first joyful mystery, the joyful mystery *par excellence*.

Mary's most pure flesh, like the flesh of Jesus raised from the dead, is the source of our life. Mary's flesh is wholly spiritualized from the moment of her conception by her privilege of being the Immaculate One, and the Holy Spirit will overshadow her more and more until the supreme invasion of the divine maternity, until the final glorification in the mystery of her Assumption. This flesh belongs to her human children just as it belongs to her divine Spouse. It was for us that she conceived and gave birth to a child.

When the angel spoke of Elizabeth, he said to Zachary: "She will bear you a son," for it is Zachary who will beget the child at the same time as she. To Joseph, who is not the father according to the flesh, he does not speak in the same manner. He did not even say that Mary would bring forth the child for herself. This could be said since she is the real mother. He simply said: "She will bring forth," because she brings forth the son, not for Joseph nor for herself, but for the entire world. The angel will say to the shepherds:

"He is born to you," and that is why Mary's great joy, which had been announced to her by Gabriel in the first joyful mystery, will be for all the people in the third mystery of the Nativity.

The virginal and maternal heart is our treasure. Thus there should our heart be and dwell. Never will we find this treasure in sufficient joy, never will we keep it with enough security, nor certitude, nor with an embrace which is sufficiently strong. This embrace is the embrace of faith. From it proceeds a divine policy destined to render that faith more and more conquering, to induce us to permit it to invade our interior domain first and then, little by little, to invade all that is exterior to ourselves. To prepare these triumphs of our faith, all things concur in the designs of God: Joseph's doubt and anxiety which are in no way culpable, as well as Thomas' and Zachary's doubts which are filled with imperfections and faults, and, far above all the rest, the blessedness of Mary's joyous faith.

Joseph's Affirmation of Faith

We ask and we have the right to ask a thousand times: "Lord, increase our faith." Nothing can be more useful or more necessary for the development of our spiritual life, which springs from the roots of faith. But if we ask for this increase of faith sincerely, we must courageously accept in advance the means and conditions which are almost always very hard. There will often be doubts and anguish like those which crucified Joseph.

St. Thomas borrows a very curious viewpoint from the Gloss: the angel appears to Joseph during his sleep because he doubts. This does not mean that doubt can never be useful; it can be useful in every order of knowledge whether it is a question of faith or of wisdom. Joseph's example is an eloquent proof of this. When it is a question of faith, it goes without saying that the doubt will not question the object of faith but the explanations or applications of faith.

Moreover, doubt can only be a temporary and a slightly abnormal state of the mind in spite of what the Cartesians, the skeptics, and the partisans of systematic doubt may say. It is not a strong, vigilant state; it is never without a certain diminution and intellectual inferiority, without a certain defect. The intellect which doubts is not necessarily bad, but it sleeps and it must be awakened before too much delay in order to be illuminated by Christ. Doubt must remain within certain limits if it wishes to remain as perfectly virtuous as Joseph's. If it escapes these limits it is fatally lost and deserves to be censored like Thomas' doubt or punished as Zachary's was. It could happen, in certain cases, that it may remain legitimate for a long time and then suddenly or gradually cease to be without our having been fully conscious of it.

If Joseph doubted, the purpose of this doubt and of the angelic revelation was an affirmation of his faith. We may add: It was also to increase our faith. Joseph merited that revelation which put an end to doubt. Every increase of faith must be merited, bought with a great price. This is true whether it is a question of an intensive increase common to all the virtues (a gradual conquest of the subject by a valiant struggle and by victories which are often painful), or whether it is an extensive increase which embraces new objects or objects which have been newly explained.

We have here the explanation of so many misunderstandings, crises, and cruel trials which, in the body of the Church, crucify certain of its members on the eve of a new establishment of doctrinal truths. These are fruitful sadnesses, similar to those of the woman who is about to give birth, and they will be recompensed by the supreme joy of lights which are increasingly bright.

Nothing is more directly opposed than the intellect which doubts and the intellect which is made firm by faith. And yet they have this in common, that in neither case is the intellect made fast simply by the force of the object. From this spring certain strange affinities between doubt and faith. These affinities explain how doubt, as in Joseph's case, when it is entirely virtuous, has the power of causing merit and of preparing for an increase of faith. This sad fluctuation can, indeed, be a gift to the just from God, but it is not the final gift; it will not last forever.

How difficult that trial of Joseph's was! How deep was the thrust of the two-edged sword! St. John Chrysostom tells us that it separated Joseph's heart from Mary's. Joseph had reached an act of the will, had reached the decision to send Mary away. In his heart he had already sent her away.

The angel of the Lord had arrested the sword in Abraham's hand before it reached Isaac's heart, but not before Abraham's heart was transpierced. In the same way the angel of the Lord prevents the sword of division from completing its exterior effect, from bringing about the physical separation between Joseph and Mary. But interiorly it had pierced to the extreme limit, had cut the vital line between Joseph's heart and Mary's, had reached the extreme sorrow even to death. St. John Chrysostom tells us in slightly different words: "He had not rejected her from his house but he had rejected her from his heart." What martyrdom for this heart thus stripped, empty of all that made up its life!

To dare to speak of this martyrdom of Joseph, we must look beyond Abraham towering over the altar and its victim in all the heroism of his faith and his abandonment to God. Before the agonizing heart of Joseph we call to mind the words of Gethsemani: *pavere et taedere*. At the first sorrowful mystery, the angel of the Lord appears to comfort Him; to Joseph also, an angel appears to comfort him: "Fear not."

To understand all this we must understand the incomparable love of these two spouses; we must consider the mystery of Eden—the only one which deserves to be compared to it—and the mystery of Adam's and Eve's love before the sin, even the mystery of their sin if, as certain theologians think, the fear of being separated from the guilty wife was part of the motive for the sin of the first husband.

Our piety tends to unite more and more the hearts of Jesus, Mary, and Joseph. It should think more about their union in suffering, in the sorrowful mystery, for there are three broken hearts. Union in suffering, union also for suffering. The fearful operation of the sword of division effected a still stronger union of the hearts of Mary and Joseph.

This is what happens whenever the thrust truly comes from above, as St. Jane de Chantal said, and whenever it is received in a perfectly virtuous manner. Now, there is nothing but virtue in the just man, even to the depths of his anguished doubt. Because of his unalterable fidelity and invincible prudence he was the one "his Lord hath appointed over His family" of Nazareth and over His universal family, the Holy Church.

Also, who can describe the martyrdom of the heart of the faithful Virgin, the Virgin most prudent, whose heart was never separated from Joseph's heart? Who can describe Mary's suffering during the silence that she felt willed by God while she was condemned by a love which doubted her and had the right and even the duty to judge her? We venerate the Mother's compassion for the transpierced heart of her Divine Son, the Son of David; let us not forget the wife's compassion for the holy heart of her human spouse, the son of David.

The Visions of Joseph and Mary

Joseph's vision came to him during sleep, by the exercise of the imagination; Mary's vision appeared to her in a state of wakefulness; she saw with her eyes and heard with her ears. Why are the external senses used here and not there? St. Thomas responds by a very delicate doctrine based on St. Paul: Prophecy is a sign not for infidels but for believers, whereas unbelievers have need of a miracle. Prophecy is given to the faithful, miracles to the unbelievers. "It is during sleep, properly so called, that the revelation called prophetic takes place." Sleep is a passive state and is therefore more favorable to certain superior communications on condition that the dangers of illusion can be set aside in some way or another.

"Since Joseph was just and faithful, the angelic apparition sent to him was the type proper to believers. . . . On the contrary, corporeal apparitions, exterior, which are visible to the eyes, have something of the miraculous about them and are therefore not proper to Joseph because he believed and was faithful."

Let us endeavor to understand this doctrine fully. What is addressed to the exterior senses is more miraculous in itself and is addressed less to the faithful than to those who, in some manner or other, are presented as unbelievers. Thus, for Zachary and Thomas very tangible testimonies were required, striking the external sense of touch or of sight. Such testimonies will be necessary for all who merit the reproach made to the disciples of Emmaus, who are "slow to believe."

St. Thomas contrasts Isaias' words, *Audite ergo domus*

David, and the weighty reproach which follows, with the first words of the angel sent to Joseph, *Joseph, fili David, noli timere,* words full of consolation. For the house of David the virginal birth is the miraculous sign given by God Himself.

To those more or less incredulous, more or less slow to believe, let us compare those to whom nothing is lacking by way of faith and good will, but who are but slightly endowed with knowledge, intelligence, and imagination. Persons like these need to have their external senses come to the aid of their other faculties of knowledge; they need to be forcibly struck and aroused. They are not slow to believe; they are simply awkward and slow in their intellectual steps.

Such were the shepherds of Bethlehem. This remark, like several of the following, belongs to St. John Chrysostom himself. The herdsmen were rugged and coarse. The great news had to take strong hold of their external senses; their eyes had to be struck by radiant lights and their ears by marvelous canticles.

What we say of those shepherds of old, we could also say of the dear little shepherdess so near to our time, Bernadette Soubirous. She needed to see the Lady of the grotto in all the beauty of her countenance, to hear her in all the sweetness of her voice. This is the saying from the Canticle: "Shew me thy face. Let thy voice sound in my ears; for thy voice is sweet and thy face comely." She needed to hear the Lady with her ears, this little peasant girl with whom the Queen of the Angels conversed in the dialect of the mountains. One of her biographers tells us that Bernadette had no imagination. Nothing had cultivated that faculty in her. Reality alone struck her childlike intelligence and she was not capable of adding anything to it.

The reasons just given are all subjective, in the sense that they are derived from moral or physical infirmities of the subjects. But there are other reasons which are wholly objective. Faithful little Bernadette found herself confronted with great things which were suddenly revealed to her, revealed to her first and to her alone, great things quite new and unforeseen. This was sufficient reason for appealing to the external senses of that child, placed first and all alone to witness the brilliant glory of such things. St. John Chrysostom gives the very same reason for Gabriel's apparition to Mary: "Because she (Mary) should have been instructed first about the greatest conceivable things."

If we can call great the objects presented to Bernadette by Mary, we should call very great the objects presented to Mary by Gabriel. If Joseph is the *servus fidelis*, Mary is the *ancilla fidelissima*. For her, everything must be pushed to the superlative.

St. John Chrysostom tells us that Joseph, because of his fidelity, did not need an apparition as striking as the one accorded to the shepherds. Therefore Mary, one could object (and St. Thomas does object), needed it still less. He answers, while keeping within the most formal line of this entire doctrine: "The mystery of the Incarnation was revealed to Mary from the beginning, when it was more difficult to believe. That is why the apparition of Gabriel should be addressed to her external sense of sight as a visible apparition."

Mary was not the only one instructed in this mystery by an angel, for Joseph was also instructed in the same way. However, Joseph was not instructed before, but after the mystery had already been realized, and dependent on the revelation made to Mary. Joseph was neither the first nor the only one to receive the news and therefore he did not have the reasons that Bernadette would have for receiving it through her external senses. He was not the first, therefore he did not have the reason Mary had. In his case, an imaginative vision in the course of sleep sufficed, as did the vision of the ladder presented to the imagination of the sleeping Jacob.

It is not stated that Jacob was troubled any more than Joseph was, whereas St. Luke says positively that Mary was troubled (*turbata est*). In other words, what St. Thomas calls *apparitio visibilis* is and should be more impressive for the reasons we have stated.

Imaginative vision must not be underestimated. Undoubtedly, this vision can seem inferior to one addressed to the external senses, especially from the point of view of utility or special necessity. It is less strong and it gives less indication of the *fortiter* of divine wisdom. But by making an approach through more ordinary channels does it not respect the *suaviter* of the more common order which must never be abandoned except for grave reasons? It could be said that it is more normal and therefore, by itself, more recommended. It sufficed in Joseph's case, St. Thomas has pointed out; let us conclude: Therefore it was preferable.

The Order of Divine Annunciations

Let us now consider another objection raised by St. Thomas.[7] Divine revelations are given to angels immediately, without the intervention of any creature, as Denis remarks. But the Mother of God is elevated above all the angels. Therefore, it would seem that the annunciation of the mystery of the Word made Flesh should come to her directly from God without passing through an angel.

To answer this objection, let us first observe that the principle taken from Denis holds all its value and all its truth only in the purely natural order. In the supernatural order, the highest angel of all can receive, and does receive, marvel-

[7] *Summa theol.*, IIIa, q. 30, a. 2.

ous illuminations which pass through the humanity of Jesus and through Mary herself.

Mary, undoubtedly, is exalted above all the angels as to her dignity as Mother of God but during her earthly life, when her state was the same as ours (except for sin), St. Thomas affirms that she was inferior to the angels in this respect. Jesus Himself, as regards His transient and mortal life "was made a little lower than the angels." But Jesus united within Himself the state of a wayfarer and the beatific state. He could not need any angelic instruction whatsoever in His knowledge of divine things. But the Mother of God was not yet in the beatific state. She could therefore be instructed by angels and we have seen how and why it was fitting that she should be thus instructed at the Annunciation.

Mary, we have said, was not in the beatific state—we cannot insist enough on this word and this notion of state—but there was nothing to prevent her from receiving the beatific vision in a transitory manner, as was granted to Moses and St. Paul, according to St. Thomas. More and more theologians refuse to deny to Mary any of the marvelous graces which other saints enjoyed. It was eminently fitting, then, that she also received this grace, which is the highest of all.

We have seen that at the moment when guilty humanity is about to be exiled from Eden, God sets every intermediary aside and Himself becomes the Prophet of the redemption. The angel intervenes later and the law of his mediation is thus safeguarded, but he no longer manifests the decrees of justice; he is merely an agent of execution. Again it must be stated that by accepting the false mediation of the serpent, which was the instrument of the bad angel, Eve, and through her Adam, had abused that angelic mediation and in a more general way the mediation of every creature.

Except in extreme cases, God always respects the common order which He instituted and which we can call the sweetness of the ways of providence. This will again confirm the response to the fourth objection of our article, which states that "the dignity of the heralds should increase in proportion to the dignity of the matter announced. But the mystery of the Incarnation is the greatest of all things announced to man by angels. Therefore, if it was by an angel that this should be announced, it should be an angel of the highest rank," by the highest seraphim and not by an archangel if, in agreement with certain Fathers of the Church, archangels are lower in rank than certain other celestial spirits.

To support our response, let us insist on a remark from Cajetan commenting on the response of St. Thomas himself. The doctrine is identical but its practical applications could be so fruitful in bringing everything and ourselves back to our proper place! If we consider only the dignity of the Son of God who is about to become incarnate or the dignity of His glorious Mother, undoubtedly the highest of seraphims should be dispatched to her. But, that the sweet orderings of divine providence may be perfectly respected, every announcement of the divine word, whatsoever it be, should be confided to those angels who are messengers and heralds by reason of their place in the celestial hierarchies.

This remark of Cajetan's could be applied advantageously to the human and terrestrial hierarchies. The most favored from the point of view of substantial divine communications are not always the ones charged to communicate and announce these communications to other men. It suffices that they be more favored from the point of view of charisms and graces which facilitate transmission. It would be a dangerous illusion to confound these two orders of favors and to measure one against the other.

The great principles from the treatise on the angels can

be found in human matters in a veiled manner, less distinct and almost blurred. This beautiful treatise is useful for us because it causes these principles to shine before our eyes in all their brilliance. Many things in the government of the Church and in all wise governments, contrary to the more or less foolish objections of those who believe themselves wise, are solved immediately if one recalls these great principles to which we refer.

False and True Mediation

Let us come to the second argument of the body of the article.[8] If the false mediation of the serpent—namely, of the bad angel—in regard to Eve had caused the avenging God alone to speak in Eden, that false mediation also demands reparation through the mediation of the good archangel in regard to Mary. According to the Venerable Bede, everything in that reparation is marvelously adapted and everything corresponds perfectly.

The angel is sent by God to the Virgin who is about to consecrate her divine maternity. The first cause for humanity's doom was the sending of the serpent to the woman whose seduction was desired by diabolical pride. The economy of these two scenes must be compared even to their least details and their parallelism must be discovered. They clarify each other by contrast. One results in Eve's act, a supreme act of pride and disobedience which surpasses man's act and is surpassed only by the pride and disobedience of the bad angel. The other results in Mary's supreme act of humility and obedience, an act which surpasses the acts of all pure creatures and at the same time that it lowers Mary before all, it exalts her above all.

By virtue of this contrast we see better why and how in the great nuptial annunciation in Eden ("This [is] . . .

[8] *Summa theol.*, IIIa, q. 30, a. 2.

flesh of my flesh") everything depended on the man because everything in woman was ordained to him. We must understand to what extent Adam, the husband, was all for Eve and she, in turn, was all wife. Everything consisted in her relation to her husband and there was nothing outside that relation, even her virginity. Her virginity was then only a privation and not a perfection such as it is now. Complete in her relation to her husband, she was also through the husband complete in her relation to her children and hence a complete wife and mother.

Outside of this relationship, which can be called single or double, according to one's point of view, Eve was nothing; she did not exist. One single straight direction led by way of the husband to the children. This is of primary importance to understand her entire being, to understand also the sin of maternal pride which claims our meditation and will claim our attention throughout this work.

Now all this is completely changed. The young Christian girl finds herself before a crossroad. Two paths are offered her, very different ones, almost opposed: Shall she remain a virgin? Shall she become a wife? Rather, let us say, shall she give herself to an earthly spouse in order to go through him and with him to God, or shall she give herself immediately and solely to the Spouse of the celestial Eden? In contrast to the picture of Eve completely a wife and mother, let us show with love the picture of Mary, completely a Virgin and Mother.

Undoubtedly even in Eden a certain collaboration of the woman with the man would have been very useful. It was fitting to allow her liberty and facility. But everything should end in the husband. All good, all definitive truth, should come from him or through him. He was the first prophet. All evil, all error begins for Eve as soon as she detaches and isolates herself from him by usurping the supreme intellectual act which is reserved to man. We shall soon return to these considerations in speaking of the mystery of iniquity.

One observation, a very curious comparison, imposes itself here. Eve replaces the *ordo per virum* by the *ordo per angelum*. This order becomes bad by the very fact that Eve chose it against the divine will and not solely, we are going to see, because the angel hidden within the serpent is a bad angel. But replacement of the husband by the angel with this sole difference that the angel is good, is exactly what God did for Mary in the mystery of the Annunciation. Augustine's words must be repeated here: There was present in Eve's sin beforehand almost a sort of perverse imitation of what God was to do later.

How excellent when God Himself reverses the normal order. But when Eve—or any other creature—does so on her own authority, everything is fatally upset. This is what happens to us every time we pervert an order established by God.

It matters very little, moreover, that the being used by us be bad in itself (in this case, the serpent and behind him the fallen angel). The use that is made of this being, even though it is good or excellent, if it is against God's intentions, renders it bad so far as it becomes the instrument of our rebellious will, even sometimes against the being's own will. Such a being then becomes all the more dangerous, since its appearances and intimate reality are better, but in our hands, which abuse it with a more or less grave malice or perhaps without any malice, the effects will be pernicious. In certain extreme cases they can go as far as to become irreparable catastrophes.

Again, we will upset the divine plan not so much by making use, in an undue manner, of what should be an instrument in God's hands and which, in our hands, becomes an instrument of sin, but by more or less consciously usurping a role which was not destined to us. No matter what mandates we may believe we have, we thwart the designs of God. Nothing is more lamentable, nothing more pernicious than these unfortunate interventions of the creature who does not know how to keep his own place.

Long ago Deborah's war chant proclaimed this truth ever new: The most subtle dust here below like the most sublime stars up above can efficaciously battle for the God of Israel on the condition—without which there is only disorder—of remaining faithfully and unchangeably in their true place, the place marked out and willed by Him.

We have seen how the annunciation *par excellence* sheds light on all the others. Through it the first prophecy from Eden which itself announced what Christian marriage will be and what the Church, Christ's spouse, will be, is better understood. The words of God Himself are better understood, rending the veil of the future and announcing in advance the great redemptive victory won by a woman.

Nazareth

Let us return to the mystery of total joy which is so fittingly called the first joyful mystery: the Annunciation. Let us meditate on that incomparable scene and consider it in the most striking manner. Let us pass from the exterior to the interior, first looking at the setting, the place where the two characters are located and where they meet.

The setting? It is no longer Eden's splendid setting. However, something in the name seems to recall Eden, for Nazareth is a paradise-like name. At any rate, it represents the only form that Eden can assume after the sin, an Eden which would seem stripped and impoverished to others but which to our Christian eyes appears charming and bedecked with flowers. What flower from Eden's fields, what lily from its valleys, could rival the flower which springs from the stem and root of Jesse?

It is to Nazareth, in calm and peace, that the angel comes. There is no rest other than there, in the only Eden possible after the first sin. The house of Nazareth is the house of prayer; the house of prayer is always the house of God; and the house of God is always a paradise, even in the midst of our poor exile. Mary gives it fragrance with the perfume of her prayer. It is the marvelous aurora, the springtime endlessly revived. Flowers have appeared in our land, making it again a homeland. This land which bore the curse since Eden's abandonment by the fugitives, this land cursed in the work of man, is blessed a thousand times in that prayer which is the work of God more than the work of man. Thanks to the budding of this miraculous springtime, the thorns will flower after the winter has gone. After the glacial silence, fruit of sin, the voice of the turtle-dove will be heard, the voice of prayerful souls chanting in the afflicted Heart of the Crucified, in the hollow of the rock.

Whatever our profession or our dwelling, it depends on us to make an Eden of our homes. I desire that my place of work and rest become a paradise on earth. Then angels will approach, they will descend into this desert which has flowered again. They are always attracted where the perfume of prayer rises, the perfume that they waft up to the throne of the Eternal One.

The house in Nazareth at first seems a very narrow and pitiful setting, but actually it is made to the measure of the height and breadth of divine things which are made manifest there and which will be accomplished in Mary. These marvels can be compared to those chanted by the first prophet and first spouse in the midst of the splendors of Eden. At Nazareth, the splendor is completely interior. Mary, by enclosing herself in her little house re-creates her spiritual Eden by the life of prayer and duty accomplished in its fullness.

In the first of all the prophecies the prophet is the man, but man in such a state of perfection that he resembles the angel. He is a true prince of the celestial court since he converses so easily and familiarly with God. Adam, Eden's prophet, is very near Gabriel, Nazareth's prophet.

The prophet in Eden speaks only of the husband and wife. Gabriel also predicts espousals but wholly spiritual espousals. No longer is it a question of the flesh even in its primitive splendor; now it is the coming of the Spirit, the virtue of the Most High. Here there is no longer the will of the flesh nor the will of man; nothing but God. Only Mary's virginal flesh is associated with these espousals of the Spirit. That is why we dare and should say: Mary, daughter of the Father, Mother of the Son, is the Spouse of the Holy Spirit. Here alone can virginity blossom into maternity.

Eve caused us to be lost along with her by her conversation with Lucifer, undoubtedly the most beautiful of creatures, but fallen so low! Mary saved us by her conversation with another archangel. This dialogue begins with the *Ave Maria* and ends with *Ecce ancilla.* Mary's conversation is totally celestial, spoken in the very midst of heaven; Eve's is totally foreign, totally that of the enemy, totally infernal. Lost by Eve's pride, we are saved by Mary's humility.

That the Annunciation should take place in that little house, in that little village, is an immense consolation for us. It proves that we can always do God's work, however humble our setting may be. Mary, the little working girl, did her work and accomplished her task. Jesus accomplished His task as a carpenter better than anyone. Jesus and Mary were in their place and they did not leave it. They accomplished what represented the will of God more perfectly and more simply than anyone has ever done or will ever do.

Let us take note of two aspects of Nazareth. Along with the positive and charming aspect there is another, a negative aspect, and even one of privations. Nazareth, this Eden we have just mentioned, is totally different from the Eden which we shall describe later. This land which is so truly ours is a land of exile. It produces nothing but thorns and thistles. This house of God, this house of prayer where so many marvels flourish, is the narrowest of prisons for our pride, which can only waste away and die. For Mary, who is humility, Nazareth is all joy. For us, who are pride itself, it can become the place of humility only by becoming the place of humiliation, which is always sorrowful. If flowers are the recompense of our lives of generous prayer, these cruel, but sanctifying, thorns are its merit, its safeguard, and its indispensable proof.

Mary and Gabriel

After the place, let us look at the characters. Let us ask ourselves who Mary and Gabriel are. This will give us some views on one of the most difficult problems of theology: the relationship between the natural world and the world of grace. We shall see the contrasts which separate and the harmonies which unite these two worlds.

From the point of view of nature, who was Mary? A young girl, performing a little task in a little house. This is often seen and is not very extraordinary. And it took place in a little village, in a little country which has nothing striking about it! Later, people would smile when speaking of Him: "Can anything of good come from Nazareth?" This small market town was in Galilee. This province, very "provincial," was already a cause for laughter. The Greeks and Romans laughed at the Jews who seemed strange to them in their manners and in their customs; the Jews took it out on the Galileans who in turn took it out on the people of

Nazareth. There are localities of this sort everywhere which everybody makes fun of although no one knows exactly why. The Gospels strongly insist on this point. Therefore a precious lesson, very necessary for our pride, must be hidden there. The little working girl in this little and despised country, in this tiny village dwarfed even more by the quips and contempt of men, amounted to very little from the natural point of view.

From this same point of view of nature, who was Gabriel? Gabriel was an angel. St. Thomas says that between the lowest of the angels and the most sublime of human geniuses the distance is greater than between a coarse peasant and this same sublime genius. Our pretensions, even those which seem the better justified to us, would make the angels laugh heartily if they possessed, as did Shakespeare, the irony of mortals. What is certain is that Mary was of very little consequence when compared to the great archangel who visited her, this prince of the celestial court, this Gabriel, strength of God. Almost an infinite distance separated them and he is not astonished that Mary is troubled at an apparition of such splendor. Here may I say that I imagine that the archangelic attire must have been the object of a very special care since it was a question of paying court to the one whom we shall shortly proclaim the Queen, *Salve Regina.*

Who was Gabriel from the point of view of grace? A very great saint, one of the blessed. With the angels the degree of the light of glory is rigorously proportioned to the perfection of nature. They are, in the supernatural order, at the level that they occupy in the natural order because in one sole act they gave themselves entirely. They have not, like us, at least two acts of which the second can, in whole or in part, retract what was given in the first. They have only one act, fully deliberated, in which they give themselves entirely, whether for good or for evil. The more lofty an angel is by his nature, the more perfect is his act, the greater his merit, and the greater his glory. If he falls, he becomes so much the more detestable, so much more damned, and so much more horrible since he had been more beautiful. Dante has said it magnificently: *Tanto bello fú quant óra è brutto.* Gabriel, great by the splendor of his nature, is also great in the supernatural order. And Mary, so little and humble, what is she in that supernatural order?

With Mary, it is no longer a question of the angelic nature but of human nature opening different perspectives and offering new possibilities to the interventions of divine grace. With the angels, a sort of distributive justice portions God's gifts according to the hierarchies of their natures. There is an exact equilibrium between the two and the greatest will always remain the greatest if he freely chooses to give himself to God.

Nothing like this is found with men. Divine wisdom puts itself, so to speak, at the service of pure mercy. We witness baffling and marvelous games whose formula only the Gospels can give us. The first shall be the last; the littlest shall become the greatest; the littlest of all shall become the greatest of all.

This law of humanity controlled by grace imparts such an impetus to Mary that it projects her beyond all the angelic summits. Because she was completely little, she pleased the Most High, and it pleased the Most High that everything be thus reversed and upset through her and on account of her. Before the folly of wisdom obeying mercy, one place alone is suitable for us; we can only take our refuge in the depths of the silence of adoration. This abyss is attracted by another, the abyss of complete littleness. God becomes dizzy in the presence of complete littleness. As soon as He finds it, He hurls Himself into it.

Let us contemplate that mysterious affinity between humanity and mercy, between that created nature and that divine attribute. By virtue of such an affinity, Jesus, from the height of His cross proclaimed one person Mother of men and, from the depths of their exile, all Eve's sons salute her as the Mother of Mercy: *Salve . . . Mater misericordiae.* This is the whole secret of her royalty. *Salve Regina.*

Humanity in the Hands of the Divine Artist

Human nature, that youngest member of the family of spirits, becomes the favored one of divine art because it offers a certain suppleness and incomparable passivity to the all-powerful Hands. Among sculptors, certain great masters use clay more readily than white marble because it obeys the marvelous caprices of their genius with more docility.

By virtue of the characteristics proper to our poor humanity, nature and grace, instead of being rigorously modeled one upon the other as in the case of angels, can present a maximum difference and also a maximum indetermination, not only between salvation and damnation but also between various degrees of grace almost to infinity. Divine pleasure will profit from this in order to express itself with a sort of exuberance.

If we place ourselves on the side of our liberty and its role, also a pre-eminent one, we may say that the angels have the choice between salvation and damnation as we. But they have not, as we, the choice between a more or less profound degree of sin and its eternal punishment.

Let us apply this entire doctrine to the case of our holy Queen. Mary received from the beginning, through God's good pleasure, a degree of grace which surpassed the ensemble of graces accorded to all men and all angels. This grace, a pure gift, she raised in value by the free cooperation of her perfectly constant and faithful will. Her treasure of grace grew unceasingly. The case was not the same for her as for her divine Son, in whom grace always remained universally perfect from the first instant because He is infinite. These accumulations of spiritual riches constitute the royal dowry given to Mary by the Lord in view of her espousals to the Holy Spirit and in view of her divine maternity. It is good for us to try to take inventory of these treasures of graces for at the same time that they are the nuptial dowry they represent our Mother's heritage. They are ours, since we are her children.

In the supernatural order, therefore, there was a continual growth in Mary in virtue of her ardent tendency to the perfection of an ever greater charity. This tendency animated her, penetrated her, devoured her, made her the prototype of the religious state. Mary grew unceasingly in order to become that giant figure standing at the foot of the Cross, being well proportioned to the Cross. Therefore she possesses a formidable sanctity from the moment of the Annunciation, and Gabriel is very little by comparison. But he is happy for his littleness for, after charity, no other virtue sparkles more joyously than humility.

Gabriel is one of the blessed plunged into the light of glory. Thanks to the beatific vision, he intimately penetrates into the marvels of the supernatural order far above all those of the natural order. When he arrives before Mary, who is completely humble, he sees—and here this word must be given its full force—he sees the immense treasure of graces accumulated in her. He is the one who trembles, for he is before his Queen. He sees, but his vision is almost blinded by the splendor of the object, and he is completely suffused in the depths of a ravished admiration. Gabriel too asks the great questions of the friends of the Spouse concerning the well-beloved in the Canticle: *Quae est ista . . . quae as-*

cendit de desertis? Who is she who is always rising, always being elevated higher and higher, farther and farther from the arid deserts here below toward Eden? And he trembles with love and with respect.

Among the masterpieces of Catholic art I cannot forget an incomparable *Annunciation* by de Vinci. But I must admit that all the works of my brother, Fra Angelico, touch me still more. Angelico alone has succeeded supremely because he alone has understood this scene in its whole theological meaning. The Virgin and the angel are in each other's presence. They look into one another's eyes. Mary, the little girl, trembles with respect and fear before the splendor of this being whose nature so far surpasses her own. Gabriel, before that royal sanctity, is seized with a respect which tends to make him withdraw, and at the same time he is impelled toward Mary by an invincible attraction.

One would have to have a power with words to explain this mixture of respect and tenderness, fear and love; these two contrary sentiments which at the same time oppose and complete, act and react upon each other. Mary and Gabriel waver between what attracts them and what keeps them at a distance, caught between two forces which seem from the first to be neutralized for an instant by silence in an unstable equilibrium. Then the great spark, the flamboyant lightning, the shaft of union which joins heaven and earth again, flashes forth. It is the *Angelic Salutation*, the miraculous star fallen from the sky into the furrows of our somber earth like a seed of light, to fructify it and unite with it. The words are so beautiful that we shall repeat them until the end of the world; rather, according to Lacordaire's happy expression, we shall say them always without ever repeating them. The *Angelic Salutation* is the Rosary confided to the angelic order. The angel's great voice contains and envelops all those human voices which will be raised after his in the course of centuries until the ultimate consummation of all things.

Mary, Full of Grace

Ave, gratia plena. An explosion of admiration and enthusiasm before the fullness of grace that is in Mary. In these three words of the angel, there is only the question of grace. Gabriel sees only that and he says only that.

In St. Luke's Greek there is a sublime play on words which gives the term "grace" a unique importance. We cannot quite translate it into another language. In place of the "Hail, full of grace," it would be necessary to say, "Grace to you, full of grace," as if the salutation to Mary could only be the rebound of grace that God had placed in her. We would have to be able to fathom the primitive Semitic expression of which the Greek of St. Luke is only a translation. We may have here, and many have thought so, the very secret of Mary.

In the presence of Mary, completely humble, the great archangel forgets his natural superiorities. Everything is absorbed in this ocean of grace which ravishes him and before which he becomes as nothing by an act of joyous and fervent humility.

The wretched conditions of earthly existence would not permit us, says St. Teresa, to endure without dying the clear vision of a soul in the state of grace. Like the eagle, the blessed one plunges and fixes his gaze directly on the sun, into the burning furnace of divinity, and can contemplate grace as it actually is: the participation of divine life in the depth of souls. This gaze puts everything in its place and therefore grace is infinitely above everything else. Moreover, what we ought to force ourselves to do here below is to see only grace, to judge only from the supernatural point of view. The priest especially should see only souls and, in the souls, God's grace. Let us at least try to be prudent and not judge principally and solely from a natural point of view, else we shall expose ourselves to singular blunders or at least to misunderstandings.

We must not be content to pass before this marvelous world, the world of grace, but we must enter in and live there. The people passing through Nazareth who merely caught a glimpse of Mary scarcely suspected that they were before the Queen of the world. However, it is true that Mary is the Queen of angels and men and also the Mother of men. I believe the angels must envy us when, speaking of "Holy Mary, Mother of God" and of "us, poor sinners," they say: "She is their Mother."

We must always return to the three words which reveal Mary's maternity to us: *Ecce mater tua.* They are extremely simple but they have a sovereign efficacy. "Here is your Mother, your own Mother." This "you" is addressed to each one of us, to each man, to each Jew, to each executioner who blasphemed at the foot of the Cross. All became her children, and she brought them forth in sorrow. She lost her Only-Begotten Son to become the Mother of all. She lost her own only good to become the common good of all, the personal good of each one.

I like to recall that she is the Mother of all but at times I also like to forget it. It is enough for me that she is my own Mother. With what depths have the saints experienced the effect of this saying, its caress and its fire, the sacred realities of Mary's maternity! They have lived and they have died in the ecstasy of these marvels.

"The Mother of God is my Mother." I have the right and the duty to experience with her all the intimacies, all the tendernesses of a child toward its mother. She is my Mother because she gave birth to me at the foot of the Cross. She is the Mother of the living and the dead, of the souls on earth, in purgatory, and in heaven, of all, even those who, here below, are far from God. She persists in being near each bed of agony. A Mother, she wants to save her child. I often find again at the depths of my memory among the souvenirs of my first years, these three verses of a hymn which has lulled me to sleep many times:

"The just man is her child, o'er her heart he has all power;
But over the sinner, night and day she watches.
He also is her child, the child of her sorrow."

Mary's Conversation with Gabriel

After our meditations on the place where the scene of the Annunciation was unfolded and on its two characters, let us pass to the dialogue itself. St. Thomas stresses the perfect order of that conversation.[9] In the *Sed contra* he gives us the proof for this order. A perfect order always reigns in everything that is from God, according to St. Paul's text as presented by St. Thomas. But Gabriel's mission was from God. Therefore that mission must present a perfect order in all its entirety, even to the least details.

To make us cognizant of the perfect order in the conversation between Mary and Gabriel, Cajetan proposes a very fortunate division, using three words which explain the three intentions of the archangel: *attentio*, he wants to arouse Mary's attention; *instructio*, he wants to instruct her on the mystery that is about to be accomplished in her; *consensus*, he wants to obtain her consent to this mystery.

And at the outset, to make Mary attentive to the consideration of such great things, he salutes her in a new and unusual manner. According to Origen, she could not find anything analogous to it in her knowledge of the Scriptures. He adds that Mary would not have been troubled if from

[9] *Summa theol.*, IIIa, q. 30, a. 4.

her biblical knowledge she could have recalled similar salutations. Let us also listen to St. Ambrose: "Mary was astonished at this new formula of blessing. No one had ever heard it spoken. This salutation was reserved to Mary alone." We earnestly recommend meditation on these last words to all Mary's privileged ones, all those who are fervent in their devotion to the Rosary.

In his salutation, Gabriel first proclaims the fullness of grace which gives Mary a sort of fitness or adaptation to her divine maternity. Let us refer to a sermon on the Assumption that was attributed to St. Jerome. We read in the sermon: "Yes, it is indeed she who is full of grace. To others grace is given only partially, in Mary the fullness of grace is poured out entirely and almost at once. Then through her, truly full of grace, the Holy Spirit is poured out in huge waves and every creature is engulfed."

The text passes on to a commentary on the phrase: "The Lord is with you." He who sent the angel to the Virgin was already with her; the Lord preceded His messenger. In saying, "the Lord is with you," says St. Thomas, the angel explains the conception of the Incarnate Word which is about to take place. He explains it in a veiled but striking manner. The Lord has always been with Mary's spirit but He is going to begin to be with her in a totally new manner, in the flesh.

When the priest turns to the faithful to address his paternal wish to them: "The Lord be with you," the faithful answer: "And with thy spirit." The created spirit is never sufficiently with God nor God sufficiently with it, except the spirit of Jesus and the spirit of Mary. To be able to express to Mary the wish that the Lord be even more with her who already possesses the fullness of grace, it is imperative that the divine presence suffuse the spirit, superabound in her immaculate flesh and invade it. Then she who even before could sing as she will sing in her *Magnificat:* "My spirit hath rejoiced in God, my Savior," can exclaim with the Psalmist in a sense which pertains only to her: "My heart and my flesh have rejoiced in the living God." Mary alone can add: "In the God living in my flesh and of my flesh." Jesus in His fullness, divinity and humanity, is with Mary wholly and entirely, soul and body, spirit and flesh.

"O Mary, He was in your heart and now He is in your virginal womb. He filled your spirit and now He fills your flesh."

Let us recall the beautiful text found in St. Augustine's *De sancta virginitate:* "It was ordained that He who is our Head should, by a signal miracle, be born corporeally of a Virgin, to signify that His members would be born spiritually of a virgin Church." He deposits the members of His physical body in the flesh of the Virgin Mary as He deposits the members of His mystical body in the virgin Church. Let us note here the admirable agreement in the Augustinian doctrine. The real presence of Jesus' body in Mary and His real presence under the species of bread, are signs of the most profound and most mysterious realities of the life of the Church.

After announcing the new but hidden presence of Jesus in Mary's flesh, the archangel predicts the brilliant glory and unending honors which shall be reflected on His Mother: "Blessed art thou among women." To that proclamation by the archangel, Mary's *Magnificat* echoes: "All generations shall call me blessed!" Vibrations flow from the angelic voice and gradually invade all humanity's domains to their final limit in space and time, to the consummation of all horizons and all centuries.

The archangel awakened and aroused Mary's attention, but Mary was troubled. This trouble could not be avoided. It often happens that what attracts attention cannot do so without troubling us. Then to make up for it we must be re-assured with all possible delicacy, sometimes by introducing a certain nuance of intimacy. This is what the Venerable Bede notes so well and in such a touching manner. The archangel did not use, did not dare to use, the human name of the great Queen of grace, the sweet name of Mary, at this particular moment. *Ave, gratia plena.* The archangel saw that the Virgin was troubled by the unusual salutation which placed her so majestically above him. Now he draws nearer to her and addresses her more intimately. With the ineffable sweetness of a pure spirit he says to her: "Do not fear." In these words a tenderly imperious nuance is apparent, due to the double superiority which the angelic nature and the divine mission confer on him. Thus human weakness is always comforted whether it be in Mary's troubled state in the first joyful mystery or in Jesus' agony in the first sorrowful mystery.

Why should Mary not fear? Because she found grace before God. Why did she find grace before God? Because she is humble. Humility is the first and, with charity, the last. We have tasted, with the Venerable Bede, all the sweetness of the flower; let us taste, with St. John Chrysostom the strength of the spiritual fruit. "One who has found grace before God has nothing to fear. That is why the words follow themselves: 'You have found grace before God.' But how could one find that grace if not by humility? God, who resists the proud, gives His grace only to the humble."

Mary's Consent

After arousing Mary's attention and freeing her from the troubled state which accompanied it, the archangel informs the Virgin of the mystery which is to be accomplished in her. "Behold thou shalt conceive in thy womb and shalt bring forth a son." According to a patristic Greek text cited by St. Thomas in his *Catena*, the word "behold" indicates the immediate accomplishment of the conception and the words "in thy womb" show that the Word takes His flesh from her virginal womb and is therefore of the same substance as our humanity.

Just as at the end of his first salutation the angel proclaimed Mary's dignity, so at the end of the second salutation he proclaims the dignity of Him who, while being the Son of Mary, is at the same time the Son of the Most High. Living from the eternal dawn in the bosom of the Father of all glory, He becomes for nine months the guest of the womb of the most humble Mary, Seat of Wisdom and Mother of the Word. He has yet another throne here below. Son of God, Son of Mary, He is also Son of David. God will give Him the throne of David, His father. At the same time that He possesses it by human birth, He will possess it by right of divine gift: "He will reign in the house of David and His kingdom will be forever."

In speaking of Mary's faith, we must soon return to the question posed by her to the archangel: "How shall this be done?" The archangel answers it plainly, with splendor and grandeur. The question and answer were so complete that Gabriel had but to seek and obtain Mary's consent, and this was the archangel's third intention. It is in Mary, in her flesh, that the adorable mystery is about to be accomplished.

Let us note that the angelic words present to us, in a powerful abridgment, all the fullness of human knowledge and all its elements of certitude. At the summit is a great metaphysical truth, a great principle bursting out like a *Hosanna*: "No word shall be impossible with God." At the foot is a concrete fact, accessible to the exterior senses and imposing itself on them; a blessed fact which comes in the name of the Lord to teach us and to reassure us. All the conditions required for an easy establishment of fact are realized in it.

A miracle had already been performed in Elizabeth and since the conception of the Precursor in the womb of "her that is called barren," enough time had elapsed for the miracle to be evident without any doubt.

St. John Chrysostom makes us admire the "industry" of Gabriel, strength of God, coming to the aid of the weakness of human intelligence. The great Doctor's words perfectly corroborate St. Thomas' principles concerning our sensible knowledge. The spiritual wonders of the future, here described by the archangel, far surpass the range of human understanding. He must of necessity descend to more humble realities, to sensible and familiar events which are as close as possible to present experience. That is why Gabriel does not refer to such remote facts as the miraculous fruitfulness of the sterile Sara, Rebecca, or Rachel. These facts are, beyond a doubt, guaranteed to our faith by the word of God, but their remoteness in the past removes them from our senses. Proximity in time and space of the proposed facts truly fortify and reassure the mind. The example of Elizabeth was sufficient. But St. Thomas points out,[10] in case this example would not be a sufficient argument, that the archangel next proposes a completely efficacious argument derived from divine omnipotence: "No word shall be impossible with God."

Mary's Faith, Humility, and Obedience

Mary gives the consent which is asked of her, and her consent is an act of obedience. What obedience? Soldiers obey their officers; children, their parents; but this is not the same obedience as a handmaid's. Here there is a mark of inferiority or lowliness, a mark on which Mary insists. That is why the words of the *Magnificat: respexit humilitatem ancillae* (sometimes translated very exactly by the word hu-

[10] *Summa theol.*, IIIa, q. 30, a. 4.

mility and sometimes by the word lowliness), can be applied to Mary's gaze at herself as well as God's gaze on Mary. Her blessedness, proclaimed by all generations, comes as much from this gaze upon herself as from God's gaze upon her.

All generations, from century to century, will know how difficult such a gaze upon self is to human nature, impossible without divine grace, but beatifying as soon as grace has triumphed over nature. But as long as grace is not in the state of fullness, there is necessarily a struggle before the victory. The remarkable and indisputable proof of the fullness of grace in Mary is that immediately and without any struggle she is installed in that blessedness.

The Most High looks only upon the humble in heaven and on earth. Total humility is very lowly and the humility of the handmaid is also very lowly. That is why it attracts the gaze of the Most High, and it will attract His virtue and His shadow. The gaze of the Most High seeks Mary. Mary, very humble, is not afraid to show herself and to draw this gaze to herself.

In a very beautiful text Eusebius points out for our admiration the eminence of Mary's virtue and the marvelous virtualities contained in that eminence. It is like an endless plain where all the movements in Marian souls can be displayed at ease. "In Mary's response—'Behold the handmaid of the Lord,'—each soul can stress that particular aspect which most appeals to him. One will prefer to emphasize her constancy; another, the promptness of her incomparable obedience. Another will see that Mary is not dazzled or overwhelmed by the marvels which the archangel presents and promises to her. Others will observe her perfect self-restraint and the absence of any solicitude, thus avoiding Eve's levity and Zachary's disobedience. As for me, the depth of her humility seems no less worthy of astonishment and admiration."

Among so many echoes resounding from all parts of the
Latin Church, St. Ambrose's beautiful words exalt Mary's
humility and her devotion. *Vide humilitatem . . . vide
devotionem*, exclaims the great Bishop of Milan. She herself
uses the word handmaid. She, chosen as Mother, is not exalted by such an unforeseen promise. She who was to bring
forth Jesus, meek and humble of heart, was obliged, like
her Son, to prefer humility to everything and to be the first
to serve as its model. By the very fact that she proclaims
herself a handmaid, she lays no claim to any of these prerogatives that furnish her so many graces. Let us listen to
her, for she not only obeys but she accomplishes what is
commanded her. That is why she adds: *Fiat mihi secundum
verbum tuum*. Let us attentively consider the function that
Mary reserves to herself: "Behold the handmaid of the
Lord," and the wish that she expresses: "Be it done unto me
according to thy word."

Three great virtues—faith, humility, and obedience—
shine forth here and will be beatified in the second joyful
mystery. In the *Magnificat* everything will blossom forth
that still remains in bud in the Annunciation. Let us recall
that humility and faith are the two fundamental virtues.
The one, almost negative, clears the ground; the other assures and establishes the foundation at a depth that is
greater in proportion to the height which the edifice must
reach. This law of essential equilibrium is imposed on the
roots of trees, which insinuate themselves in the soil to conquer it and to be installed there. The "roots" of inert rock,
the foundations of our edifices, cannot do this. To establish
them, a hard and obscure preliminary work of excavation
and clearance is necessary.

From the outset the marvelous vitality of grace in Mary
gives to her humility all its triumphant spontaneity. In us,
the vitality of grace, feeble because threatened and warred

upon by so many enemies, is obliged to struggle constantly against a nature in which pride is so active. If we remain filled with self, it is impossible to sink the angular rock of faith deep enough or to establish it firmly enough. We must hollow out a place for it by means of humility. Another comparison will make us better understand that this work is never achieved once and for all but always needs to be taken up and begun again. The alluvium which incessantly descends from the summit of our pride exacts a work of tireless dredging. We are not immaculate; let us try to accept humiliations with courage. They are the only efficacious means, says St. Francis de Sales, of acquiring that humility without which nothing can be attained.

Attention Aroused by Astonishment

The answer to the first objection of our article [11] will give us still another practical lesson in humility. At the same time, the objection states one of the greatest controversies in Marian theology. What precedence must be established between the two aspects of Mary's sanctity: the aspect of sanctifying grace which makes her, more than any other creature, the daughter of God participating in the intimate life of the whole adorable Trinity, and the aspect of the divine maternity by which Mary conceives and brings forth in her flesh the humanity to which it has pleased the Eternal Word to be united in time?

Here are the terms of that first objection as presented by St. Thomas: "The dignity of the Mother of God depends upon the divine Child she is to conceive. But it is a general principle that the cause should be manifest before the effect. Therefore, the angel should have announced that conception to Mary before expressing her dignity by saluting her as full of grace." He should not have manifested so clearly

[11] *Loc. cit.*

in the *gratia plena* that dignity which is only an effect, but should have hidden the cause in the *Dominus tecum*. This sort of chiaroscuro between the full light from which the *gratia plena* bursts forth and the shade which envelops the *Dominus tecum* seems to obscure the relation of cause to effect that should have been emphasized in the economy of such a mystery.

It could also be said that instead of speaking of the dignity of the Mother at the end of his first phrase, *benedicta tu*, and of the dignity of the Son at the end of the second, *hic erit magnus*, Gabriel should have inverted the order. The sanctity of Mary is but a flowing from and a participation in the sanctity of Jesus. Hence, the *Dominus tecum* would have to be said before *Ave, gratia plena; hic erit magnus* would have to be said before *benedicta tu*.

To answer the objection it will suffice to repeat that Gabriel wishes before all by saluting Mary to make her attentive to the announcement of so great a mystery. But nothing is more efficacious for making the mind attentive than astonishment.

Let us insist on this principle, so important for our spiritual life, by some instances taken at random. Anyone incapable of being amazed will never know anything since, according to the Philosopher, amazement is the beginning of all knowledge. This is of primary importance for the exegesis of divine annunciations. It may happen that one or another of these annunciations greets us at first with surprising *Aves* which provoke astonishment from which it is difficult and sometimes impossible to separate fear. There are too many affinities and close relationships between astonishment and fear to be without fear under such circumstances. If we were to analyze certain annunciations differently, we would encounter insurmountable scandal.

In an analogous manner all this is true of the miracle. It

does not suffice just to give proof, but it must often astonish as well. This accounts for the strange character of certain miracles, especially those which open up an unexpected series of supernatural things.

Voltaire claimed that it was sometimes more important to strike strongly than to strike accurately. This can be true in one sense. It can be relatively easy to rectify an impression which from the first was not entirely accurate. After the event it is always difficult to attract attention when it has already begun to lag. In fairs a great deal of fanfare is made to attract the attention of the loiterers, an attention which is dispersed in every direction. The crowd does not know where to turn. True good must condescend to compete with the false. For this reason there must be as much and even more fanfare in announcing the good. If the good of a superior order has too great a repugnance for imposing itself by means of these noisy tactics, it is defeated beforehand by earthly uproars.

We would almost dare to reproach St. Thomas for not taking our feebleness into account and for presenting as clear and easy, things which are scarcely easy for us. When he says, *manifestum est quod, patet,* and other expressions of this kind so frequent with him, it is true for him but it is much less true for us. It would perhaps be useful for us to be a little more astonished in order to become much more attentive. One of the great services of commentators is to warn us that the ease is only apparent and that we must take care not to be too quickly satisfied that we have understood.

These applications, so important in intellectual matters, are also important in mystical matters. The very gentle breeze in which Elias felt the Lord pass is often too subtle for the grossness of our spiritual faculties. It explains the sweetness of the divine wisdom very well, but sometimes a violent wind, fire, and the trembling of the earth will be more successful in making an impression on us than this hardly perceptible breeze and it is in these forces that we shall more easily find the Lord. The contrary is universally true only for the saints or for contemplatives, those who are truly so in virtue of their temperament or formation. This is all the more true since what should hold our attention is of the spiritual order and is therefore less obvious. We say "hold" because our attention, while attracted and fixed for a time, is always a little wavering and uncertain. The supports that we are forced to lean upon must be guaranteed a certain continuity.

Three Typical Cases

In the human sphere we could describe some forms of astonishment and subsequent attention and also the various ways of producing this astonishment. The world of art is prolific with suggestions but we do not have time to explore it. The moral world offers us violent oppositions between vice and virtue. It abounds in contradictions. Among the causes of astonishment we shall see that one of the principle ones will depend on pride or humility. Let us study in particular three significant cases to which all the others are more or less immediately referred: the case of Eve, still innocent; the case of Mary, very humble; the case of ourselves, poor sinners, or, if you prefer, the case of our pride.

With Eve who has not yet sinned, the serpent maneuvers very cleverly. The unexpected arrival of the spirit of evil is mysterious and perfidious, surrounding the woman with the shadow of the lowest of spirits, who is about to be condemned to crawl and to devour dust. The insidious question, swollen with the poison of satanic pride, is astonishing enough to attract and fix Eve's attention.

The serpent does not need to begin by praising or criticizing Eve by a salutation or any *Ave*. He directs Eve's attention at once to the precept and to the seducing fruit. He strikes strongly rather than accurately, according to the counsel of Voltaire. He points out how the precept itself is astonishing and scandalous, since Adam and Eve will not die, but their eyes will be opened and they will awaken to a true, intense life, the life of complete and perfect knowledge even concerning evil. All this will be theirs if they consent to eat the fruit on which, in virtue of this astonishment, their attention is concentrated. Moreover, Eve sees nothing but the fruit. The serpent detracts her attention not only from himself but also from herself. She was still full of grace and possessed the integrity of original justice. The Lord was still with her and she was blessed. Above all, no portion of this blessing must be lost and at no cost must she allow herself to withdraw from God to whom it is good to adhere and in whom alone all hope must be placed.

Neither must we permit ourselves to be alienated from this supreme good for any good of heaven or earth. So St. Thomas advises us when speaking of the salutary effects of the gifts of the Holy Ghost. The soul that receives them is the only one to know them. It becomes more and more astonished by them and becomes more and more attentive to the visits of the Spirit. These gifts, moreover, by the profound taste of the spiritual fruits of the enclosed garden give us infinitely more than the serpent could promise. A thousand times more than the fruit which seduced Eve, these spiritual fruits are "sweet to taste, beautiful to behold, desirable for acquiring an understanding of divine things."

The gift of knowledge shines mysteriously for us on this depth of nothingness, of ever possible evil which is so often present, although more or less hidden in every creature. By salutary tears, this gift terminates the enchantment in which we are held captive and disarms it from the dangers and illusions with which it threatens us. It is the only knowledge

of evil which is good and beneficial. The gifts of understanding and wisdom give us here below something of a
taste of the fruits which blossom forth on the tree of eternal
life.

On the part of the serpent, the least word of praise or
criticism addressed to Eve would have risked forcing her
back on herself, of rendering her attentive to this most precious grace still residing within her, and of putting her on
her guard against the dangers which could threaten her.

To see ourselves clearly, to will for ourselves what God
wills for us while tending to complete our filial resemblance
with Him, and to take cognizance of the gifts that He has
given us and will give us more and more, this is the life-
giving knowledge which is both magnanimous and humble.
God's gifts are infinitely more precious than all others, but
what are the most sublime gifts of God in comparison with
God Himself? Who is like God?

In Mary the gift is double, as we have already said. She is
God's daughter by grace, but she is also the Mother of God.
These blessings are unfurled before Mary's eyes first by
Gabriel's voice and then in the silence of her humble and
joyous meditations. "If thou didst know the gift of God,"
is said to each one of us. Mary knows this gift and she alone
knows it in all its splendor. How "sweet to taste" is the fruit
of her womb in His real and mysterious presence! How
"beautiful to contemplate" He will be in the third joyful
mystery! She knows that all is God's gift and she recognizes
that is a pure gift, for she is fully conscious of her own nothingness, which is why the *Magnificat* grew so slowly in her
heart.

Gabriel speaks to Mary of Mary. Any good angel would
have spoken to Eve of herself, of the grace of God in her,
and thus would have saved her. Often temptation seeks to
distract us from ourselves, to reject ourselves, to push us

gently toward some fruit of seduction, to alienate us little by little from the Divine Word, and to make us finally revolt against the divine precept. We are then at the antipode of Mary's saying: *Fiat mihi secundum verbum tuum.* This is the consummation of apostasy in the most literal sense of the term and, for Eve, in the most essential sense of faith. She allowed herself to be distracted and this constituted the "levity" of Eve which we will come back to again. Mary is attentive to all things, to herself, to the grace of God and His words, to the blessed fruit, to every mystery which is incarnate in her.

It is extremely dangerous for us not to be vigilant, not to pay attention to everything. When attention falls asleep, the enemy enters.

Gabriel's Conduct Toward Mary and Zachary

The serpent attracts all Eve's attention to the fruit and the precept. He says nothing to her about herself, we have just seen. Let us also note that he says nothing to her about himself. The serpent hides himself, and he is truly dangerous only when he is hidden. Once he shows himself, it is easy to wound him and to wound him mortally. Gabriel says nothing about himself to Mary, but he speaks about himself to Zachary. Why that apparent resemblance between the serpent and Gabriel in the case of Mary? Why that difference between Gabriel's way of addressing Mary and his way of addressing Zachary? Let us try to understand all this and to draw precious lessons from it.

Let us first note in St. Luke's text a contrast which should astonish us and therefore attract our attention. We are offered a profusion of indications on the surroundings in which John the Baptist is going to be born and on his parents, whereas Mary and Joseph are hardly even named. Undoubtedly the beginnings of the New Testament must be powerfully attached to the rites, to the remembrances of the Old Testament, to Aaron's priesthood, to Elias' prophecies. Mary and Joseph are wholly directed toward the Christian future, toward the already present Emmanuel, the "God with us." Likewise, at the commencement of the Annunciation, Gabriel is uniquely designated as envoy; everything else disappears in the splendor of the dawn which is Mary and of the Sun which is Jesus. Everything in Gabriel's words is divine; "beyond anything human," remarks St. John Chrysostom, and we could add, "beyond anything angelic." Nothing comes from me in what I announce. I am only the bearer of the words of the Master who sent me. All the goodness and the only goodness of the envoy as such consists in not giving anything which does not descend from above. The sublime sanctity of Mary and Joseph is fully adapted to this humiliation, to this absorption of the envoy in his role. Those who are imperfect—and Zachary is still imperfect—are not satisfied with the pure values of instruments. They wish to know persons and things as they are in themselves. That is why Gabriel reveals his name, his celestial function before God, before speaking as evangelist and also as avenger as regards Zachary. "I am Gabriel, who stand before God and am sent to speak to thee."

We cannot refrain from thinking about another archangel, the one of healing and consolation whose words are almost identical: "I am the angel Raphael, one of the seven, who stand before the Lord. . . . When I was with you, I was there by the will of God." Here again the terrestrial mission is indicated after the angelic name and the celestial function. This terrestrial mission fell under the senses. It is a question of elevating the witnesses to a higher cognizance of the one who has multiplied benefits for them and who, moreover, has no reproach to make to them.

In this marvelous archangelic diptych, let us note the

identity of celestial function and let us say with St. Gregory: "When angels come to us, they accomplish their external mission without losing anything of their intimate contemplation. The angelic mind is restricted to know only God. That is why the angels, even when they are sent forth, remain before God, who is omnipresent. It is in God and without leaving God that they accomplish their most distant missions."

Zachary's "How shall I know this" could almost be placed on Eve's lips and in her heart in echo to the promise of the serpent that she would know good and evil, but for her this question is resolved beforehand. Through the serpent she already knows that the means of arriving at the knowledge of good and evil is to eat the fruit. She heard the tempter, she believed his word, and now she sees. She sees that the fruit is beautiful and she foresees that it will be sweet to taste, desirable for her senses, desirable to acquire knowledge. She loves this fruit first of all because it is the means of attaining this seductive knowledge of good and evil, and then she loves it in itself because it is beautiful and sweet.

How many things we begin to love for their utility and then little by little we love them for themselves, because of some indefinable charm, real or apparent! Zachary is punished by the heavy chastisement of dumbness until the birth of the one who "shall be called the prophet of the Highest." Eve also is punished by silence. Zachary, because he did not believe the words of Gabriel; Eve, because she believed the serpent, and therefore was silenced in the Church. This great silence will last until the consummation, until the day of the Lord when all things shall be accomplished.

To that transitory punishment of the Precursor's father, to that definitive punishment of the mother of the living, let us oppose the blessing by Elizabeth of the one who "hast believed, because those things shall be accomplished that were spoken to thee by the Lord." She will not have to wait until the birth of the Son, to sing her *Magnificat*. Mary was humility itself and nothing could more efficaciously attract her attention than to hear herself praised. It was therefore necessary to begin by means of praise, St. Thomas says. Let us follow Cajetan's admirable commentary to penetrate the nature of humility. It makes the soul utterly astonished at the praises it receives. A truly humble soul is preoccupied with its own imperfections and the treatment it deserves because of them. To hear great things said of it, seems to the soul to be novel, unprecedented, strange, and therefore a cause of astonishment. We have here a sure means of understanding ourselves just as we are and of knowing just what our humility is worth. If the praises heaped on us do not cause any astonishment, we can see by that fact how far we are from being truly humble.

This is indeed our case, we poor sinners. We are astonished when we do not receive any praise. Nothing is less astonishing to us than praise. Therefore if we are to be astonished, other means must be used. Reproaches, for example, succeed better. Compliments would make no impression, for we take it for granted that we merit them and that we are merely given our due.

In contrast to Mary (let us admit it in all simplicity), we are all proud creatures. That is why, in their diverse annunciations, supernatural beings and divine things must often begin by humiliating us sometimes in the most repulsive and the most offensive way for the purpose of catching our attention and to astonish us. Thus they assure us all the more effectively of the impossibility of escaping lessons imposed on us for our greater good. Yes, Lord, it is good for me that You have humbled me; only thus shall I learn in truth what is no longer mine but Yours.

How Shall This Be?

After humility has made the excavation, faith builds. If pride reaches its limit, faith weakens or disappears. But when humility has done its work completely, faith can begin and perfect its own.

Let us ponder the terms of the second objection of our article: [12] Where nothing is doubtful, every proof becomes useless and should therefore be set aside; but where a doubt can be raised, proof must be given immediately, in order to prevent this doubt. The angel's announcement to Mary, "Behold thou shalt conceive in thy womb and shalt bring forth a son," can arouse a doubt since it arouses a question: *Quomodo fiet istud?* Therefore the proof should have preceded and not followed.

We answer that the question here is one of the exegesis of the word *quomodo*. According to St. Ambrose, Mary did not doubt. He compares her answer to Zachary's: *Unde hoc sciam.* The first two words, *Unde hoc,* of Zachary's question remind us of the *Unde hoc mihi,* with which Elizabeth will humbly respond to Mary's salutation. The last word, *sciam,* brings an aftertaste of the first sin, of its fruit and the fatal tree, of the *scientes bonum et malum* hissed by the serpent into the willing ear of the mother of the living. In Eden, man's pride did not go as far as the woman's. Here the priest's humility cannot go as far as the Virgin's. For want of humility, Zachary's faith is hurt like Eve's faith but in a much less grave manner. In Zachary's words a sort of negation of his own faith is present, since he seeks to rely on other reasons that he claims and seems to exact.

In Mary's words, on the contrary, there is a kind of profession of faith. If one limits one's inquiry to asking how

[12] *Loc. cit.*

something will be done, one does not doubt that it will be accomplished. Much could be said on these words of St. Ambrose. Let us confine ourselves to stressing the curious fusion of the *scire* and the *credere*.

St. Ambrose has cautioned us that two stumbling blocks are to be avoided and Mary avoids them both at once by the marvelous simplicity of her *Quomodo fiet istud*. One would have to avoid not believing or of not sufficiently believing the words of the angel, not to fall into what Eusebius called the disobedience of Zachary. Nor ought we ever to put our hand out with too much temerity toward divine things that are offered to us. This is what Eusebius calls "Eve's levity." He also remarks that Mary knew equally well how to avoid these two excesses. She is inviolably faithful to the straight line of perfect virtue.

According to the mysterious saying that David deciphered on the wall, how many of the sons of Eve weighed in the inexorable balance have, like their mother, been found too light! According to Jesus' reproach to the Jews, how many of the sons of Eve are thrilled for but an instant when the ardent torch of a sermon passes by! It succeeds only in casting a fleeting light in their eyes without piercing the darkness and without penetrating their hearts.

If Eve is too light, Zachary would be too heavy if he were weighed in the great balance. That is why the punishment of a crushing silence weighs heavily upon him until the birth of the son who was to be a word of the Lord. It would be more exact to say of this son as do the other prophets: *Factum est verbum Domini ad eum.* "The word of the Lord is made to him." He announces and prepares the coming of the Word *par excellence*, of the Word made flesh.

The Fathers of the Church point out for us the lessons that the silence of Zachary implies for himself and for others. "He whose words lacked faith, learns to believe by keeping silence." By his silence he teaches what he had experienced in the secrecy of the temple. Until then there were only vague opinions and incoherent rumors in the crowd which awaited his return. He became deaf, the just chastisement of his disobedience, and dumb, for his contradiction in his response to the angel of the Lord. The obstacles that Elizabeth's sterility opposed to generation are set aside so that John the Baptist could be born, but Zachary's tongue was tied in punishment of his lack of faith, more grave for a priest than for any other.

These texts are brought together by St. Thomas in his marvelous *Catena*. Like him, we add nothing to them but limit ourselves to recommending them to the reader's meditations. We also point out a fruitful comparison between the faults and the punishments of Moses and Zachary, both of whom were lacking in docility to the action of the Holy Spirit. Let us also call to mind the cry of the Psalmist: *Credidi propter quod locutus sum*. The words spring from faith. By a just return, the words are lacking to him who lacked faith. Not only is there no longer any eloquence but there is complete muteness. It is the great silence broken by Elizabeth's fervent exclamation and the chant of Mary's *Magnificat*.

Let us listen again to St. Ambrose. "Mary had read in Isaias that a virgin would conceive and bring forth a son, but she had not been able to read there how this would be accomplished. That is why she answers the angel by asking: 'How can this be?' The marvelous 'how' had not been revealed even to so great a prophet as Isaias. It was expedient that it be announced not by the mouth of a man but by the mouth of an angel. Until the angelic annunciation took place, Mary had as the object of her faith only the fact of the conception and birth. The 'how' is not yet the object of an act of faith and therefore it can only be the object of a question, provided the question be virtuous. Until then, Mary had asked nothing. She whom we call Seat of Wisdom shows herself to be wise in those words which had become necessary as the silence which preceded them."

Let us not leave St. Ambrose without having gathered from the lips of the magistrate turned bishop one of these original profound sentences whose secret he possesses. "All souls are not like Mary, who conceived of the Holy Ghost and proceeded to childbirth. There are certain spiritual miscarriages which do not permit the Word to be born in us and do not allow Christ to be fully formed in us." These words of St. Ambrose remind us of those of St. Paul, *donec formetur Christus in vobis,* and the role he assigns to the apostles in the issue of supernatural fruitfulness. For souls to be able to give birth to Christ, they must themselves have been born by apostolic solicitude. That sentence of St. Ambrose is at the same time a denunciation and a condemnation of many miscarriages in every human domain. Let us mention for the moment the domain of art, so symbolic and so significant of all the others. How many powerful conceptions there are, sketches full of promise, but from which nothing definite can proceed because of physical or moral weakness which had not been prevented or corrected in time!

The exegesis of St. Augustine seems to be opposed to that of his master St. Ambrose: "To the hesitant Mary the angel preaches the possibility of her marvelous conception." But St. Thomas points out that this apparent doubt holds only astonishment without any incredulity. What shows this to be true is that the archangel does not preface the sign and proof he is about to give to Mary with any reproach or amendment such as he did to Zachary. The sign and proof given to Mary do not aim to suppress incredulity but simply to dispel astonishment. Astonishment does not have to be punished; it is not in the least guilty but can be good and useful when it arouses or strengthens attention. But Gabriel could address to Zachary Jesus' reproach to Peter: "O thou of little faith, why didst thou doubt?"

It is always bad for faith to be small and paltry in an apostle and a priest. It should superabound in him since he has the office and duty to produce or strengthen faith in others. That is why certain restrictions or hesitations in faith, certain undue searching for proofs or confirmations which could be excused in others should not be excused in a priest. Jesus' voice always reproaches him for it in the depths of his heart, and for such faults the punishing angels often inflict severe, cruel chastisements.

Mary is blessed because she believed that the words spoken to her by the Lord would be accomplished. (Note that expression. Gabriel spoke, but Mary heard only the Lord.) She is recompensed by this accomplishment itself. A priest is always unhappy when he does not believe sufficiently in God or in His instruments. It is only just that he be punished and sometimes even to the hour of the accomplishment of the divine predictions that he had not listened to with sufficient docility.

After the rigors of justice all too well deserved, "let us consider," says St. John Chrysostom, "how mercy is manifested in the words addressed to Zachary: 'Until the day wherein these things shall come to pass, you will be dumb.' God seems to say: 'When I show you by the events which I come to announce to you, when you yourself recognize the justice of your punishment, only then will I deliver you from it.' The cause of that punishment is explained by what follows: 'because you have not believed my words, which shall be fulfilled in their time.' "

"In their time." Let us insist on that last nuance. We do not find it when Elizabeth speaks about Mary to Mary: "Those things shall be accomplished that were spoken to thee by the Lord." Here, to Zachary, the angel adds: "shall be fulfilled in their time." Is there not on these words almost a reflection of the great words of the Ascension: "It is not for you to know the times or moment, which the Father hath put in his own power"? In any case, these few simple words of Gabriel refer in advance to all the impatience of detail which is ordinarily mingled with defiance of faith and obedience. One does not know how to stand erect, sustained only by the words of the Lord: *Sustinuit anima mea in verbo ejus.*

Eve believed the bad angel; Zachary did not sufficiently believe the good archangel. Gabriel gave Mary as a proof and example that which Zachary had objected to him about: Elizabeth's sterility. What is an objection for the imperfect can become a proof for the perfect. That well-known sterility of Elizabeth, aggravated by her advanced age, causes the miraculous character of her conception to be manifest in an irrefutable manner.

Elizabeth will proclaim the blessedness of Mary's faith, she who had ascertained the imperfection of Zachary's faith and suffered from it. She will herself repair that imperfection as is becoming to a faithful spouse, according to St. Paul. It will also be amended by the sanctity and sermons of the son, John the Baptist.

The Magnificat

From the temporary silence which was a heavy punishment for Zachary will spring the *Benedictus*; from habitual silence, so dear to Mary, will rise the *Magnificat*. Supreme sayings spring from silence as light from darkness. This is one of the laws of every true sermon. As Elizabeth's ardent outcry precedes and announces Zachary's *Benedictus* and John the Baptist's preaching, so Mary's *Magnificat* precedes and announces every sermon from the Gospel. Again, St. Ambrose remarks profoundly that woman precedes man in good as in evil. Eve's sin preceded, in every sense of the word, the sin of Adam. It preceded it in time and in gravity. In the words of the Bishop of Milan: "Sin had its beginning in women. True good also begins with them. Therefore it is not without reason that Elizabeth prophesied before John the Baptist and that Mary prophesied before the birth of the Lord. The more Mary is perfect personally, the more perfect she will be as a prophet." It is therefore necessary to measure the sublimity of the *Magnificat* with the sublimity of the sanctity of Mary, of one who is *propheta plenior* because she is *gratia plena*.

The *Magnificat* is the resumé of the whole Old Testament, as has often been remarked, and also the resumé of the whole New Testament. Materially, it is a collection or a bouquet of flowers gathered from everywhere in the widely diverse regions of the Old Testament, chosen and harmoniously arranged with a delicate and profound art. This material is given its form by the spirit of the New Testament. The astonishing marvel, dependent at this point on the ancient texts, is that it could be animated by a breath of life which depends so little on the past and is steeped in the present and future.

In an analogous manner, if we may be permitted this comparison, human nature can be the connecting link between animal nature and angelic nature, communicating through matter with the inferior beings and through the spirit with the celestial hierarchies.

These characteristics of the *Magnificat* would perhaps be manifest in a more striking fashion if it were compared with the canticle of Anna, the mother of Samuel. It is an admirably beautiful canticle with all the rude and almost fierce beauty of the Hebraic antiquities. Much of this canticle is contained in the canticle of Mary, but in an infinitely serene and gentle atmosphere. The winter and the rains have passed and everything is the springtime of the Canticle of Canticles. We are truly in our own land, the sweetest flowers have finally appeared, and the voice of the turtle-dove can be heard.

We must constantly have recourse to the *Magnificat*. It is the commentary of everything that is hidden in Mary, the woman of silence. Her other brief words are like flashes of light in the night, whereas the *Magnificat* is a beautiful, radiant noon.

In the *Magnificat* Mary herself blesses her humility and her obedience. The blessedness of her faith did not have to be inserted in the *Magnificat* since we find it in the sentence immediately preceding it, which is like an antiphon on Elizabeth's lips. The first joyful mystery is itself the preface of the *Magnificat*. What we call the mystery of the Annunciation is the "tidings" of the *Magnificat* which could itself be called the annunciation of the whole New Testament, the charter of the kingdom of heaven and of the Queen of the angels, the charter for angels as well as for men. This charter proclaims the great laws of sanctity. The essential condition for all sanctity, for every supernatural exaltation, angelic or human, is the condition that the Gospel proclaimed: "He that shall humble himself shall be exalted," and that St. Paul applies to Jesus Himself: "Because He lowered Himself to take on the form of a slave, God has exalted Him above all things."

Regarding the conditions essential for us all, angels or men, let us cite Cajetan, commenting on the *Magnificat*: "In these appellations of the proud, the humble, and the rich, not only men but also the good and bad angels are included. First of all there are the proud angels who have been dispersed, wrested from their lofty places. But the angels who were humble and hungry for divine glory have been exalted and filled with good things." We find in Holy Scripture, adds Cajetan, some striking examples of proud men stripped of their temporal splendors (Nebuchodonosor, Saul, etc.). These men are "signs which attest how much pride displeases God and how much humility pleases Him."

Does the *Magnificat* contain, as Cajetan thought, an allusion to the mystery of the Redemption in these words: *in Deo salutari meo?* If there had not been a Redemption, and even if there had not been an Incarnation and in Mary's womb the Word had not been made flesh, the great laws of every elevation to the supernatural order would continue to be applied and proclaimed and promulgated by the *Magnificat*. Let us conclude, therefore, with these decisive words of Venerable Bede: "Above all thought of personal good, Mary is elevated and turned toward the divine judgments envisaged in their vast generalities. She describes the state of the whole human race."

The Blessedness of Poverty

The *Magnificat* is the answer of the sinless Eve to all persons and to everything. As regards the other Eve, we have only the answer to the why of the serpent, and then the excuse to God against the serpent. After that she must be silent in her sin, to be silent with a great silence, the fruit of seduction.

But here is the marvel: the radical impoverishment of all the spiritual riches of the state of innocence, the fearful, heart-rending poverty of spirit, can become the first beatitude preached on the mountain. The tribulation of a spirit led astray and turned away from God by sin can become a sacrifice to God as soon as it is offered to Him with a contrite and humble heart in a sincere conversion. The evil tribulations of the spirit can be transformed into purifying penances. The spirit troubled by tribulations of the flesh, an inevitable consequence of the state in which sin left us, the multiplication of maternal sufferings predicted in Eden by the anger of the Judge, all this, by becoming the object of a fervent and generous *fiat*, can give access to all the riches of the Redeemer. Magdalen the sinner can become the sublime contemplative. For this it suffices for her to cling to God with all her strength, to "place" in Him all her hope, so that after the wretched intoxications of the flesh she no longer desires to know anything but the exultations of the spirit in God, her Savior.

When priests lack faith as Zachary did, they are cruelly punished by impoverishments of the spirit and especially of words, sometimes by the humiliation of a complete silence. And yet, while praying for Peter, Jesus prayed for each of them in particular so that the faith of each of them would not fail, for such failures in the case of priests always entail other falls. They are very guilty since, despite the protection of that prayer of Jesus, they allow themselves to be exiled from the interior word of God and from their own word as priests. May they at least accept the pains and anguish of this double exile as their poor mother Eve accepted the punishment of her definitive silence in the Church. But may they be anxious to return to the double homeland of the fullness of their prayer and its overflow in their sermons. Their vocation always maintains for them a sacred right to this return when they desire it with all their heart.

St. Thomas teaches that the blessedness of spiritual poverty under the influence of the gift of the fear of the Lord is the last word in humility. Mercy recompenses all fear of the Lord, not only the fear of His terrible justice, but also the fear of other attributes. Each of them is terrible in its manner and it is, alas, so easy for us to offend them. Mercy is like an oil-stain which penetrates from generation to generation all those who fear the Lord. In order to have treated this subject of the blessedness of poverty in a complete enough way, let us carefully note that here again the Immaculate One is the object of an exception and a privilege which are proper to her alone; her poverty of spirit will be incomparably superior to all others since her spirit does not bear any of the consequences of original sin.

Of the beatitudes of the mountain, the beatitude of the poor in spirit is not the only one which is opposed to the nothingness where the rich are abandoned. This nothingness is also opposed to the beatitude of those who hunger and thirst for justice. The opposition of the rich to the poor is too evident to be raised. The *Magnificat* insists on the opposition of the rich to the hungry, an opposition more delicate and more mysterious than the preceding one. It can hardly be translated except by these words: "sent away with empty hands." But not only the hands but also and above all the heart.

Blessed, cries out the Psalmist in his turn, is the man who fears the Lord, who walks in His paths, who turns away from all the others, who does not know and does not desire anything outside of the paths of the Lord. He abandons himself to the caprice of the Divine Master and lets everything be determined by the infinite art which is exercised in him and around him. He is humbly astonished and amazed at unforeseen initiative, humbly attentive to the least signs which are always easily recognizable to those of good will. He is a living *fiat*. He rectifies each of his thoughts, words, and actions according to the indications which come to him from God. Little does it matter to him what instrument God employs, provided that he has the certitude of its quality and its role as instrument. Constantly restored and restoring all things to his profound peace, he is never turned away from God, never dissipated as the proud are in the thoughts of their heart and the works of their hands. Detached from miserable exterior goods, he joyously distributes them in the magnificent gift of alms. He loves the poor, being himself poor in spirit. As for spiritual goods, he knows their inestimable price. Gathering all things in the heart of God, he is always laying up a treasure and wastes nothing.

Exaltavit humiles. These two words sum up universal history in a still larger interpretation than the work of Bossuet; the history of the whole world of spirits, pure spirits and spirits united with matter. If there is true humility, all the rest follows. From this point of view it is indeed the very first virtue since faith itself, the fundamental rock, can only be set in its place after the excavation which humility alone can effect.

We have said that God fixes his attention on true humility. Apparent humility often attracts the attention of men while the attention of God is repulsed. It attracts men's notice precisely because it is apparent. Men see only appearances. God looks at the heart, or rather, in the heart at humility. The truly humble, remarks St. Augustine, do not want to be praised by men. They want only God's praise. Their spirit exults only in God their Savior and not in the things of this world.

Faith and humility are the two fundamental virtues. A strange thing and full of great mysteries is that the blessedness of Mary's faith is proclaimed by what we have called Elizabeth's "antiphon." The blessedness of Mary's humility is also proclaimed, like an echo, by the immense choir of all generations. No longer is it solely Elizabeth who exalts her blessedness but all the nations of the faithful.

Mary, like Jesus, is humiliated, annihilated even to accepting the form of a servant. That is why God exalted her above all and gave her the name most holy after His own, which is infinitely holy. If we cannot say that at the sound of this name of Mary every knee should bend in adoration, let us proclaim that every head should bend and incline in a gesture of incomparable respect from the highest heavens to the most profound depths of hell.

Blessedness of Mary and Malediction of Eve

Mary made herself very little and she loves to make herself the handmaid of the little ones. That is why He who is mighty has done great things to her. To these blessings accumulated in Mary let us oppose the malediction from the sin of Eve. The first mother knew how to rise from sin to a penitent and dolorous sanctity. But in how many of her sons does the mortal malediction blossom and bear fruit! Woe to her who was so rich in spiritual treasures, who willed criminally to enrich herself and her children, who filled her hands with forbidden fruit and was sent away with empty hands! The proud thoughts of her heart have been scattered. She has been torn from her throne of splendor for she willed, like the fallen angel hidden in the serpent, to be like unto God, according to the fallacious promise: "You shall be as gods." She is not content to be gathered up with the Lord, to be wrapped in contemplation with Him, but she willed to gather the fruit of knowledge which God had forbidden her. Believing the serpent, like him she willed to enrich herself with a false treasure. There, in this treasure of nothingness, she imprisoned her heart. By not fearing the Lord, she surrendered all claims to the beginning of wisdom. During the time of the temptation neither the precept of the All-Powerful nor the threat of

terrible chastisement nor any other reversal could re-
establish equilibrium in this strayed spirit who, believing
that she was turned toward a new orient, fell "in darkness
and in the shadow of death."

Let us connect the virtue of obedience with the blessedness of the peaceful, blessed because they will be called the
sons of God. A person who does not consent to abdicate
cannot remain at peace with superior powers unless he himself consents to obey. Necessarily one or the other must
capitulate. This is the profound meaning of Job's words:
"Who hath resisted Him and hath had peace?" This is true
of all authority conscious of itself and faithful to its essence.
It must not astonish us that this may be even more true
of the authority from God. Pride's resistance to God, a
deep-seated resistance and the root of all the others, is
denounced by this verse from the Book of Job and doomed
to final and definitive failure. Indeed, if God is resisted,
there will be no peace. War will ensue and sooner or later
God will be victorious. God resists the pride of His creature. "He hath shewed might in his arm: He hath scattered
the proud in the conceit of their heart" and outside of them.

"He hath received Israel His servant, being mindful of His
mercy." He received Israel in the most vital way, the most
divine and at the same time the most human way, according
to His word and by His word. He spoke not only to the
father of Israel, Abraham, but to his entire race throughout
the centuries. And it is a supreme blessedness to hear this
word, to penetrate its meaning completely, to dwell in it
even to perfect obedience. But in order to revel in this
blessedness the obedient person must condescend to allow
himself to be led like a little child, even like a little lamb.
Not only do lambs follow the gestures of the shepherd but
they hear his voice.

Let us take the three virtues, faith, humility, and obedience, and raise them to a greater coherence of doctrine. Virtues in us are always mingled with imperfection. On the contrary, Mary's virtues were in a state of perfection and fullness. Gabriel proclaims that fullness as regards grace, the root of all the virtues: *Ave gratia plena.* The supreme acts of the virtues under the rule of the gifts of the Holy Spirit which confer on them still more strength and perfection are, according to St. Thomas, none other than the evangelical beatitudes. Mary communicates her virtues to us by her maternal influence. She is truly the Mother of this supernatural life which, according to the Apostle, springs entirely from faith, of this life whose primordial conditions are humility and obedience. She is the Mother of the living. Poor Eve is also, alas, the mother of the living, but of those who live a natural life, a fallen life.

When we speak of Eve there is no longer a question of blessedness but of adversities. By opposition, but also by a sort of mysterious correspondence to Mary's blessedness, Eve's adversities are at the state of fullness in her, even if we compare them to those of Adam. He is less of a sinner from the point of view of faith and therefore, it seems, from the point of view of humility and obedience.

The mother gives life. Food also gives life. Are there not great mysteries concealed in such simple words of the Sacred Text whose very simplicity runs the risk of misleading us? The woman is the one who "took" the fruit, who "gave to her husband who did eat." Let us note well these two words: "took" and "gave." She is the one who "communicates" to him by a kind of maternal influence exercised on him. Undoubtedly she is not the head, she is not the authority, and from this point of view St. Thomas informs us that Adam's sin is graver than Eve's. If the authority had not capitulated in Adam, sin would not have been transmitted to his descendants. Eve's sin is nevertheless the very first human sin.

In another way, what is from the mother in good or in evil always affects the children in a greater or less degree. If we are exiled from certain marvels of Eden, it is perhaps above all as children of Eve. A kind of primacy can be recognized in the order of material causality. Although the mother is not the first principle of generation, often she is the one who seems to explain the most things which are difficult to determine in the children, namely, the lines of descent coming from the father.

Let us here make a rapid allusion to the Thomistic theory of generation which dominates more than one of our views. In spite of certain sensible appearances and scientific developments which command these appearances, we are rightly forced to respect the essential of this theory under pain of not being able to safeguard the metaphysical unity of the generating act. We know that in this theory the orderings of which we speak are reduced to material causality, and it is in this order of things that many maternal influences seem to be disclosed, just as those of the father are more clearly attached to formal and final causality.

Mary's Beatitudes, Remedy for Eve's Adversities

The beatitudes of Mary can be also considered as remedies to the adversities of Eve, inherited by us from her. Mary alone holds the efficacious remedies for these maladies or wounds. Her obedience repairs the first great disobedience which operates again in all the disobediences that are actual sins. Her maternal humility makes reparation for the pride of life as it is manifested in the mother of the living. Alas! Eve is too alive in this respect. She makes us live by her proud exaltation which at first is purely spiritual but after the fall is made heavy by the whole weight of the flesh bent more and more toward earth and she leads us toward all those more sensible forms of pride in which so much jealousy and sensuality are mingled.

Let us traverse the descending gamut of temptations from the summits to the dregs, from the nearly angelic mother down to her faraway descendant, the young student of Faust! Goethe is too optimistic a disciple of Spinoza; that is why old Mephistopheles is but a deficient copy of the ancient serpent. But here as always he whispers the same words into willing ears: "You shall be as gods, knowing good and evil." Eve, in her false joy, believed that she led us to definitive knowledge. At the price of numberless sorrows, Mary's maternal humility leads us to true wisdom. She will always be able to make us prefer wisdom to knowledge, contrary to the essential tendency of original sin.

In her pride and disobedience, Eve communicates the same kind of fault to Adam. But the sin which wounds faith is peculiar to him. That is why, by contrast, it is the blessedness of Mary's faith that Elizabeth proclaims. Adam did not lack faith, and Jesus had no need to practice it. The beatitude of faith is proper to Mary's blessedness as the ruin of faith is proper to the malediction of Eve.

Blessed are they who do not see but for whom faith alone suffices! Blessed are they who do not see with the eyes of the body, and this is already very hard for beings whose entire knowledge depends on the senses! Blessed are they who do not see with the eyes of the spirit, and this is harder still for beings whose proper knowledge is intellectual! Blessed are they who cannot perceive by means of the intellect the words that God speaks to them, words that they love and would wish to penetrate! Let us not forget that this last torment is that of the greatest saints, particularly of Mary and Joseph as regards the word of Jesus, their Child, which have been preserved for us. But like them the great saints profit from that blessedness of not seeing in order to plunge themselves deeper into the abyss of faith, and the Child Jesus holds out His little hand to them on the way back to the humble Nazareth.

Eve sinned in believing the serpent. Men, and especially women, must always believe in something. In the measure in which faith in God's word lags, another faith and another word irrevocably take the upper hand. Women believe the serpent more easily than men. They are more easily deceived.

Mary removed Eve's unfortunate and guilty faith by the blessedness of her faith. Let us now listen to Bossuet: "To achieve the mystery, Eve, deceived by the devil, is forced to flee before the face of God, and Mary, instructed by the angel, is made worthy to bear God. Eve has offered us the fruit of death; Mary presents us with the true fruit of life so that, in the words of St. Irenaeus, the Virgin Mary became the advocate of the virgin Eve." The Mother of Mercy is made advocate for us all, pleading for us particularly as children of Eve, and we can say, pleading through us for our poor mother Eve. All this is invoked and taught in the intimate logic of the incomparable *Salve Regina*.

Would this not be the most ancient form of devotion to Mary in the Church, considering her as acting as another Eve? Therefore it is not useless to make these meditations on that intimate relation which is so deeply rooted in Catholic tradition.

5

False Annunciations:

MYSTERY OF INIQUITY

The Lord thy God shalt thou adore, and Him only shalt thou serve.

THE Lord said: "I will put enmities between thee and the woman, and thy seed and her seed." We saw woman's first defeat. Let us see the first victory of the one who is *par excellence* the woman's Son. In both the former and the latter instances the enemy makes use of divine words. In the latter, he cites them without daring to disguise them in any way. In the former, he cites the precept that God imposed, but he envelops it in a "why" and makes it the object of an insidious question: "Why hath God commanded you?" In the latter, he lays snares at the Son's heel; in the former he had addressed himself to the woman's head. The woman, led by pride to curiosity and presumption, had usurped man's role. Instead of bending toward him in a gesture of appeal and request, she straightened up in a movement of revolt. The Son covers Himself with His Father's words as with a shield;

Eve does not know how to use this shield, and she lets it fall into the enemy's hand and exposes herself to the venomous darts. She does not know how to use these words which also are a sword, as St. Paul tells us. If one abuses the word of God or if one through his own fault does not use it well, it wounds or kills. The sword will always pass, either for the salvation of many, as in Mary, or for the loss of many, as in Eve.

Our present state is no longer the state of Eden but a state of fall and of redemption. In the pages of the Gospels devoted to the temptation of Jesus, the great struggles for the life of the spirit are announced and summarized as well as the victories over the race of the serpent. The serpent is stripped of appearances, but the terrible reality of the enemy who was hidden in him remains. St. Thomas intimately joins to this temptation the remembrance of the temptation in Eden. The similarities and contrasts between these two temptations can be fruitful for us and can project much light on several different problems, primarily the problem of solitude.

The Problem of Solitude

The problem of solitude is always posed for man in all the states of his nature, but in very different ways according to the different states. What distance between the *vae soli* of Scripture and the *beata solitudo* of the great contemplatives! What a vast difference between the isolated and the solitary! One who gives himself up to solitude is soon abandoned by men, but once one is a solitary, he is no longer alone.[1] The problem is to avoid the curses of isolation without losing the blessings of solitude. St. Thomas says that

[1] *"Kann ich nur einmal*
   Recht einsam sein,
   dann bin ich nicht allein." (Goethe, *Wilhelm Meister*)

solitude, any more than poverty or fasting, could not be the very essence of perfection; it can only be an "instrument" of perfection. But the efficacy of any instrument depends on the usage one makes of it; the instrument does not act by itself.

Of which of the two great forms of human life, active or contemplative, can solitude be the instrument? It is impossible to exaggerate the importance of this question and the answer which is short and to the point: "Solitude is not an instrument conducive to action, but to contemplation." In an inverted sense, Aristotle had affirmed with the same vigor that wealth is an instrument not of contemplation, but of action. It is important to note with St. Thomas that solitude is not compatible with the various forms of the active life, neither the form which is totally absorbed in exterior occupations nor the form which is found in the mixed life, which is dedicated to the teaching of the sacred sciences or to preaching and is raised above contemplation as an overflow. Any action, properly so called, necessarily supposes at least a recipient on which it can act. For contemplation, a purely immanent act, solitude can be a very efficacious instrument, but under the terrible condition that the contemplative be perfect. It is indispensible that to the lofty notion of contemplation be added the loftier notion of perfection. In other words, the solitary ought to be self-sufficient, that is, he should be able to stand alone.

Let us remark in passing that man can, at least from a natural point of view, endure solitude and profit from it more than a woman can. The perfect man is the man to whom nothing is lacking according to the line of perfection considered. The perfect contemplative is the man to whom nothing is lacking as a contemplative. But this perfection is possible to human weakness in only two ways: either by an exceptional grace, such as the grace which enabled John the

Baptist while yet a child to remain in the desert, or by the laborious exercise of the virtues which, according to St. Paul, gives man a sharpened sense for the discernment of good and evil.

Man is powerfully aided in the practice of virtue by the society of his fellow men. He is aided as regards the intellect by receiving instruction in the objects and methods of his contemplation; he is aided as regards the affective part of his being by the example and correction of others.

We can therefore say that social life is usually necessary for the practice of virtue, as St. Thomas teaches. He adds: "If solitary life is attempted without having been preceded by the practice of the virtues, it is very dangerous unless a divine grace supplements what is generally acquired by this exercise, as happened in the case of St. Anthony and St. Benedict." Considered in itself, the solitary life should be put above the social life as "one who is already perfect should be above that which tends or strives to be perfect."

The principles we have just examined explain the preeminence of the solitary life and the dangers which threaten it. Let us now consider other principles and other dangers which equally claim our attention. St. Thomas asks whether Christ should have been tempted in the desert.[2] Was the desert, where so many men flee to escape the temptations of the world, a fitting place for the temptation of the Man-God? The question could be put in a more general way: Where does the enemy attack us with more advantage, in the midst of the world or in solitude?

The first fact to be taken into consideration is that "the devil prefers to attack the man who is alone, for it is written: To the enemy who has prevailed against the solitary man, two men are the measure of resisting." That is why, when Christ went to the desert, it was like going to a field

[2] *Summa theol.*, IIIa, q. 41, a. 2.

of battle to be tempted by the devil. St. Ambrose even goes so far as to say: "to provoke the devil there."

Christ could conquer His enemy only if he consented to fight. Therefore it was necessary to urge him to combat. What is true for our Chief should also, in a certain measure, be true for His soldiers. Man should not fear the desert and, by this very fact, He invites the enemy and his attacks. Undoubtedly, a man must not directly provoke the devil, but sometimes in the performance of great works he gives an occasion to the devil. St. Thomas says that this is not dangerous, indicating the limit that one can go and still be conducted by the Spirit of God, but one must not go too far.[3] To obtain or defend a higher good, enemies could be provoked who are not the devil himself. We reflect on David provoking Goliath, St. Ignatius of Antioch provoking the wild beasts who grind with their teeth the members of the martyr bishop, the wheat of Christ.

St. Ambrose gives a reason for Christ's temptation and it is impregnated with a mysterious symbolism: Christ wanted to deliver Adam from his exile, who had been driven from Eden into the desert. Another reason, again from St. Ambrose, is of the moral and exemplary order: The devil in his envy is always attacking those who exert themselves to do more in the spiritual order. Through this envy of the devil, Scripture tells us, death entered the world. We cannot sufficiently take into account the ravages of envy to explain human misery. We especially do not attach sufficient importance to the envy of our principal enemy.

Distrust of Self and Confidence in God

Here we are stopped by the second objection of the article in the *Summa*: It seems that Christ ought to have been exposed to temptation, for He is our Model in everything and

[3] *Summa theol.*, III, q. 41, a. 2, ad 2um.

hence He should have suffered temptation to give us a more efficacious example. We have to follow our divine Model in every respect and therefore we must throw ourselves into the great adventure of temptation as He did. On the other hand, we must also be prudent and we are commanded to avoid occasions in the matter of temptations!

To answer this objection, let us recall one of the great principles of Christian ethics. We must humbly distrust our human nature because of our state of fall and extreme weakness and at the same time must maintain a magnanimous confidence in the all-powerful grace of God. We can, with St. Thomas, distinguish between occasions of sin. Certain occasions are such *ex parte hominis,* that is to say, derived from our nature dangerously inclined toward evil. The dizziness which would precipitate us into the abyss of evil must never be augmented by our approaching the precipice, by leaning over it. Not only must we never look in the direction of Sodom but, as Lot was commanded, we must not even live in the low regions which surround the accursed city. "Save thy life. Look not back, neither stay thou in all the country about; but save thyself in the mountain, lest thou be also consumed." To lift up one's eyes, according to the counsel of the Psalmist, toward the mountain where help will come to us, is not sufficient here; we must begin to ascend this mountain and elevate ourselves as much as possible. Thus, we avoid the perils down below.

Other dangers await us higher up, and they will grow in proportion as we ascend. The envious rage of the enemy will unleash itself against us with all the more fury as we become imbued with a more exalted ideal and strive for it more energetically. These are the dangers of sin *ex parte diaboli,* according to St. Thomas' expression. But with the attacks of the enemy, the help of divine grace which is never lacking will also increase more and more. From this point of view the religious state is a state of permanent and growing struggle. Indeed, instead of striving toward perfection in a languishing or intermittent way, the true religious strives for it constantly and always with more ardor and without any wavering of his ideal. Let him be well aware that he will never escape that struggle and that he will be plunged into it more and more.

The envy of the infernal brigand will multiply his assaults and his artifices, but we must never be astonished nor slacken our step nor let our ardor weaken. Sometimes it is necessary to wait for him firmly and sometimes to outrun him; in any case, we must never hesitate, either at the foot or on the side of the holy mountain as long as the summits are not yet conquered. How unceasingly the two "whys" resound in our ears that Dante, to chide our discouragements and lassitudes, puts on Virgil's lips at the beginning of his journey: "Why return to so many annoyances? Why not scale the delightful mountain?"

St. John Chrysostom tells us that it is not only Jesus who is led into the desert by the Spirit, but all the sons of God who possess this same Spirit. They remain idle, seated in sloth and indifference like the workers in the parable whom no one would hire. By the very fact that they are in the service of the Holy Spirit, they are already delivered from that slavery of indolence. Furthermore, this divine Spirit, their Master and their Guide, presses them to undertake great work. It is the urging of the charity of Christ, of which St. Paul speaks, which does not leave us to our wretched liberty.

To enter into this intention of the Spirit and the execution of His great work is, "from the devil's point of view, tantamount to placing oneself in the desert, creating a void and stripping oneself of that injustice in which he takes delight. Every truly good work can be called this desert, not only as regards the devil but as regards the world and the flesh, since it is not according to the will of the world and the flesh. He goes into the desert," St. John Chrysostom continues, "who exiles himself courageously from the restrictions of the world and the flesh. By that very fact he avoids many temptations."

As for the occasions of temptation which we give the devil by burying ourselves in solitude, St. Thomas dares to add that they are not even dangerous, since the help of the Holy Ghost, the Author of good works, is greater than all the attacks of our enemy. "He who is in us," says St. John, "is greater than he who is in the world." We muse here about the maternal encouragements which St. Therese lavishes on little souls urged by the Spirit toward the desert of prayer and whom Satan tries to frighten with outbursts of his impotent rage. He knows the harm they will do him and he tempts them by every possible means in order to stop them. He even transfigures himself into an angel of light so that these dear souls, already charmed with the first light of the dawn, cannot arrive at the overwhelming brilliance of the great noonday of contemplation.

We see that this doctrine is clearly a doctrine of humility and holy distrust in regard to what St. Thomas calls the occasions of sin *ex parte hominis*, but at the same time it is a doctrine of absolute and magnanimous confidence when it is a question of the attacks which come to us directly from the devil, from the occasions of sin *ex parte diaboli*. Let us therefore disregard the latter, but let us not disregard our poor nature. It is much too dangerous. Its weakness is, if we may use the expression, too powerful for us to dare to disregard it. This is one of the meanings that may be derived from the words of the Apostle: "When I am weak, then I am strong." Our weakness is often the strongest force within us.

Christian and holy magnanimity elevates us to the level

of everything of which divine grace makes us capable and worthy. Let us measure our efforts by the immense horizons which grace opens to us and not limit them to the shabby perspectives of nature, for we would then become the miserable victims of pusillanimity or false humility. They can hardly be distinguished from each other and both merit the glorious contempt with which St. Teresa crushes them. We must always go forward, always attack; then, without flinching, endure all the weight and sustain all the exigencies of great works bravely undertaken. These are the two principal acts of the virtue of fortitude, and we shall find that fortitude in the word of God.

The Example and Help of Jesus

Jesus goes to the desert and therefore to the enemy to serve as an example for us. "He offers this example to us along with His help," says St. Augustine. And St. John Chrysostom says that when God does not prevent us from being tempted, it is because He wishes in this way to inform us and teach us that we have become stronger. In fact, He never permits us to be tempted above our strength. Temptations are also permitted, adds St. Thomas, so that our strength may increase still more, as soldiers are strengthened by experience in combat. It is an honor to be tempted by the enemy of all good, since it is the normal consequence of spiritual progress. The Christian thus realizes his higher dignity because the devil attacks saints.

But if Christ was tempted as an example for us, that example should be proposed in a clear way and therefore it should not have occurred in the desert, since in the desert Jesus was seen by no one.[4]

Let us reply that Christ is undoubtedly proposed as an example to all but that this proposal is made by faith, of

---

[4] *Summa theol.*, IIIa, q. 41, a. 2, obj. 1.

which He is the Author, according to the words of St. Paul. It is by faith that He dwells in our hearts and it is by faith that he wishes to be known. But according to St. Paul, faith proceeds from hearing and not from sight. Not seeing is an essential condition for believing as such. "Blessed are they that have not seen," was said to Thomas. The greatest possible number must be assured the merit of not seeing, the blessedness of hearing and not seeing. These blessed ones are the privileged ones. Finally, verification must be assured the very small number who cannot be dispensed from seeing, especially for the benefit of others. To exact more would be to misunderstand the profound economy of the supernatural life and to diminish it in its dependence on faith. Let us think of those who have but little faith and are completely entangled in doubts.

Two affirmations require our attention. The first is that everything in the Gospel is example and that Jesus is our Model in everything and for everyone. The second is that since He is our Model in everything, He must lead the common life of humanity and not a solitary life or a life full of austerities. But, if He is everyone's example, He must also be the example for those who give themselves to the contemplative life or to its superabundance by preaching. He cannot neglect those who lead the highest life. There will be times in His own life when He will isolate Himself. "He went out into a mountain to pray; and He passed the whole night in the prayer of God."

As for preachers, He shows them that this sublime office cannot be embraced without the rude preparation of the desert. Undoubtedly when the preacher returns to the world to make the word of God heard, he should, like his divine Model, lead a communal life and communicate easily with those he has the difficult mission of teaching. But of necessity this must be a return, and this return cannot be fruitful if it has not been prepared by a period of purification, of perfection in virtue. He must have first made himself what he intends to make others. Jesus Himself gave the example of these indispensible periods of austerities during the time between His baptism and His public life. He did not have to subdue His flesh as we must, but He became an example for us.

Christ did not need to fast for Himself, but for us. We should be well aware that we need to prepare ourselves for combat by fasting and other mortifications. Moreover, they are not sufficient to preserve us from temptation. If this is true for all Christians, it is even more so for those who wish to make others better Christians, for preachers. They should chastise the body and bring it into subjection, lest, according to the threat of the Apostle, after having preached to others, they themselves become castaways.

Let us summarize and apply what has just been said. Solitude has no moral value in itself any more than fasting does. Everything depends on the end that we strive for and the use we make of it. One of the Fathers of the desert said that solitude should be loved and sought because it leads to purity of heart. St. Thomas adds that the same must be said of fasting and other austerities of the same kind. Let us not forget that this purity of heart is a beatitude: "Blessed are the clean of heart; for they shall see God." They will see Him in heaven where nothing impure or sullied can enter; they will see Him in a certain way here below in their contemplation. Solitude can be the best means of that vision of God, for it suppresses the temptations of the world and almost all those of the flesh.

But here, the doctrine would be incomplete and even dangerous if we did not hasten to add: Solitude does not suppress the temptations which come from the enemy; rather it attracts that enemy. Solitude deprives us of the help of others against the devil. It also deprives us of their help for the exercise of the virtues. God could say: "I shall lead the soul into solitude and there I shall speak to her heart," but the enemy can also say this and can very easily mimic God's voice. Like the woman, solitude can give place to active and passive deception and become the instrument of the devil. Eve did not have the reasons that we have in our fallen state for fearing solitude, for the grace of her state of original justice sufficed for the particular graces which St. Thomas requires of the solitary. Nevertheless, Adam was for Eve in this respect what Christ is for us and it would be a contradiction for us to isolate ourselves from Christ under the pretext of finding God more readily. We would then fall into the error of the *Alumbrados* whom St. Teresa scourges.

The Mystery of Eve's Solitude

St. John Chrysostom says rightly: The devil tempted Eve, finding her without her husband. But he seems simply to state the fact without a formal condemnation of Eve's isolation. The first human couple of Eden led the contemplative life, the highest human life of all and most conformable to their sublime state of innocence. They led it together in one spirit, with a certain sharing of roles and functions so that duality did not represent something purely material. Their contemplation had been organized by God Himself and nothing short of sin could disturb its intimate economy. Often it was the woman who brought certain communications to man, angelic or otherwise, because in woman's temperament there is a greater passivity and hence a more subtle receptivity.

It would be well to recall here a doctrine of St. Thomas. He recognizes in the state of sleep a kind of relative superiority over the state of being awake, in the sense that sleep renders us more passive and can therefore be more favorable to certain mysterious communications. On the contrary, for judgment, the supreme and definitive act of the intellect, the waking state is required. This state alone assures the continuity of all our knowledge in the knowledge of the exterior senses, a continuity which is the principle and guarantee of the legitimacy of the judgment. Its proof is in the fact that upon awakening we usually perceive some error in the evaluations that the state of sleep had suggested to us.

Woman can also enjoy a sort of relative superiority as regards the reception of extremely delicate impressions, but it is man who holds the light of the definitive judgment. He alone, therefore, has the right and the duty to exercise it and without usurpation. Adam, furthermore, possessed infused knowledge which augmented his authority still more. These two roles, about which we have just spoken, agreed in an admirable manner, and such perfect harmony was a source of joy for the husband and wife. According to St. Thomas, this is the true meaning of the Biblical expression: *adjutorium simile sibi.*

Eve failed the order and hierarchy instituted by God by isolating herself in the definitive judgment such as we have defined it. She usurped it, since this judgment was reserved to man. This essential point must be fully grasped; everything leads back to it or is derived from it. Eve was guilty of the crime of agreement with the enemy. She betrayed because she did not go immediately to authority and did not subordinate herself to it purely and simply. Isolating herself in judgment, she exposed herself and was no longer sufficiently armed as she was before.

It is different with us because our state does not protect us in any way. Ours is a state of fall and our nature is frailty personified. The question: "Why hath God commanded you, that you should not eat of every tree of paradise?" is a question which would be too terrible for us. We could perhaps save ourselves by responding: "Do not question! Since God commanded it, that is sufficient." But if we have the misfortune of listening and wanting to answer, we are lost. We are led into temptation much more quickly and easily than Eve, who was in the state of innocence. Because of this the request in the *Pater: et ne nos inducas in tentationem*, takes on another shade of meaning for us. Because of this we are compelled to take different precautions, to flee the adversary or immediately to break off any conversation which would involve us. This terrible "why" of the devil is the very death of obedience. Obedience is an order and we must not deviate from it. We must be like the soldier. He has his orders. Do not have words with him. He has been told: "No one shall pass," and if you pass, he will run you through with a bayonet. Why? Orders. We, too, should answer: "I have orders." If we listen to the devil's "why," all is ended. He is more cunning than we. He was more cunning than Eve. He triumphed over her, who was so strong, and he will triumph over us, who are frailty personified.

The sentinel, who is under pain of death to fill his role correctly, must be isolated to a certain post, otherwise he will be of no use. But it is only a question of a physical isolation. He must never isolate himself morally from the chief's orders. We insist on these points which are so practical for us. They are the only ones which explain the first sin and, furthermore, they explain almost all other sins. Let us not forget that according to St. Thomas, Eve had not sinned before the serpent's persuasion, or rather, before the act of pride which was its consequence. Therefore, she had not committed a sin of imprudence before this persuasion, which would be at least a venial sin, for she could not begin by a venial sin. If she was imprudent, it was in the judgment itself which was not her concern. Furthermore, she did not put the judgment of man between herself and the tempter and was lost by that very fact. She discarded the normal instrument of divine aid.

Eve could operate without imprudence only when it was a question of the *acceptio specierum*. (We prefer to keep St. Thomas' expression, difficult to replace and difficult to translate.) The mother who was and could have remained the mother of the living, gathered from the vegetable and animal world precious impressions which could prepare for Adam's definitive judgment, better than he himself could have prepared it. Adam knew this and consented to it, provided that his role was respected and remained intact. For this *acceptio specierum*, not only could woman do very well, sometimes better than man, but the angels could even help her. It is said of the angels that, after Jesus' temptation, they drew near and ministered to Him. From this Gospel passage Cajetan deduces the argument, with respect to St. Thomas' doctrine, which admits an acquired knowledge in Christ. If the angels intervened in this way for bodily nourishment, it is much more reasonable that they could do likewise for necessities of spiritual nourishment.

Why, in an analogous fashion, had not these singular facts been offered by the angels to the intellect of the first mother? This ministry of the angels to woman would be comparable to the ministry of the woman to Adam. Now that she has listened to the bad angel, the good angels, contrary to what they do for the victorious Son, withdraw from her, and instead of surrounding her joyously, they fall back toward the gates of Eden where they will mount guard to prevent her from returning there. Through Eve's fault, a state of war has replaced the state of peace. Sin armed the angels against us when they would have loved to remain at the service of our innocence.

Imprudence as a Result of Pride

Eve committed a fault of imprudence and usurpation but this fault was a result of the movement of pride which formally constituted her first sin. Adam's movement of pride will likewise admit of a bad judgment, less bad, however, and less perverted than Eve's. Thus, we see that woman, in certain cases, goes more easily and more quickly to the very depths of evil and error.

According to Cajetan, Adam's desire was conditional, whereas Eve, believing the serpent, desired purely and simply. Eve scorned the divine will explicitly; Adam did so only implicitly. Adam's judgment remains more reserved, does not go as far. Something stops man as we read in the book of Job: "Hitherto thou shalt come, and shalt go no further. And here thou shalt break thy swelling waves," waves of your pride. Certain gates stay closed, certain salutary obstacles, discarded by woman with an audacious and impatient gesture, are respected by man.

Because Eve isolates herself internally in her judgment, the delicate organism of psychological prerogatives is cut at the root and collapses. It was totally ordered to the definitive judgment of man, as the imperfect is ordered to the perfect, and it is of value only in preparing and orientating itself toward that judgment. The danger, always the same in hierarchies of this kind, is that the inferior does not know how to keep its place, but invades and usurps the domain of the superior. From the threshold where it should remain and where its role would be marvelously useful—irreplaceable perhaps—it presumes to advance too far, attempts too many things, and spoils the whole work.

Fenelon says in one of his sermons: "The error of a soul intoxicated with self is soon punished by a thousand other errors. See her pursuing the idols of her own invention. Do not believe that this soul is docile; at least she is docile only to flattery. One says to her: 'Read the Scriptures; judge for yourself; prefer your opinion to all visible authority. You will understand the text better than the entire Church, from which you receive the sacraments and the Scriptures. The Holy Ghost will not fail to inspire you by His internal testimony. Your eyes will be opened and by reading the divine words in this spirit, you will be almost a divinity.' These words are spoken to the soul and she does not blush at believing them. Does the heeding of these poisonous words of the serpent represent docility? No; it is presumption, for there is no submission to authority. On the contrary, it is a trampling under foot of the greatest authority that Providence has placed under heaven in order to set in one's own heart a supreme tribunal."

We think, by contrast, about Bréal's marvelous memoir for the rehabilitation of Joan of Arc. He so carefully safeguards liberty and spontaneity of souls in their reception of supernatural revelations but at the same time he energetically upholds their duty to adhere to the judgment of the Church! He makes us relive the case of the dear little Saint in her Eden of Domremy, closed to all the rest and open so wide to the great pity of the kingdom of France.

Solitude and Community Life

We also think of the application of these principles to the domain of art, and one of the most beautiful *Lieds* of Goethe comes back to us (*Wilhelm Meister Wanderjahre*):

> *Zu erfinden, zu beschliessen,*
> *Bleibe Künstler oft allein.*

When it is a question of new inventions, of decisions to be made, the artist must often remain alone, but if he wishes to profit by and enjoy his isolated action, let him hasten joyously toward the unity of the group:

> *Deines Wirkens zu geniessen*
> *Eile freudig zum Verein.*

There only, in the totality, can a complete view, a full consciousness, a full experience of the course of his own life be taken:

> *Hier im Gamzen schau, und erfahre*
> *Deinen eignen Lebenslauf*
> *Und die Thaten mancher Jahren*
> *Gehn dir in dem Nachbarn auf.*

The activity of long years past suddenly reveals its secret in a smile or gesture of someone who has, by chance, been brought near us. We have such great need of others for knowledge and fulfillment! Undoubtedly, certain operations of the artist will be better accomplished in solitude, but these very operations need contact and social fusion to be profitable and enjoyable. In any case, certain other realizations will remain dormant and semi-conscious in us as long as that indefinable something which we need fails to appear before us in something or someone. If we had remained alone, without this precious contribution, we would have done no more than dream for long days and long years of what it is now given us to accomplish.

These are the laws of every human art, or rather, of human nature itself. We have said: "every human art," therefore, feminine art as well, which can gather flowers and fruits with a delicate and subtle gesture, which can display them in a bouquet or on a table with a rapid dexterity in a way that a man could never do.

Let us refer again to the text, so simple and so profound: "She took of the fruit thereof, and did eat, and she gave it to her husband who did eat." He eats of it only because he is with her, and because she took and ate of it first. Man copies the woman's gesture, and a copy never has quite the value of the model. A man's gesture never has the total skill or, I was going to say, the elegance of a feminine gesture. This constitutes the captivating seduction of woman for good as well as for evil. The child, stubborn in his caprice, will eat only if his mother is with him, if she takes and eats before him and in front of him. The husband is an overgrown child who acts likewise. His attitude is sometimes comic, sometimes tragic as in Eden, but always faithful to these profound laws.

In the mystical domain, many deeds due to woman's initiative and initiated by woman might easily fall under these laws. There is a Teresa of Avila, who in her clear and concise way, was the first to rectify and smooth the paths of the Lord in the desert of the contemplative life. She is the great voice which cries out in this desert and will people it with multitudes attracted by her example. In these ways, into these paths, she not only attracts her daughters but her sons, John of the Cross and others. There is a Jane de Chantal whose vigorous influence was felt around her, far and near, by her daughters and by all, even by him who had shown her the ways and taught her the paths. He had begun by tracing them and then had made them his own by patient study and virtuous practice.

These things initiated by woman are so precious and so fecund that it is to the interest of man to respect them, to humor them, and to favor them as much as possible by allowing them full liberty and spontaneity. He must be very careful not to diminish them or impede them under pretext of directing them. Later, his true role will come, that of judging, and then his truly legitimate authority will be exercised. Before this, he should loosen the reins and not be too much concerned with guiding. The principles indicated here should be very useful keys for opening certain issues in feminism and for closing certain others.

If these delicate nuances in the psychological relations of man and woman are found everywhere, we should be able to find eloquent expressions of them in the prototypes of humanity, Adam and Eve. Certain of these aspects will be manifested in a still more striking fashion in the true Adam, Jesus, and the true Eve, Mary. What Adam is for Eve cannot be fully equivalent to all that Jesus is for Mary. Among Adam's attitudes toward Eve, we sketched the attitude of an overgrown child which, moreover, is transitory. But the attitude of a little child is precisely the first that Jesus takes in His relations with Mary, an attitude which Catholic piety and art like so much to represent.

If we admit with St. Thomas the acquisition of human knowledge in Christ and an actual growth in wisdom and in age, we admit in Mary, by the same token, certain aspects of the mother's role as an educator. Christ can have no master, but His Mother, as well as His angels, can develop around Him a ministry of touching efficacy. Certain words from the Gospel, certain actions quietly indicated, suggest this preliminary and preparatory role that we recognize in woman even when Jesus is no longer a child, at the beginning and during the time of His public life, at Cana or elsewhere. "They have no wine," Mary says to Jesus. "Whatsoever He shall say to you, do ye," she says to the servants. "The Mother of Jesus was there," St. John reports to us. She is always there. We are always at Cana. We have only to act accordingly.

Woman could often find moments of solitude useful for penetrating into the impressions and "discoveries" from which man will later benefit. She will return again with a joyous haste to the common life, to the participation of the goods that man alone can communicate to her. He alone possesses the definitive light of judgment, the most precious of these goods. Woman fatally deprives herself of it by the fact that she would desire to isolate herself in this act, which should be the most noble act of their common life and in which her strict duty is to be subordinate.

Indeed, we have said "solitude" and not "isolation." Eve begins to isolate herself in the act of judgment; before that her solitude is perfectly legitimate and justifiable. Isolation is the punishment of sin, and here it is sin itself because it is division. Up to this point unity reigns and solitude does not hinder unity. It even favors unity with God. We are isolated only by sin. As long as there is no sin, we can always say with Jesus: "I am not alone, because the Father is with Me." "Christ dwells in us through faith." "We are temples of the Holy Ghost, who dwells in us." The whole adorable Trinity comes and dwells within us. There was only solitude and not isolation for Eve, even without Adam, as long as God was there. There was solitude in all its grandeur. After the sin, even with Adam, nothing remained but isolation and then exile.

As regards the virtuous exercise of our activity, St. Thomas says that the last practical judgment, which gives action its impetus, should be preceded by an act of counsel. These two acts are very different. The good counselor, who should always soar above the question to suggest many combinations without settling down too soon, is very different from the judicious person who, so to speak, instinctively swoops to a dead stop on the sole means which is the best of all. Such diverse qualities as those of the good counselor and the judicious person correspond to the multiplicity and unity of the moral object. When the decisions are grave, then especially they must have been considered thoroughly from every point of view. We must not neglect to examine the information of others, many others in fact, for they can furnish us with material for richer information. Whence the adage: Counsel is so much the better in proportion to the number who contribute. Furthermore, not only the intellect but all our faculties should cooperate in this counsel: the external senses aided and completed by the internal senses which elaborate on the data in the most subtle and delicate manner. Suffice it to say that woman especially will be an excellent counselor in the role that we have recognized as hers, which appears in the preparation of the definitive decision, of the last practical judgment. There is greater advantage in referring judgment to one person, and it is better if it devolves upon the man.

In speculative material, Adam, more than other men, was independent of woman's contribution because of the infused knowledge that he possessed from the beginning and which merited for him, St. Thomas tells us, his role as master and head of the entire human race. But from the very first, Adam was capable of instruction and direction which looked at concrete realities. In practical matters it was to his interest to utilize the relative superiority of the woman, to let her gather and bring the flowers and fruits to him, as long as it was not the fatal fruit which he knew was forbidden by God. As regards other fruits, he must have encouraged her to take of them, to profit by them when she was alone and to cause him to profit by them when he was with her. While gathering them for him, she was still morally with him even in moments of solitude. But as soon as that blessed unity was injured and destroyed by sin, nothing but dispersion remained. The rebel dispersed everything, she dispersed herself, and she was dispersed by the vengeful God in the proud thoughts of her heart.

In the measure that the mystery of unity is fully respected, so the moral presence lives. Eve can absent herself corporeally; she can even linger in solitude. The arms can move the hand away from the head and they must do so if the hand is to accomplish certain of its offices. As a result, the hand does not participate less in the vitality of the head, in the service and the unity of the entire organism that the head commands. According to a charming comparison of St. Francis de Sales, little children, especially in the mountains, tighten their hold on their mother's hand in the measure that the flower they are going to gather is nearer to the edge of the precipice. Should the hands be unclasped, the danger which did not exist becomes mortal.

Eve could not know how to profit from what could have been a test of her faith. If she had known this, faith would have directed itself in her toward the blessedness that Mary will enjoy. For us, in similar cases, the first fault, often venial, is often a fault of imprudence or of grasping greed or another fault. We do not necessarily begin through pride as Eve did. Eve could only begin her sad adventure with a mortal sin and this sin could only be a sin of pride. Thus, there is a double difference between her and us. Sin could only enter by that sole gate and death followed. In us, sin and its companion, death, still know many other ways of entering and taking up their abode.

The Mystery of Mary's Solitude

Opposed to the mystery of Eve's solitude is the mystery of Mary's solitude. The mystery of solitary Eve, without her husband but with the serpent, could be compared with the mystery of the angel Gabriel sent to a Virgin espoused to a man named Joseph. It might also be compared to the mystery of the distinct annunciations to Mary and to Joseph. In the first of these two annunciations, absence of the husband; in the second, absence of the wife.

Mary is never seen in the presence of Satan, nor is Adam. Why does Satan, who did not dare to address man in Eden, dare to address the Son of man in the desert? Perhaps because the Son of man is also the Son of woman, and Adam was not, for he is the only man who is not of "the race of the woman." The enmity is between the serpent and the woman's race.

Furthermore, let us not forget that Adam is head of all humanity in the natural order. That is why he does not have to grow, like Christ, in wisdom at the same time as he advances in age, though he could undoubtedly grow in acquired knowledge, as all men can. St. Thomas recognizes in him from the beginning all that was necessary or useful to him as master of other men. Scripture's words on the angels also apply to the first man. He is full of wisdom from the beginning, with the sole difference that this fullness befits the angels in virtue of their nature, whereas it befits the first man solely in virtue of his dignity as head. Let us not say in virtue of his state, for then it would also be suitable for Eve. This fullness of wisdom makes Adam capable of commanding all beings, all men who are to come, and all the animals of the earthly paradise. He summoned them, as it were, by his right as chief and head, and imposed their names. He is elevated above all for the purpose of commanding. How could he pay attention to a voice other than the voice which came from God, except, alas to the voice of his spouse? Satan does not dare to strike against this rampart, to attack this stronghold directly. To become master he must change his tactics, he must concentrate his infernal strategy on one who is very near and dear to Adam and who is, moreover, weaker than he. He must begin with the woman.

Christ is Chief and Head in the supernatural order. From the point of view of the natural course of humanity, He follows the common order; He mingles with His brethren and the crowd. He is in the midst of them, and that is why they know Him not. By his hunger after the fast, He emphasizes and proclaims the common human conditions and voluntarily offers Himself to temptation as later He will offer Himself to suffering and death. His fullness of wisdom and knowledge in the supernatural order is hidden from Satan, who makes every effort to find Him out and test Him.

He is King, but His kingdom is not of this world, yet this does not prevent Him from being King of this world. He calls the devil "prince of this world," reserving to Himself the title of royalty. The Scriptures appropriately call the devil "king of the sons of pride," namely, king in the order of sin. Only there is the devil truly *princeps* or first; and he insists on being the first.

God clearly affirmed that Mary was Satan's enemy and that she was to crush his head. But Satan does not tempt her; he seems to ignore her. She is too hidden, Grignon de Montfort would perhaps tell us. It is not impossible nor is it a contradiction that Mary could have been tempted by the devil. What is certain is that Satan approaches Mary's Son. He seeks to deceive, not the woman, but the Son of woman. Moreover, he no longer appears under the form of the serpent, but he assumes a form more in conformity with his true nature.

We must study the advances that the false prophet makes to the Son of man in order better to understand both Satan's ruse and the way to answer him and foil his plans. In the "annunciations" contained in the words of the devil and the answers of Jesus, the entire future is comprised. The adversary betrays himself in spite of himself and informs us of his plans and tactics. Let us note that the temptations of the Son of man by Satan are, much more than those of the innocent Eve, connatural to our present state of fall and similar to the ones to which we ourselves must submit. This is quite normal. If it were otherwise, Jesus could not serve as an example and model for us. In these temptations we shall point out in particular the aspects which pertain to the great virtues about which we have spoken: faith, humility, and obedience. The fact is that Satan addresses himself to all the aspects and states of our poor nature with the consummate art of a dialectician who cunningly varies his points and methods. "You do not know that I am a logician," he tells one of Dante's characters. We should know it only too well, yet we never know it well enough.

The enemy approached Eve only when Adam was not with her. He approaches the New Adam only when the true Eve is no longer with Him. Mary was like a rampart, even for Him, which Satan did not dare to attack; a frontier which he did not dare to pass. For us, she must always be there. Such separations and such isolations would be dangerous and culpable. For Jesus, they are the condition of His terrible and victorious duel. Jesus sets Himself apart from all, even from Mary. This separation of Jesus is holy, whereas Eve's would be culpable and imprudent for us.

The Temptation of Eve and of Christ

Let us come now to the exegesis of the temptation of Christ. Here and there, the text of St. Thomas seems to present some divergences which are rather baffling at first, but they ultimately furnish a doctrine which proves precious in its applications.[5]

St. Thomas treats first of the mode and order of Christ's temptation. First of all, the question of mode. The temptation which comes from the devil is made by way of suggestion, as St. Gregory has remarked. Suggestion can succeed on two conditions which seem, at the outset, difficult to reconcile. In the first place, it will rely on the deepest instincts of our nature; in the second place, to insinuate itself

[5] *Summa theol.,* IIIa, q. 41.

more easily, it will begin with what is less grave, advance to what is more grave, and end with what is most grave.

St. Thomas declares that he finds an analogy of all this in the first temptation in Eden. The devil first inquired about the interdiction on the eating of the fruit; "Why has God forbidden you to eat from all the trees in paradise?" In the second place, the devil proceeded to the subject of vainglory: "Your eyes shall be opened." In the third place, the temptation was extended to pride: "You shall be as gods." The devil followed this same order in temptation when he addressed himself to Christ. The greatest attention must be accorded to all the terms set forth here by St. Thomas. Was the eating of the forbidden fruit truly the very first object of the temptation and the sin? Do we, from all points of view, find the same order in the temptation of Eden and in the temptation of Christ?

Let us refer to the doctrine that we find in other parts of the *Summa*. St. Thomas states that various movements can concur in one and the same sin but that that alone will be the reason or formality of the first sin in which we observe a disorder.[6] Then he demonstrates that in the first human temptation the first sin could only be one of pride because of the state of original justice.

In the second objection of the same article St. Thomas quotes a text from St. Ambrose according to which Christ's temptation followed the same order as the temptation which the first man had succumbed. Now, of the three temptations which comprise the great temptation of Christ, the first one is formally a temptation of gluttony. "Command that these stones be made bread." Therefore, the first sin of the first man was not a sin of pride but of gluttony.

St. Thomas answers that gluttony had its place in the sin of our first parents, for the woman saw that the fruit was

[6] See *Summa theol.*, IIa IIae, q. 143, a. 1.

184

good to eat and she took of the fruit and ate it. Nevertheless, the goodness and beauty of the fruit were not the
primary motive of the sin. It was rather the terrible persuasion of the serpent: "Your eyes will be opened and you shall
be as gods." The woman desired that and there was the sin
of pride. Hence, the sin of gluttony was only a consequence
of the sin of pride.

In proving that the mode and order of the first temptation was fitting, St. Thomas says that in every sin we find
the same order as in the first sin. He explains this by stating
that the concupiscence of sin is first presented to the sensuality, represented by the serpent. The enjoyment is afterward presented to the inferior reason, represented by the
woman. Lastly, consent to sin is given by the superior reason, represented by the man.[7]

All these comparisons are from St. Augustine and project
a profound clarity on the three characters of Eden's scene
by distributing the roles and indicating the characteristics
proper to each. The same holy Doctor sketches in a striking
way the scene between the serpent lying in wait for the
woman's heel to lay snares for her, and the woman lying in
wait for the serpent's head in order to crush it. The serpent,
comments Cajetan, tries to engage our inferior reason in
the enjoyment of sensible things, appealing to the woman
that is in each of us, that part of us which remains invincibly
feminine in the most virile being. La Fontaine would say
here: "I know well in this regard a good number of men
who are women."

While inferior reason (symbolized by the woman) can
become detrimental and even fatal when it intervenes over
and above its legitimate domain, it can also be beneficent,
useful, and even necessary when it respects its limitations
and asserts itself without over-stepping them. The Book of

[7] *Summa theol.*, IIa IIae, q. 165, a. 2.

Job offers us a striking example of the excesses to which woman's judgment can be carried. Instead of the compassion and consolation which would have been normal when the husband was mysteriously stricken, she aspires to raise her judgment against her husband and, as an inevitable consequence, against God. "And his wife said to him: Dost thou still continue in simplicity? Bless God and die. (In the Greek of the Septuagint: Say one word against the Lord and die.) And he said to her: Thou hast spoken like one of the foolish women." Here we see *stultitia* or foolishness as St. Thomas defines it, as opposed to *sapientia* or wisdom. The inferior reason always results in foolishness when it is obstinate and refuses to submit to the superior reason enlightened by wisdom. Wisdom is represented by the attitude and the impeccable words of Job: "If we have received good things at the hand of God, why should we not receive evil?"

The Tempter's Allies

In the body of the second article of the question we are discussing, St. Thomas recalls that man is a composite of intellectual and sensitive nature. These are two different supports or allies for the tempter and he will lean sometimes on one, sometimes on the other, or on both at the same time. In every human intellect there is a desire to know, which can become all the more imperious in the measure that the person is more noble in virtue of his personal temperament or given circumstances. Drawing as near as possible to divine knowledge, penetrating more profoundly not only in the knowledge of good but also of evil, this tendency is found everywhere and the enemy profits from it as much and as often as he can. The deep-seated needs of our intellect do not suppress but sometimes arouse the multiple appetites which are rooted in our sensible nature and of which the temptation will take as complete advantage as possible, counting on success in the measure that the objects that it proposes have more or less affinity with us. Such is human nature such as we experience it in ourselves.

Let us recall that in Eden, in the integrity of the state of innocence, everything was a unified whole. Unity and peace were safeguarded by the perfect submission of the sensible part to the spiritual part and could not be menaced as long as that submission lasted. A direct and immediate attack of the enemy against the sensible part was not even possible, so invincible was the stamp of the spirit. It could be attacked only from above. But once the unity is destroyed and the domination of the spirit has disappeared, the state of fragmentation which results makes man susceptible to all the initiative and schemes of the tempter. He can undermine and attack any point whatever, because everything is stripped of protection.

As regards the sin of our first parents, it was impossible for it to be anything but a sin of pride. It was impossible for the enemy to attack by means of sensible objects before attacking by suggesting the objects of pride. Whatever preceded was only preparatory, which does not mean unimportant and without influence, but it did not itself constitute sin.

As to our own temptations and the temptation of Christ, to which He willed to submit Himself, it is just the contrary. The priority of temptation by sensible objects, even by gluttony, is of the physical order. Things succeed themselves in time, starting from below, and ascend the slopes of the spirit more or less rapidly.

In his *Commentary* on the Gospel of St. Matthew, St. Thomas says [8] that Scripture, mentions three kinds of

[8] *Super Evangelium S. Matthaei,* cap. IV, 1.

temptations. Sometimes God Himself tempts man, but it is always to instruct him; thus it was said in Genesis that God tempted Abraham. Sometimes man tempts man, and it is to instruct and to learn or to be taught or informed. For example, it is said that the Queen of Sheba, interested in questioning the celebrated wisdom of Solomon, came to tempt him by riddles. On other occasions, the devil tempts man and it is always, at least in the final analysis, to deceive him. St. Paul aptly calls him "he who tempts."

The more clever the temptation, the more it is directed at the outset to what is common to us all—what is strongest in us—our most vulnerable points. St. Thomas says that the common vices of the human race are vices of the flesh, principally gluttony. These last two words are astonishing and instructive. Let us recall that in the treatise on temperance, eating and drinking are the first matter of concern, for the preservation of the individual is of primary importance. This enables us to understand why in Eden the very first sin, necessarily and formally a sin of pride, will not present itself without an allusion to "fruit good to eat." He who wants to besiege a stronghold begins with the weaker part.

St. Thomas continues by saying that man has two parts: carnal and spiritual. The devil always tempts the weaker part. That is why he first tempts on the matter of vices of the flesh and, for our first parents, it is on the matter of gluttony.

The rest of St. Thomas' commentary projects a vivid light on the explanation of Eve's sin. The astuteness of the tempter is astonishing. He attacks directly on one point but in such a manner that he reaches another obliquely and, moreover, a much more important one on the spiritual plane. He persuades Eve to eat the fruit of the tree. Such an action, isolated from all the rest, would be only a sin of the flesh, and among the sins of the flesh would be a sin of glut-tony. But in a hidden manner, an indirect and oblique man-ner, he urges and pushes the woman and involves her in spiritual sins, especially sins of pride and disobedience. The promise: "You shall be as gods," indicates in a very sig-nificant way that the object in view is wholly spiritual: pride. No longer has this anything to do with the flesh; it is elevated infinitely above it. Christ's first temptation will suggest to us analogous remarks.

The Effect of Gluttony on the Spirit

Certain faults seem to have but little gravity and in reality they do have little gravity if considered only from the point of view of the flesh. However spiritual we may be, we always remain, according to the essential law of human knowledge, strangely dependent on the senses. What is slightly grave in matters of the flesh runs the risk of appearing slightly grave to us in all respects, but behind the more or less insignificant carnal mask there is always the spirit with its faults and possible errors. Between the flesh and the spirit, so distant from each other in appearance, there is a greater reciprocal influence than we can imagine, for the good reason that both together form one and the same human nature. The tempter's ruse consists in con-centrating on that trivial carnal speck and in casting a shadow on the spiritual disorder of pride or disobedience.

Let us beware, moreover, of the prevalent idea that sins of impurity are the only sins of the flesh which truly count and that those which concern eating and drinking are of hardly any importance. It is true that the sins of impurity are generally much more grave, but it is false that they are greater sources of temptation than any other faults. The question here is of the preservation of the individual, al-ways more interested in himself than in another. Thus, there is a great tenacity in the appetites which derive from the instinct of self-preservation. Moreover, absolute chastity, a radical and simplifying solution, can be practiced, whereas a complete abstinence which would eliminate all eating and drinking cannot be attained without a miracle, which was granted only to a few saints. The very fact that the borders of mortal sin are far away when it is a question of drinking and eating does not obviate certain perils. We do not take precaution, and the tempter, under the guise of slight venial faults, can insert certain suggestions which would have unforeseen consequences in our spiritual life.

It is worthy of note, St. Thomas says, that many men consent and yield a little to certain carnal vices because they think that this slight concession will not cause them to lose their state of spirituality. This temptation would have little serious effect if it could be consented to without great spiritual damage. As for the temptations of Eve and Christ, the tempter went still further, since he promised spiritual goods and made them attractive before their eyes by means of the sensible goods toward which he urged them.

Apart from the prohibition in the spiritual order, there was scarcely matter for a venial sin in the fruit which was good to eat and fair to the eyes. For Eve, because of her perfect state, this could not be the first step in the descent toward evil. But for us things can begin to be spoiled by misfortunes of this kind. It frequently happens. It is by compromises and concessions that the tempter makes an effort to attract the Divine Lord fasting in the desert. What St. Paul so forcefully calls the concupiscence of the spirit against the flesh loses something of its vigor. The spirit already has such difficulty in maintaining itself intact in the midst of our frailty! It is somewhat disarmed. The concupiscence of the flesh against the spirit, whose accomplice our nature always remains, profits from the least bit of lost ground and entrenches itself there.

We see in what sense and with what distinctions we can make the beautiful words of St. Ambrose our own: "The devil attacks Christ at the point where the defeat of Eve had begun." The difference, we have seen, is that Eve could not be attacked by successive maneuvers; all must be overthrown with one stroke. For us and for Jesus who wills to be one of us, the effort must be aimed at some particular point. This point should be chosen with all the more care since a more spiritual being is the object of the attack. But the ambushes which triumphed over the woman shall not triumph over the Son of the woman. Instead of the serpent's victory, the victory belongs to Him who had consented to be tempted in order to teach us how to conquer the tempter. Jesus teaches us not only to expose the ruses of the enemy, but to turn them against him. The supreme elegance in the order of the attack leading to victory is worthy of imitation. "The first human couple succumbed in the same way that Satan succumbs to the New Adam whom he dared to tempt." It is difficult to give an exact translation without losing something of the rigorous brevity of St. Gregory: *Quibus autem modis primum hominem stravit . . . secundo homini tentato succubuit.*

In analyzing Jesus' temptation we have the best opportunity to predict what the enemy's first insinuations will be in our regard. There is one thing that men, even the most spiritual, cannot keep from desiring because they absolutely need it: the nourishment of the corporeal nature. Union with matter is essential to man and he would be foolish to want to exempt himself completely from it. But the more spiritual a man becomes, the more he tends to reduce the temporal to a minimum. St. Thomas has noted that this is what constitutes the virtue of poverty if it is fully understood. It also consists in looking after this minimum to preserve it in a good state as a sufficient and efficacious means. The spiritual person, by definition and by temperament, is always somewhat maladjusted and tends to become so more and more in virtue of his age, his state of fatigue, or malady. He can be tempted to come to the aid of this physical and moral misery. The enemy will tempt spiritual souls all the more as he discovers in them these small and great miseries.

Certain actions of Jesus manifested the power of His divinity; others showed the weakness of His human nature, such as His hunger after the forty day's fast. St. Hilary even goes as far as to say that the devil never would have dared to tempt Christ if he had not seen in Him a human nature suffering the weakness of hunger. Satan knows that he is confronted with a man who is at least very spiritual. He therefore speaks only of what is completely necessary: bread.

These are his tactics: to speak first only of necessary things and to suggest only slight faults. To deal with that which is important from the physical point of view and slight from the moral point of view. To tempt a spiritual man, the devil stresses grave necessities of the physical order which involve the possibility of slight faults in the moral order, such as what concerns nourishment. The spiritual man is accustomed to deprive himself of what is not necessary and to recoil before the least thought of a grave fault. In matters of purity the tempter is less likely to succeed, for the sexual instinct concerns the necessities of the species, and since such sins become grave very quickly, the spiritual man is accustomed to avoid the objects and their occasions. With anyone but Jesus, the tempter would perhaps insist on points which they would consider necessary in this matter but which in reality are only apparently so, although these may sometimes involve us more than real needs.

The First Temptation of Jesus

If Jesus accedes and commands the stones to change to bread, Satan will know that Jesus is God. It is God's prerogative to command nature, to bring about all that He wills by His word alone, according to the words of the Psalm: "He spoke, and all was accomplished." Satan will be in the presence of a divine action as such, and cannot be mistaken. "If thou be the Son of God." The question here can only be, according to Cajetan, concerning the Son who is consubstantial with the Father and not the metaphorical meaning of "son of God." A mere man has no right to play with a miracle as God can. If, under this latter appellation, Jesus attempts the miracle, the devil has been successful, for he would then know that Jesus is but a man and he has made this man fall into sin.

As St. Leo remarks, Jesus responds not by manifesting His power, but by hiding it. The enemy remains in his ignorance. His effort was shattered against the rock of the divine word. He is punished even more, St. Leo adds, being conquered not by God, but by this man about whom he continues to know nothing definite. Thus, all humanity is honored by the victory that one man wins over the enemy of the human race.

In the first and third temptations, Jesus is the only one who makes use of Scripture; in the second, both make use of it. The devil makes use of it only once, but it turns to his disadvantage.

St. Gregory the Great develops the great example that Jesus gives us here. "Whenever we suffer anything because of the wicked, this example should teach us to have recourse to doctrine rather than vengeance." Such retaliations are not only the most beautiful but also the most efficacious. The intellect is the highest of our faculties and it is always more honorable and profitable for the intellect to settle the accounts of the other faculties.

The very text with which Jesus opposes the tempter proves that it is the virtue of faith which should intervene and save us. It is derived from a beautiful passage from Deuteronomy: "He afflicted thee with want and gave thee manna for thy food, which neither thou nor thy fathers knew; to show that not in bread alone doth man live, but in every word that proceedeth from the mouth of God." Let us recall another great text: "The just man liveth by faith," that is, by the object of faith, which is every word of God.

The just man lives by faith; faith lives by hearing; and what is heard is the word of God. All these scriptural terms are closely connected, and we can proceed from one to the other with rigid logic—from the notion of life and the word of God. This will be true of every word of God. *Fiat mihi secundum verbum tuum.* This acceptance is tantamount to a *fiat* of life. Since my soul lives in the word of God, it is also in His word that it will be able to support everything and endure everything. It is also in His word and in faith in His word that I shall be able to find the strength to resist everything. If Adam himself partially resisted Eve who was weaker in her faith, it is because he was stronger in faith. It is only because of that strength and that faith that he did not go to the limit of the sin of his spouse; that he had not, like her, believed the serpent.

The Second Temptation of Jesus

The devil was not conquered by our Lord's answer. The object of the first temptation was of the sensible and material order. It was rather easy for any man to be aware of it and consequently to evade the snare. The object of the second temptation is wholly spiritual. Furthermore, the terms, "vanity" and "vainglory" clearly indicate that it is of extreme insignificance. It therefore escapes us very easily. From these two points of view it differs from the first temptation and is more dangerous. The devil leads Jesus to the pinnacle of the temple. St. Gregory asks why it should be astonishing that Christ permitted Satan to lead Him to the temple and the mountain when He permitted Himself to be crucified by Satan's tools.

We have seen that faith is necessary to the spiritual when it is a question of a material and temporal minimum which it is impossible to do without. Let us add that it is very difficult to determine the quantity and quality of the temporal goods which we must use for our own needs.

Now let us see what great humility is necessary in the purely spiritual domain where everything is more difficult to apprehend, where the appetites become excessive so easily and are upset by all the forms of pride and vainglory. This is one of the reasons why God permits all sorts of trials and even temptations, so that we do not allow ourselves to grow proud because of the grandeur of His gifts. For this necessary humiliation, God even permits the sting of the flesh and the attacks of the devil.

There is a kind of progression between the first and second temptation. Truly spiritual men, who are hardly ever attentive to the things of the flesh, sometimes act with a certain ostentation and give way to vainglory. The devil attacks them on this point, not only when he has conquered them in the inferior domain, but even when no faults have been committed and they have resisted valiantly. There are, according to Cajetan, many men who have shown themselves full of energy and constancy before faults, such as those of the flesh, who find themselves strangely feeble when it is a question of sins of the spiritual order such as vainglory. How many excellent people know how to resist everything, except a compliment! One need not try to take them by force, for they are disarmed by flattery in a twist of the arm. Others, Cajetan adds, impregnable to flattery and vainglory, will allow themselves to be dazzled by the offer of a kingdom. According to Caesar's words, they will violate their oath only to reign. But this is the third temptation which we shall speak about later.

In themselves, spiritual goods cannot be desired too much. The excess of these desires is exterior to their intimate goodness, to which one could not be too attached. But if this excess is accidental to them, it is only too easy for spiritual men to be attracted to it and fall. As elevated as our degree of spirituality may be, we always feel the effects of the state of fall which no one escapes. Adam and Eve, too, were spiritual because of their state of innocence, and such a perfect state preserved them from faults which are proper to our misery and are characteristic of it. We must never forget the similarities or the differences between us and our first parents. We must remember it particularly when we compare the way in which they were tempted and the way in which we are tempted.

Balance is difficult for us for we are especially unstable. Our clumsy and awkward gropings, the gestures and words which explain them, are an inexhaustible source of petty sufferings and ludicrous situations. We must be resigned and know how to smile. We must try to "be an angel," since this spiritual life is in itself "more angelic than human." Let us courageously and joyously accept being victims in some measure. It is easy to laugh at contemplatives, but our Master defends them from the mockeries of those who do not understand their difficulties, their sufferings, or their merits. They have chosen the better part and they have chosen it with all their heart. This part will not be taken away from them.

To perform a miracle, not for the necessities of hunger but simply to manifest the omnipotence of God, would assuredly be vainglory. The same thing is true of anyone who exposes himself to dangers without necessity. Satan proposes this vainglory in a very adroit way: "Cast thyself down."

Very often, says St. Thomas, a kind of spiritual glory and exaltation in the order of spiritual goods is sought by means of external humiliations. This is almost a perversion of the saying from the Gospel: "He that humbleth himself shall be exalted." One does more than descend, one casts oneself below corporeally, and the spirit, ceding to an unconscious pride, rises in its own estimation or endeavors to rise in the estimation of others. This is the profound meaning of the second temptation.

Again, according to St. Thomas, the proud man voluntarily submits to an inferior as soon as the manifestation of his excellence profits thereby. "Cast thyself down." The devil's intention is always to cast us down as he himself was cast down. His voice, St. Jerome says, can well cry to us: "Cast thyself down," and urge us to do so, but it can do no more; it cannot cast us down.

St. Thomas analyzes the sin of precipitance, which is so easy and so dangerous for certain temperaments. One has not the patience to pass through all the intermediary degrees, prudently to descend all the steps of the stairs, but one hurls oneself head first. Nothing attracts more powerfully than the intoxication of glory. This is Tacitus' famous saying: *In ipsam gloriam praeceps agebatur*. This is the fall. Thus St. John Chrysostom says that certain spiritual persons, after having conquered the flesh, fall into vainglory.

Undoubtedly, in cases of this kind, the question is rarely

of final ruin, of that mortal pride which was Eve's first sin. This vainglory is too vain, too slight, too small a thing to end ordinarily in sins graver than venial sins. It is the buzz of annoying flies which fill the air around us. After a moment they fall dead, as Scripture tells us, in the ointment which attracted them and whose loss they cause because they spoil its sweetness. The perfume of spiritual works evaporates. It no longer mounts up to God, nor even to one's neighbor, who is disillusioned by the ridiculousness of a vainglory which is paraded too much. For the unhappy spiritual man himself, it causes a sort of nausea, of interior distaste which will threaten to stop his progress and paralyze his flight.

Jesus' Temptation and Peter's Trial

"Cast thyself down." This cannot be a prayer; it is a strange command addressed to the Most High by the most low. Because of his sinful state, he always urges that one cast oneself down.

Let us compare this scene, which is enacted on the pinnacle of the temple, with the scene at the lake. Here is a saint still imperfect in regard to his faith but for whom Jesus prays that his faith may not fail, for on the rock of that faith He will build His Church. Simon Peter "casts" his prayer toward the divine apparition which appeared on the lake.

The prayer, St. Thomas tells us, is also a kind of command, rising from low to high, from the little one exerting his influence on the great, from the imperfect to the perfect. All the strength of one's petition is in the strength of his faith. Peter's faith is still "little," as Jesus reproaches him about it; therefore he is also "little" in the power of his prayer of petition. It suffices however, thanks to divine mercy, to call forth the all-powerful command: "Come to

Me on the waters." This command was the object of the prayer: "Bid me come to Thee."

Let us meditate well on this divine mechanism in which our weak intervention brings infinite strength to our aid and puts it at our service. The prayer was as weak as Peter's faith and yet God yields. What counts is the end toward which Peter is called: "to Me." "Whatever the element in which I reveal My actual presence, you must have the courage to join Me there, according to the words of the truly faithful disciple: 'Master, I will follow Thee whithersoever Thou shalt go,' and according to the action of the virgins who 'follow the Lamb whithersoever He goeth.'" Little matter the strange and new element in which it is necessary to be plunged or on which one must walk, and little matter what dear and familiar element must be renounced and left behind. All that is secondary. What matters is that it is Jesus who calls us and who commands us to go to Him.

We must cast ourselves in the water, whether to swim, which is the natural mode of advancing in the water, or to walk on the water, which is the miraculous mode. Peter will later use the natural way of going to the risen Christ who stands on the shore of the same lake. Then Jesus will not call Peter nor will Peter ask Jesus to call him. It will be sufficient for the Beloved Disciple to say: "It is the Lord." Then Simon Peter will cast himself into the sea while the other disciples approach in the ship. Peter cannot wait for the boat, weighed down by the miraculous catch. He listens only to the impatience of his love and his desire. A few strokes and a few steps in the shallow water and he is near the Lord.

For fishermen the boat is the tradition of the family which is transmitted from father to son. It is a human tree marvelously put together to yield to the movements of the waves and yet resist their invasion. For the born fisherman the boat is truly the father's house which he must leave to follow the imperial call of the divine vocation: "Come, follow Me." Whether it is a question of Abraham or of the apostles the command is always the same and it must be followed without reservation: "Go forth . . . out of thy father's house and come into the land which I shall shew thee." For Abraham it was a land, because land is the base of the building of great peoples. The Church is built on rock. But the exercise of the apostolate is better symbolized by water. The apostle's place is on that element. He must walk on it bravely to go to Jesus and to souls. It is almost impossible that, like Peter, we do not begin to sink a little. But the steps will become firm as the heart grows strong. Jesus' arms are there for protection against weakness and fear. At any rate, we must cast ourselves out of the boat. As long as we do not leap over the edge, we remain far from Jesus who calls: "Cast thyself down."

Cast thyself down! It is not far from the edge of the boat to the surface of the water, especially when the sea is agitated by a tempest. Often even then, the water goes beyond the edge and invades the boat. But it is far from the edge of the pinnacle of the temple to the bottom of the abyss where Satan would like us to cast ourselves. Sometimes, it is true, God tempts man, as it was written regarding Abraham; but more often it is the enemy of God and man. Sometimes also it is man who tempts God.

Satan's Abuse of Scripture

Satan transforms himself into an angel of light and even makes use of Scripture. The Fathers of the Church have noted the perfidy of that use, which merits rather the name of abuse and is fundamentally clumsy in spite of all Satan's cunning. This is also what happens with the heretic. According to St. Ambrose, the heretic sets snares to trap the faithful, to snatch the prey from the true Hunter of souls. He does not teach, but he deceives. Other Fathers demonstrate the mechanism of the trap. Thus, St. Jerome tells us that the passage cited by Satan does not apply to Christ but to any holy man. Therefore Scripture is used here incorrectly.

St. John Chrysostom says that the Son of God is not carried by the hands of angels but that it is He who supports the angels by His omnipotent word. If we insist on saying that the angels bear Him up, it would not be to support Him in His weakness but to give honor to Him as sovereign Master. Satan quotes the text: "They will bear you in their hands," but he ignores the text which states that the head of the serpent will be trampled underfoot. In his pride he emphasizes the first statement but cunningly ignores the second. Thus he abuses the text of Scripture.

The perfidious counsel of casting oneself down has nothing to do with the text of the psalm. Satan simply does with greater skill, what his tools, the heretics, will always do. He mutilates the texts, takes what is favorable to himself, and discards what is against him. So Origen remarks that the mere reading of the word of God does not make people better but the letter kills those who desire and love only that. St. Cyril says that God does not accord His help to those who tempt Him, but to those who believe in Him. Jesus refused to perform miracles for the Jews who tempted Him. He merely answered: "An evil and adulterous generation seeketh a sign, and a sign shall not be given it."

The devil cites Scripture here because Jesus had answered with the Sacred Text: "Man liveth not by bread alone, but by every word of God." These words are true for every man, but especially for the spiritual man. To tempt this spiritual man who was perhaps the Son of God, the devil could do no better than quote in his turn the word of God. In this strug-

gle let us admire with St. John Chrysostom "the calm of
Jesus and His great humility in order to conform to it with
all our power. 'Learn of Me, for I am meek and humble of
heart.' Conduct yourself in the same way with men who
have become devils. . . . If you do not speak as Christ did,
you will not attract His grace or even His attention."

Jesus answers with a saying derived from Deuteronomy,
which is the preface and symbol of the New Law: "Thou
shalt not tempt the Lord thy God."

The scene of the second temptation is the pinnacle of the
Temple. The spiritual man is a temple in which the Spirit
of God dwells in a special way. Pride and vainglory are the
fissures through which rise the vapors of an incense which
should be reserved to God alone. "He who tempts a man of
God," says St. John Chrysostom, "tempts God Himself."
The more spiritual a person is, the more he is a man of God,
and hence the gravity of this second temptation and the justice of the application of the words from Scripture with
which Jesus answers it.

The Third Temptation of Jesus

The third temptation is graver in itself than the first two,
but according to Cajetan it is no longer an appeal to pride or
vainglory. The third temptation is one that is addressed to
carnal men who desire the riches and glory of the world,
even at the price of contempt of God. That is why the
temptation does not begin with the words: "If thou be the
Son of God," for it is not directed to spiritual men who are
sons of God by adoption. The first temptation emphasized
the carnal appetites and needs which still remain in a spiritual man and from which it is impossible to be freed completely. The spiritual man strives to escape from the flesh
in order to dwell in the domain of the spirit where, unfor-
tunately, vainglory lies in wait for him. He can only listen

to the third temptation if he has fallen again into that which is most alien to the spirit and if all his appetites have been reawakened.

Jesus is now tempted as the Messias, according to the expectations of the carnal Jews. The whole program of false messianism is summed up here. The Jews expected from the Messias not only victory by the sword, but also the abundance of all temporal goods. Jesus' preaching will clash with all these prejudices which are the origin of a hatred that will not be appeased and will be pursued until the death of the Son of Man.

The tempter causes Him to leave His desert, His solitude, in order to present a false Eden to Him and to try to establish Him there, just as he caused Adam to leave the true Eden for exile in a land become a desert.

The sinful parents of humanity, like the prodigal son of the Gospel, follow an illusion which apes the divine call heard by Abraham: "Go forth . . . out of thy father's house and come into the land which I shall show thee." Eden was indeed the house of the Father; the desert is the land where the tempter leads those who have had the misfortune to obey him, the land where the prodigal became the herdsman of unclean beasts.

Satan proclaims the kingdoms of the earth as his own by the very fact that he offers them to Christ: *tibi dabo*. These words from St. Matthew suffice to prove that assumed possession. All is his because he makes use of it, although he himself, as a spirit, scorns the calf of gold and the material goods of which it is the symbol. St. Luke's text is more explicit: "To thee will I give all this power and the glory of them; for to me they are delivered, and to whom I will, I give them. If thou therefore wilt adore before me, all shall be thine."

Three Transfigurations and Three Mountains

To penetrate these mysteries, we must speak of three transfigurations and three mountains. The angel of darkness seeks to transfigure himself into an angel of light. He does not succeed, however, because here he stands before the inaccessible light, inaccessible particularly for him. In vain does he try to force an approach by using the keys of Scripture. He who dares to make himself the scrutinizer of the majesty of the Son of God is crushed by the glory of the Son of God. Jesus on Tabor is truly transfigured, both in His humanity, the vestment of His divinity, and even in the vestments of His humanity. "And His face did shine as the sun; and His garments became white as snow." After His transfiguration into a being of glory, Jesus will transfigure Himself into a man of sorrows. No longer will there be in Him any beauty or comeliness. His intimates, who will succeed in piercing the veil of glory of the Risen Christ, will never quite succeed in piercing the obscure veil of the Man of Sorrows whom they will always misunderstand to some extent.

Only the word from the Cross, which is foolishness to the Gentiles and a scandal to the Jews, can dissipate the darkness of errors and dispel the fogs of illusions. Thanks to it, neither prejudices nor misunderstanding can subsist. Everything that would tend to be opposed to it can only flee and disappear before its victory. The word from the Cross in a single stroke causes all the prestige of the tempter to fall and levels the mountain of false glory. Satan tempted first to vainglory; now he proposes the false glory of the kingdoms of the world. All these glories can only be vain or false because they do not desire the final loving acceptance of the Cross, of that Cross which is not only the only salvation but also the only glory of the world such as God has

204

decreed it. Every other glory should be directed to it under pain of irremedial perversion.

The glory of Tabor is true because the conversation of the transfigured Christ, of Moses, and of Elias, concerns the sufferings and ignominies which will be accomplished in Jerusalem. The mystery of the Cross is fully accepted by Jesus and by the two witnesses who sum up the Old Testament and are no longer of this world. The other witnesses, the apostles, are still in the world and that is why they will understand and accept only little by little.

And the third mountain is that of sacrifice. The Lord said to Abraham: "Take thy only-begotten son Isaac, whom thou lovest, and . . . offer him for an holocaust upon one of the mountains which I will show thee." Here is the cross in all its horror and all its splendor. Isaac asks the question which sums up the entire Old Testament: "Where is the victim for the holocaust?" The Old Testament can only answer with Abraham: "God will provide a victim for the holocaust, my son." With John the Baptist, the New Testament responds and that response also summarizes it completely: *Ecce Agnus Dei.* Isaac accepts in silence, bends down, and stretches himself on the wood of sacrifice. But here the sorrow will end by being transfigured and converted into joy. The lamb is saved. "Abraham lifted up his eyes and saw behind his back a ram amongst the briers sticking fast by the horns; which he took and offered for a holocaust instead of his son." When it concerns His own Son, God will not spare Him. Isaac was offered but he was not delivered to the sacrifice. Jesus was delivered for us all, and by His own Father.

Listen and see, faithful soul. Forget your people and the house of your father. Forget all things so as to have before your eyes and in your heart nothing but "the land which I shall show thee." There I shall speak to your heart, and the word will be the word of the Cross, which is the strength and wisdom of God for all whom it saves. It is the sword-pierced heart that you cannot avoid. The heart of the true Isaac did not avoid it nor did the heart of His Mother avoid it. Your soul must be transpierced. The heart of the first Isaac was spared because he was to be the source of a whole posterity according to flesh and blood. But when it is a question of spiritual generation, the heart of flesh can be emptied of its blood, the flesh can be struck and die so that the spirit may be saved and live on.

Prodigal sons go away from the house of their earthly father at the call of a voice, but that voice is not the voice of the Father who is in heaven. The region to which they are led astray is always distant. One cannot fall lower than with the women of bad life who surrounded the prodigal, but sometimes the man exiled from the paternal house is attracted by the mirage of great heights and is led astray into the mountainous region of pride. Freed for a time from certain shameful compromises and proud of a solitude which makes him greater in his own eyes, he does not perceive that it is still the tempter who leads him into that solitude and will speak to his heart there. Once more, as St. Augustine says, Satan imitates God.

From the height of his pride and ambition exiled man believes that he dominates all the kingdoms of the earth. The shocking truth is that he is dominated by an invisible summit, a hidden tyranny which is exercised on all the sons of pride. He easily forgets the house of his father and believes that he is well off on the summit where his illusion attempts to create a new fatherland. The prodigal child of the Gospel can find only suffering and distaste in the mire in which he is sunk. Nostalgia revives spontaneously. The more the sensation of exile is sharpened, the more intensively the remembrance of the lost fatherland is awakened.

If the spouse of the psalm can forget the house of her father, the reason is that the house of the husband has become a still dearer fatherland. True contemplatives no longer remember anything because a definitive fatherland has absorbed all others, the celestial Fatherland of which their life is no longer but a foretaste. Betrothed with their whole being to the Spouse of the eternal nuptials, they are so detached that they do not even think of what is terrestrial. They forget the world easily, but the prodigal, chained to the impure beasts and concupiscences, sometimes violently forces himself to forget. Every desire is generative of forgetfulness and would wish to annihilate what has been left behind so that he can yield to his hunger. What is to be desired with all our hearts for the prodigal children is that the nausea of shame may be so strong that it will drive away infamous desires.

It is written that the tempter took Jesus away to a high mountain. To have some chance of success, the temptation must be elevated or seem to be elevated, at least in its surroundings. Christ cannot be tempted by vile things like the prodigal. From stones in the path the temptation rose to the pinnacle of the Temple. But edifices built by man's hand, the highest realizations of human art, even when they are consecrated to God, are small things in comparison with the gigantic constructions of nature. That is why the mountain is most suited as the place of the third temptation.

Tabor is a very real mountain, like the glory of the Transfiguration, and like the sorrows and the death of the Cross. Christ could enter into His glory which was proper to Him only by virtue of His passion. When the King of glory rises to the full height of His stature in the splendor of His definitive victory, the princes of heaven will have to raise the eternal gates. But before that time, the bloody gate is lowered toward the earth and the Man of Sorrows can only pass it by bending under the weighty reality of His cross.

The two mountains are described in the Gospel as high mountains. The mountain of the Transfiguration, says St. Matthew was *excelsum seorsum*, whereas Satan's mountain was *valde*. These are two significant strokes. The mountain of pride is extremely high, *excelsum valde*; Tabor is also high, in reality higher still, but it is apart, *seorsum*. Certain mountains are high, but are not sufficiently set apart. They are too evident and attract men's attention too much. This is not the place where Jesus will transfigure Himself and transfigure us with Him.

Ambition and Idolatry

The tempter shows Jesus "all the kingdoms of the world and the glory of them." When Satan perfectly reigns over men, says St. Thomas, he makes them glory in their servitude and in his reign. That glory is not only false, it is thoroughly evil and is the last degree of sin.

St. Thomas observes that Satan tried from the first to become aware of the divine character of Jesus. Believing that he has discovered that Jesus was not the Son of God, he dared to say to Him: "All these will I give thee, if falling down thou wilt adore me." He lies shamelessly and usurps what belongs only to God. Divine Wisdom alone can say: "Through Me kings reign and princes ordain what is just." The world is so bad that the first part of the verse could at times seem to apply to the tyranny of Satan over rulers, but that interpretation is impossible because of the second part of the same verse: "princes ordain what is just." Domination can be violently usurped by the powers of hell, but justice comes only from God and can belong only to God. When, through misfortune, the wicked reign, they can only do so by virtue of a divine permission. This evil is often nothing other than the most terrible of punishments, merited by the sins of the people, as we read in the book of Job.

Moreover, St. Jerome says that the evident proof that Satan cannot give, as he boasts, all the kingdoms of the world is that God has deigned to accord to men many excellent kings. St. Remigius emphasizes what he calls the "insanity" of Satan for promising to give earthly kingdoms to Him who bestows heavenly kingdoms and the glory of the world to Him who is Lord of the glory of heaven.

The spirit of lying and cunning has just promised something, but the spirit of pride is about to try to obtain something different. What is this something different? "Fall down at my feet and adore me." Satan always perseveres. He cannot escape from that evil will in which he was confirmed by his sin. The words that he has just addressed to Christ shed light on this sin, and tradition recognizes a description of his sin in the words of Isaias: "I will ascend into heaven; I will exalt my throne above the stars of God; I will sit in the mountain of the covenant. . . . I will ascend above the height of the clouds; I will be like the Most High." [9]

"I will be like God," proclaims Satan, and he will always and everywhere repeat it. These are his first words, which drew the thunderbolt of the avenging Michael. The words which were spoken in Eden: "You shall be as gods," are only the echo of the first, reducing the immensity of angelic ambitions to the proportions of human pride. But here again, Satan is concerned with making himself adored. To adore Satan, one must imitate him in his fall, for one cannot adore Satan without falling as he fell.

One must always fall. This is Satan's eternal request, whether it is a question of the supreme and definitive fall of idolatry, or whether it is a question of the preparatory fall of ambition. We aspire to honors which seem to raise us in the eyes of others but which in reality abase us. Ambitious men always humiliate themselves to an extreme. They al-

[9] See Isa. 14:12–14.

ways go beyond the point which tact and moderation require. They do not know how to be magnanimous because humility is inseparable from magnanimity. There, says St. Ambrose, lies the real danger of ambition. It feigns a humility which, in reality, is puffed up with pride. It puts itself at the service of others but only for the purpose of dominating them. It bows low obsequiously, but only to seek praise. Wishing to rise up and be elevated, it abases itself. Dreams and desires of splendor can be one of the most efficacious means of the activity of worldlings, but to the spiritual they are always real imperfections and easily become culpable.

St. Thomas says that in the panorama of the kingdoms seen from the mountain the allurements of riches were much greater than those of honor. The promise of reigning included that of enjoying the abundance of wealth. Therefore, we here encounter a direct and mortal threat against holy poverty, which is an essential condition for high spiritual development and its fruitful superabundance in souls by preaching.

Christ's Answer

Many abuses had been addressed to Christ and overlooked by Him. He had ignored many attacks and many invectives. He had endured the offense of many deeds and many words, but He does not endure this one. Here it is not His humanity, but His very divinity which is injured. But Jesus does not argue nor does He make known His divine secret. Without revealing Himself to the enemy, He unmasks Satan by the word of God. In like manner, when Satan recited the prohibition of God to Eve, she should have turned that precept against the serpent. But in this kind of fencing it seems that the woman cannot wield as well as a man the sword of the spirit which, according to

St. Paul, is the word of God. By wielding this sword, man, by reason of the greater strength that is his through his authority through his grace as head, more efficaciously keeps the tempter from the souls that are confided to him. Similarly, the cherubim, armed with the flaming sword, prevented the return to Eden of the sinful couple condemned to exile. A kind of "strategic withdrawal" of the woman under the cover and the protection of authority represents her preferred refuge and sometimes the only possible one.

Eve's disobedience strips her of the spiritual arms from on high, which the Holy Ghost confers on the faithful. By his perfect obedience, the Son shows us how to return to the Father, to lean on the immutable rock, and to be no longer weak and alone, for the Father will be with us. We shall participate in the unity of the adorable Trinity, in which three are one in the same spirit as, through the sacrament of marriage, two are one in the same flesh. From the inaccessible refuge of obedience we can command Satan as Jesus commands him, for one commands the most low in the degree that one obeys the Most High. The bad angel is put to flight, discomfited, and disconcerted; the good angels, who comfort us in our agonies and whose fraternal ministry surrounds us in our fatigues, are attracted to us.

When the devil retires, says St. John Chrysostom, he does not obey, but he merely gives in to the force and divine violence which dominate him. Let us not use the sacred term obedience in his regard. It is not a question here of this great virtue, for Satan never obeys any more than he practices true humility or true supernatural faith. But we can remain firm and confident in the midst of his most harsh attacks. He cannot tempt us as much as he would wish, but only in the strict measure of the divine permission. According to the touching expression of St. Paul, God, who is faithful, will not permit that we be tempted beyond our strength, but with the temptation He will provide a happy outcome by giving us the power to overcome it. This happy outcome often constitutes a true spiritual progress which consoles and rewards us. Let us apply here the words of the Sacred Text: *non procedes amplius*. As for the waves of the sea, God has fixed a limit to the waves of temptation, and they shall not pass beyond it.

"Begone, Satan!" The Gospel puts these words in the mouth of Jesus and directs them to two different persons: Satan and St. Peter. It is impossible that the meaning of these words should be the same in each case. According to St. Jerome, it is not the same sentence which condemns Peter and Satan. To Peter it was said: "Get behind Me, Satan," which means: "Follow Me, you whose will does not at this moment agree with Mine but is raised as an adversary against Mine." To Satan it was said: "Go, begone." It was not said: "Get behind Me, follow after Me," but: "Go to the eternal fire which has been prepared for you and your angels."

We are all, very often, enemies of the Cross of Jesus. We are then the instruments of Satan and deserve to bear the passing stigma of his name. St. Thomas says that Peter had wished in some way to prevent the Passion of his Master and by His harsh rebuke Jesus wishes to put Peter back in his proper place and restore him to the following of Christ. Indeed, after that infidelity of a moment, as after the triple denial drowned in the tears of repentance, Peter, perfectly obedient, will follow Jesus unto death, even to the death of of the cross. Peter was saved, as we shall also be saved, by the obedience which puts us behind Jesus to follow Him.

Jesus prays for Peter so that his faith will not fail or that the weaknesses of that faith will be, as in this case, quickly overcome. In the measure in which the man of the Church becomes again a man of the world, he exiles himself from that Eden which the prayer of Jesus wills for him. Jesus does not pray for the world, especially when this accursed term represents a weakness of faith in those who are charged with inspiring the faith in others and who should, therefore, maintain it firm and strong in themselves.

We too, like the apostles, must lead others to God, and we can do it only if we ourselves advance toward Him. This will happen only if we begin to be completely submissive to Him, with the total obedience that we owe Him. We are always forcibly led back to this obedience.

Let us note with St. Ambrose that in these "wrestling matches," in this struggle for the life of the spirit, Satan is not accustomed to resist or to hold on indefinitely. He yields before acts of true virtue. The rage of his envy is not appeased for long, but he fears to insist lest he suffer too many defeats.

St. Athanasius says that Satan came to Christ hoping to find Him only a man like the others, but he withdraws as soon as he sees that there is no sign or vestige of the race of of the serpent in Jesus. "The devil departed from him for a time," says St. Luke, that is, until Gethsemani and Calvary, when the soul of Jesus will be tempted by a sorrow unto death, as His soul had been tempted in the desert by the mirage of the pleasures of earth.

The Victory of Jesus and the Defeat of Eve

The triple victory of Jesus over the tempter corresponds to the triple defeat of Eve in Eden. As soon as she had "raised her eyelashes against her Creator" (the phrase is from Dante), everything is changed in her and around her. In a wholly different light and with wholly different eyes, she sees the seductive fruit. She sees it good to eat, fully satisfying the appetites of the flesh. She sees it "delightful to behold," satiating the proud concupiscence of the eyes, and inviting all the audacities which tempt God. She sees the desirability of responding to the ambitions of intellectual pride which promises the domination of the spirit over the world. In all this, the woman gone astray lets herself be seduced more quickly and more profoundly than man. Man is always a little defiant and although defiance may be unfortunate elsewhere, it is fortunate here.

"You will be like gods in knowledge." This "divinization" by knowledge always supposes, in a more or less hidden manner, that one falls at the feet of the prince of this world. Scripture refuses to give him the name of king; the Christian refuses to bow down before his tyranny. Instead of saying: "You will be like gods," the tempter could say with greater accuracy: "The gods will be like you, humbled and debased." The absurd and abject anthropomorphism which would condemn the gods and make them descend to nothing more than vicious men, is the ransom and the punishment of the pride of man who wanted to make himself a god—a pride, do not forget, which was first inspired by woman.

You, who were made to the image and likeness of God, will make gods to your image and likeness, the gods manufactured by the hand of men and so often condemned in Scripture. You are not content with being like the true God. You were meant to be gloriously like God, since He made you to His image, stamping on your forehead the seal of His light and the signature of His all-powerful art. You were marvelously efficacious signs as long as you consented to remain no more than pure signs. But you have willed to usurp the reality, to "be as gods" in a sense which could only be illusory. According to Bossuet's profound saying: "All became god, except God Himself."

Let us note carefully that the weaknesses of faith which we have discovered in Eve's sin but which are not found in

Adam's, have their final but normal term in the apostasy implied by idolatrous acts. Active idolatry, like passive idolatry, is the result of Eve's sin. To cause himself to be adored, to impose himself as the object of adoration, is the result of the angel's sin. The perverse imitation of God goes to its extreme limit. The idol takes its place on the altars.

Let us put the last touches to the portrait of the guilty Eve. We could not do it earlier but we can do so now that we have considered the annunciation of Eve and Mary and the temptation of Eve and Jesus. As far as Eve or Jesus is concerned, it is necessary to start with the three "precipitating" temptations on which the Gospel insists.

As soon as we escape ever so little from the captivity of matter and the senses, we find everywhere this appetite or desire for a properly human knowledge, which devours everything and believes that it is nourished with everything. This knowledge goes everywhere and always follows the insatiable illusion that any stone whatsoever can become its bread, that any stone whatsoever can become the foundation of its intellectual edifices, that everything which it touches is consecrated and by that very fact can serve to nourish and to build. That is the falsity, the essential lie! They are the cursed stones which cannot become the bread of children. They are stones that all those who want to construct in a solid and durable manner should pitilessly "reject." One can only build on Christ, the only true Rock. Christ builds His Church on Peter, whom He chose by setting him apart from all the others. As for the only true bread, it is the same for all, as the one true Church is the same for all. The only true spiritual bread is the same for angels and for men. He condescends, with all the weight of His mercy, to make Himself the Bread of pilgrims, in the Eucharist. The poor human caravan, so miserable without Him since it has been driven out of its true country, Eden, stumbles in its journey and strikes its feet on the stones of its exile, unless the angels intervene.

To this kind of intellectual precipitation must be added the precipitance of whims and acts in practical matters. The acquisition of knowledge demands the attentive respect of all the links of the chain of reason. One must raise oneself step by step, as on the stone steps of a tower, toward vaster horizons bathed in a fuller light. In the same way, when one wishes to be plunged into the concrete solutions of action, the foot must be set prudently and firmly on each of the descending steps. If one strikes them violently in a too rapid flight, one risks losing balance and casting oneself down head first to death. Such was the precipitance or fall of the first mother of the living when she replaced the *ordo per virum* by an *ordo per angelum*, full of errors and illusions.

But the most fatal and perhaps the easiest of the precipitations leading to the *mitte te deorsum* is that which humanity knows only too well in religious matters. In place of the *sursum corda* which would raise it to a conception more worthy although farther away from the divinity, it is terribly tempted to stop at the nearest solutions, which seem to satisfy most quickly the yearnings of its senses and passions. The tempter said: "To thee will I give all this power and the glory of them, for to me they are delivered." Among those things which have been given to him, or rather, which he lured from the cult of the Most High, there is much incense which rises not to God, but to the usurping idols. One can only adore them by falling down, and one can fall no lower than that, for it casts one at the feet of the most low.

Mary's Humility and Eve's Pride

From the comparison of the two scenes, Eden and Nazareth, which are the first scenes of the Old and New Testaments, springs a lesson in humility which every creature most urgently needs. Mary is this living lesson, but we can never completely understand the abyss of her humility without casting our glance once again into the abyss of Eve's pride. One statement illumines the darkness of these abysses: The pride of Eve was a maternal pride. This is for every woman a most sensitive point.

The mother of the living knew that all the destinies of humanity depended on her. As she listened to the tempting voice, a profound echo was awakened: "It depends on you alone to make your sons divine, to bring them forth joyously into divine life." What mother has never been tempted to maternal pride? It could almost be said that there would have been some extenuating circumstances if Eve's state of perfect integrity did not deprive her of every excuse.

We recall Eve's pride in order to oppose it to Mary's humility, a humility which is also maternal. The recompense of this humility will be to have a son who will not be "like God" but will be God Himself and to have other sons who will learn from Him and from her to be meek and humble of heart. Satan speaks: "Your sons will be like gods. I shall give them all the kingdoms of the earth if they fall down at my feet and adore me." This is the illusion of pride, full of lies. The Son who will be born of you "shall be called the Son of the Most High. And the Lord God shall give unto Him the throne of David His father, and He shall reign in the house of Jacob forever." This is the recompense of humility. It is authentic, definitive, and eternal.

Let us note how events occur in the terrestrial paradise. The serpent approaches Eve, whom he wishes to ensnare by maternal pride. *Cur praecepit?* It is sufficient to listen to this "why" in order to be led into disobedience. There is a "why," said the Philosopher, at the beginning of every new science. The first "why" for Eve was the first step by which she would plunge into the knowledge of good and evil. After her attention was aroused, the enemy pressed his point: "God said that, but it is not true. If you eat of this fruit, your eyes will be opened and you will have knowledge of good and evil!"

You will know. Which you? Eve or Adam? Both, and even their children. Eve thought about her children. She knew that she would be the mother of the living. She wished to make the living even more alive with an intellectual life which would be ever greater in intensity and extension. She also knew very well that she and Adam held in their hands the destinies of humanity, the whole future of their race. Adam and Eve were giants of spirituality. It is difficult for us to imagine the desire for knowledge which was perfectly proportioned to her nature. Eve could acquire this knowledge instantly and could ultimately obtain it for us all. But in doing this, she enclosed with her all the sons of woman in this circle of knowledge, so vast in appearance but still much too limited for the sons of God.

Eve is fascinated by the perspectives that the serpent's promise opens up to her. "You will know good and evil." She will be able to possess, to enjoy, to communicate this wonderful knowledge to her sons. It depends on her to make her sons like gods. The intoxication of her maternal pride precipitates her into the abyss. To many women after the fall, it is not the intellectual or spiritual horizons that the tempter offers for their children. They would prefer the calf of gold, but Eve was above such base seductions. She was undoubtedly seduced by something completely different, something very noble: an intellectual ideal.

Mary takes exactly the reverse of Eve's attitude. It is proposed to her that she become the Mother of God. Her Son will not be solely *sicut dii*, He will be *Filius Altissimi*. And to this marvelous proposition which touches her to the most profound depths of her heart, to this perspective of infinite glory, she responds: "Behold the handmaid of the Lord." She does not refuse to be a mother, but if she consents, it is to be a handmaid all the more, for no one serves as a mother does. It is only in virtue of her role of handmaid that she accepts to become a mother. The mother is the child's handmaid; the child is the mother's lord. The humility of Mary's *fiat* cures the evil which was done by Eve's proud and silent *fiat*. False spiritual maternity, presented to Eve, had seduced her; Mary consents to accept the true and total maternity which is offered her, but enveloped in the humility of a handmaid.

St. Thomas has told us that woman was deceived more easily than man. We can conclude that she is also more easily tempted, especially if it is a question of the serpent's sly and silent approaches. But the contemplative is the adversary preferred by Satan. The contemplative will attract the tempter's attention and effort by a double title. May she be aware of this, never forget it: may she watch and pray so as not to enter into temptation. The spirit of contemplatives is prompt; the flesh of woman is weak.

The mother also, as we have seen, is sometimes pursued in a very special and dangerous manner. Because of her state of innocence, Eve could easily resist any temptation whatsoever, though less easily than Adam. Let us add that certain temptations were more appropriate than others to seduce her. Would not the most formidable temptation for any woman be that temptation which joins the irresistible power of maternal instinct to the powerful attraction of pride? For spiritual men, ambition represents a culminating point. We understand, then, the serpent's tactics with Eve, making the knowledge of good and evil glisten before her eyes. This knowledge alone can give to evil, which is nothing in itself, its most seducing consistency and a sort of divine superiority to those who possess it. The tempter makes himself strong so that he may give all this, and he will give it, not only to Eve, but, in her and through her, to all her sons, for whom she chooses their destinies.

6

Other Divine Annunciations:

MYSTERY OF SORROW

And thy own soul a sword shall pierce, that, out of many
hearts thoughts may be revealed.

WE have seen Eden's gate sorrowfully close on the exiles.
We have heard from God's lips the annunciation of the
terrible and bloody war.

For the annunciations of which we are now going to
speak, there is no one but God, since it is a priest who acts
as God's representative and instrument. Whether Simeon
himself was a priest matters little; it is a question we shall
discuss later. The role which God confides to him here is, in
any case, the role which the priest ordinarily plays in the
Church. For particular reasons which we shall give, it is
sometimes convenient for God to confide this role to some
person other than a priest.

To the mystery of sorrow of Eden's gate, there is a corresponding mystery of sorrow announced to Mary in the
Temple by Simeon and, later, by the Child Jesus Himself.

In the admirable economy of the holy Rosary, the last two mysteries called joyful undoubtedly merit this name, at least in part, because of the presence of the Beloved finally accorded to the holy old man and later found again by Joseph and Mary. The *Nunc Dimittis* is the most joyous chant next to the *Magnificat*, and the joy of the *Magnificat* is perhaps surpassed by that of the "Recovery," as it was so aptly called in ancient times. But these two joyful mysteries are likewise sorrowful and are a kind of link between the joyful and sorrowful mysteries of the Rosary. Separations still more cruel, longer absences are announced to Mary. The sword begins to sink into her heart, to touch the recesses of her soul, to pierce it through and through and to presage total anguish.

Simeon and the Priest

In the fourth joyful mystery Mary is found with the Child and Joseph before a priest. Eve, before Adam, was before a priest, for Adam was for Eve God's representative and intermediary. Since the sin, the priest is no longer the husband. John of St. Thomas teaches that in the state of original justice there would not have been sacraments, but there would have been sacrifices. It is quite proper to Christ's priesthood that the priest is also a victim. Every victim can only be sorrowful, although when the victim knows how to understand its meaning, the sorrow may be a recompense and the object of an ardent desire and humble request. But the priest as such is in a state of joy, whatever the austerity or apparent cruelty of his ministry. There is in him an essential and profound joy, measured by his love for God and men. He is conscious of reconciling heaven and earth in unity and peace.

Was Simeon a priest? Cajetan responds in the affirmative, basing his argument on the fact that St. Luke relates that Simeon bestowed a blessing on the parents of Jesus, after which he addressed the prophecy to Mary alone. But the blessing of the children of Israel was a function of the priest.

Father Lagrange's opinion is completely opposed to that of Cajetan. He maintains that Simeon had the privilege of bestowing a blessing because of his advanced age. Simeon, says Father Lagrange, was not a priest and he had not gone to the Temple for any priestly function. He was led there by the Holy Ghost. The text does not say that Simeon was an old man, but it is implied. Simeon was an unknown man of modest condition, as are all the persons who figure in these events.

The priest is constituted in his office in view of a certain function belonging to worship and especially to sacrifice. But the fact of not being a priest can acknowledge all the more, in certain cases, the purely instrumental character of certain interventions. It is interesting to contrast the profusion of details given on the prophetess, Anna, with the extreme sobriety of St. Luke's text when it concerns Simeon. A whole life spent in the Temple is not indicated in his regard. There is mention only of his "waiting for the consolation of Israel," of the revelation which he had received ("He should not see death before he had seen the Christ of the Lord"), and of the movement of the Spirit which urges him to go into the Temple at the moment when the Infant is brought there by His parents. The Gospel seems to limit itself to the traits which emphasize the pure instrumentality of Simeon. Simeon is only an instrument of the Holy Spirit and very holy himself. Whatever the case may be, God alone speaks here in the Temple as in Eden after the fall.

If the priest is the man of sacrifice, the Temple is the place of sacrifice. Although God can make use of His in-

struments in all places, there is a special fitness or correspondence between the instrument of God and "the house
of God." In the Temple also the victims are led forth to receive the ultimate consecration through immolation. If the
suffering of the Heart of Jesus is about to be predicted, the
suffering of the Heart of Mary is about to begin. Never has
a victim more pure and more submissive come to be placed
under the sacrificer's knife. There is a twofold sacrifice of
Mary's heart in the Temple: Now, it is the old man, the
instrument of God; later it will be the Child-God, the
Child-Priest. Both together sacrifice this virginal and maternal heart, the holiest of all the victims who are but pure
creatures, and the most agreeable to God. Both plunge the
sword into this immaculate heart.

Whether he be a priest or not, Simeon is in any case the
living figure of the priest. He prefigures the priest of the
New Covenant to whom certain functions of the prophet
of the Old Testament will be restored. This old man, just
and God-fearing, living on the promise and the expecta-
tion, is one of God's intimate friends. He is led by the
Holy Spirit and through him the Holy Spirit will speak to
Mary. This old man will have the function of a priest in
her regard. Mary obeys him and allows him to proceed.
From the arms of the young Mother he takes the Child
into his own arms and ardently presses Him to his heart.
He receives Jesus, after the mysterious invitation of the
Spirit, as Joseph received Mary his spouse after the angelic
reassurance, and as John will receive Mary, his Mother,
after the supreme words of the Crucified: *Ecce Mater tua.*

Mary lets Simeon take Jesus. She will also let us do what
Simeon does. She knows that in taking Him from her, it is
our good that we take. He is ours as well as hers. Miserable
sinners that we are, let us dare to say that in a certain sense
He is more ours than hers by this very title of sinners. The

Immaculate One cannot claim this title, although her own redemption is still more perfect and more complete than ours since it consists of preservation from all sin. To our unutterable poverty she will always bring the alms of her infinite riches, of her Child and her God.

Simeon takes Jesus from the heart of Mary. In His place he plunges into this heart the sword of his terrible words. The serpent's head will be crushed by the virginal foot only if the maternal heart is pierced by the sword. This is the condition for the great victory.

Humility, Obedience, Faith

Let us admire how everything in our present meditations is explained by the three great virtues of humility, obedience, and faith. The first sin of every rational creature, whether angel or man, can only be a sin of pride. In the first human couple this sin ended in disobedience and, in Eve, a weakness in faith. In virtue of his role as head of the Church and in virtue of the all-powerful prayer of Christ for this head, Adam is preserved from sin against faith but he is not preserved from the sin against obedience. That is why Christ, the new Adam, cannot give us too many examples of humility, of annihilation, and of obedience even to death. The recompense of this heroically obedient humility is, as St. Paul tells us, the exaltation of the name of Jesus. Mary herself had already proclaimed the exaltation of the humble in the *Magnificat*.

Because of its special nature, obedience not only elevates to great things but also descends to the smallest things. That is why nothing is unimportant for perfect obedience, or rather, perfect obedience neglects nothing and is satisfied only when it has pentrated everything. Humility is the root of obedience. Now, it is the root which sends the plant toward the sky, the complete plant, even to the most delicate veins of its leaf, the finest shades of its flower, and the most subtle flavors of its fruit. If this is not well understood, it will never be understood how God prepared the chosen people for the coming of the Messias and why the Messias Himself complied fully and perfectly with the Law. *Non veni solvere legem sed adimplere.* Above all, the immense place that obedience holds in the law of love will never be understood. Fear is put to flight and a new soul, full of charity, is breathed into the precepts.

The angel's first sin, which can only be a sin of pride, is a wholly interior sin. The angel stops short and locks himself within himself forever. Man is more dependent than the angel on things which are external to him. When it concerns his intellectual life or his corporeal life, he must seek the necessary nourishment outside himself and assimilate it little by little. Appetite, the desire which quickly becomes excessive, emphasizes the need that it has of this food. Due to the attraction to which we refer, abuse becomes easy. The divine law ruling its usage must intervene; the natural law inscribed on the heart of man imposes itself on his intellect and will and specifies the object of obedience.

In Eden a single positive precept sufficed. After sin had weakened man's will and obscured his intellect, God multiplied the positive precepts because of the multiplicity of infirmities and needs, particularly during the long centuries which precede and prepare for the Gospel. According to the profound words of St. Paul, the law was the "pedagogue" of the race from which Christ was to proceed. The adolescence of this race, which would give of its divine fruit in the fullness of its age, needed, as do all other adolescents, to be surrounded with care, vigilant surveillance, and detailed precepts and instructions. From all this the race of Christ would be freed one day, after attaining its ultimate development.

We see how pride was to culminate in disobedience for the first spouses just as it continues to do for all their descendants in the course of ages. The fullness of pride always results in disobedience. On this point, the condition of Adam as a sinner does not differ from the condition of Eve. But it differs from it completely when it pertains to the ulterior progress of sin in regard to faith, safeguarded in Adam by the requirements of his authority and his ministry. The insurmountable barrier which is raised imprisons his intellect in the holy captivity of faith, whatever the weaknesses of his will may be. His disobedience cannot act on his faith. But it will be completely otherwise for woman. The contagion of disobedience in the will prevails over the intellect of Eve. Moreover, the faculties of woman are almost less distinct from one another than man's. They are more entangled in each other.

In every human being pride always implies at least a tendency to disobedience. But formal acts of disobedience, especially in matters of a positive precept, do not necessarily indicate a weakness in faith. If it were otherwise, Adam would have been led into infidelity as Eve was. He could keep it intact and as head of the Church he did keep intact this faith which was so wounded in Eve. Adam cannot lose the faith; Jesus cannot practice it. Eve and Mary, from two points of view diametrically opposed are the specialists of faith. Mary is blessed and is Mother of all the beatitudes because she believed in God; Eve is unfortunate and mother of all misfortunes because she believed in the serpent.

Between these two extremes are placed all the combinations of faith and incredulity, and therefore all the beatitudes and misfortunes which can be disclosed in the poor exiles of Eden, sons of Eve and Mary. The infinite complexities of these intermixtures explain so many things in the destinies of each one of us! The most eloquent and also the most anguished expression of these fatal struggles for life between the exiled sons of Eve and the reconciled children of Mary is furnished by the Gospel: "I do believe, Lord. Help Thou my unbelief." I believe with all my poor heart, with all my miserable strength, but destroy this accursed unbelief which is always too much present in me. It is the lamentable heritage of Eve and has banished me from that land.

It is well to note that from the point of view of faith the curse of exile injures us more as sons of Eve than as sons of Adam. Our heart can thus seize the whole meaning of these words: *exsules filii Evae*, so often put on our lips by the *Salve Regina*. In us, as in Eve, weaknesses in faith can be immediately traced to the spirit of disobedience, son of pride. The last result of our pride will be to believe no one but the serpent, as our poor mother Eve did, whereas the perfection of humility and obedience will lead us to the blessedness of faith, fully realized in our glorious Mother Mary.

Sensible Signs in the Divine Annuciations

All divine annunciations exact from us the most perfect obedience in the measure that they express order from above. One can no more say: "Lord Jesus, if this is not in the Spirit," than one can enter into the temple if it is not in the Spirit. This is true wherever the temple may be, the Temple of Jerusalem or the temple, no less holy, in Bethlehem, the stable of the shepherds where the star conducted the Magi and where the Child was.

One can come to Jesus only in the Spirit, but the Spirit can reveal Himself by not addressing Himself equally to all our senses, but to a particular sense, whether a corporeal sense or a spiritual sense to which the mystics refer. For unlettered men, without natural or supernatural education, the exterior senses must be strongly and sometimes violently aroused. That the angelic annunciation may strike the shepherds and make them "go over to Bethlehem," it is not sufficient that the immense flashes of light in the heavens dazzle their eyes. It is not even sufficient that the canticle of glory to God in the highest and peace on earth charm their ears. A visible angel must explain to them what the great joy is and the marvel of its universal extension to all peoples. Without the glory and exuberance of this manifestation the poor, ignorant shepherds will not understand and will not set out on their way.

For the Magi, it will be entirely different. They are wise men, astronomers, who know how to read and to whom the alphabet which shines on the immense page of the night reveals many things. Nevertheless they are men, and therefore dependent on the exterior senses. But it is sufficient that the light which is necessary for them be concentrated in a single scintillating star. The only act of their sensible faculty is to see. How do they know that their star is the star of the King of the Jews who has just been born? The Gospel does not tell us.

For the saints, educated by the Holy Spirit Himself, divine annunciations always depend much less and sometimes not at all on the external senses and their objects. The mode is more angelic than human. Here below, they are already like God's angels, as the Gospel affirms we shall all be in the future life. St. Thomas says that knowledge conveyed by signs requires the use of those things which are familiar to the persons to whom the knowledge is imparted. However, through the spirit of prophecy, certain spiritual persons have a familiarity with the internal motion of the Holy Ghost and are accustomed to be taught in that way, without the use of sensible signs.[1] It is understood

[1] *Summa theol.*, IIIa, q. 36, a. 5.

that everything that St. Thomas says and everything that we are going to say is submitted to the judgment of the holy Church.

We can never meditate enough on such a simple and profound doctrine as this. By means of it we can explain certain mysterious communications and certain annunciations whose object it is difficult to determine. Spiritual authors, imitating Holy Scripture, relate the divine communications by analogy with the external senses, such as touch, taste, and even smell. The Canticle speaks to us of the perfumes which follow in the wake of the Beloved. The saints more and more depend only on the interior world. They no longer need, like the Magi, this minimum of external light: the star which moves in the Orient. The interior abysses are more profound, more unfathomable than others, and it is in the depths of these abysses that a light springs forth to lead them. Other lights are extinguished one after the other. The Gospel proclaims the blessedness of not seeing, but it maintains the blessedness of hearing the word of God, because faith depends on hearing. And yet, for certain ones who are more tried and more holy, it can be good that God Himself be silent, that the great silence fall upon them, a silence which no longer permits anything but the activity of the lowly senses of touch and taste. The Holy Spirit deprives the soul of everything and communicates Himself immediately.

But if these are the laws of sanctity and if their application is extended in proportion to one's progress of sanctity, how is it that the Saints of saints, Jesus and Mary, seem to contradict this rule in the mystery upon which we are meditating? Why do they submit to all the humble external rites which are confusing and even humiliating, such as the Child's circumsion and the Mother's purification. Why do they submit to the requirements of Mosaic legality and to the multiple ceremonial details which will not endure?

The answer is to be found in the mysterious name given by the prophet to the Child who is now offered in the Temple. "They shall call His name Emmanuel, which being interpreted is, God with us." God, the Spirit of spirits and infinitely more spiritual than all the angels and all the saints; God with us poor men, with us all, involved in sensible things. If He came to be with us, it is to lead the common life with us, to give an example to us all, lest anyone complain that Christ's example is too far above him. We have said often enough that the most necessary example for the sons of pride and disobedience is that of humility and obedience. That this example may be given in the best possible way, obedience must be very perfect in itself, but the model must be adapted and proportioned to us so that it may be easily understood by us and make a strong impression on us. In entering the Temple, Simeon obeys the Spirit with an obedience which in itself is more perfect than that of the shepherds to the angels and of the Magi to the star, but it is a more hidden obedience and less easily serves as an example to us. Therefore, we could say with St. Paul that a hidden obedience would be even less fitting for Him who, being "in the form of God," took upon Himself "the form of a servant, being made to the likeness of men." An obedience such as Simeon's has less place in the perspective of the Redemption and in the plan of Jesus and His Mother. To counterbalance the marked disobedience of our first parents, there must be in Jesus and Mary an example of purely legal obedience, a very pure obedience in things which are good only so far as they are commanded. The same is true for the objects of pure faith. They too can be accepted by us as true only on the testimony of

God. In the case of obedience, as in the case of faith, the words of St. Paul are justified: "the evidence of things that appear not."

These principles are stated by St. Thomas when he speaks of the fourth joyful mystery. He says that "as the plenitude of grace flowed from Christ to His Mother, so it was fitting that the Mother should be like her Son in humility. . . . Therefore, just as Christ, although not subject to the Law, wished to submit to circumcision and the other obligations of the Law, to given an example of humility and obedience, . . . for the same reasons He desired that His Mother fulfill the prescriptions of the Law, although she was not subject to the Law." [2]

Humility and Obedience

Cajetan summarizes the doctrine of St. Thomas in a few words: "Just as the grace of Christ is showered on His Mother, so also is His humility poured out upon her. Therefore, in the same way that Christ places Himself under the Law, He also places His Mother under the Law. The proof of the antecedent is that God gives His grace only to the humble. The proof of the consequence is evident, as it is evident that the Mother's purification proves her humility." Since this rite is not only humble but humiliating, let us add with St. Francis de Sales that humiliation is necessary to humility, whether it be a question of acquiring this virtue, as in our case, or a question of giving an example, as in Mary's case.

Let us meditate on each of the elements of this powerful abridgment of doctrine which Cajetan sketched with such a sure hand. Jesus wills to give His Mother not only His grace but a plenitude of grace. In the divine salutation of the eternal predestination, of which the angelic salutation

[2] *Summa theol.*, IIIa, q. 37, art. 4.

is but an echo, He says to her in a sovereignly efficacious way: *Ave, gratia plena*. Since He gives His grace only to the humble and in the measure of their humility, He must first be assured of a plenitude of humility in Mary, and her plenitude of humility will necessarily lead to a plenitude of obedience and faith. Eve is the mother of the living by pride, ending in disobedience and in a profound injury to faith. Mary is the Mother of the living by humility, orientating herself, by the practice of this virtue, to the beatitudes of her obedience and faith.

However, St. Thomas raises an objection to the fittingness of Mary's purification. Purification, he says, presupposes uncleanness. But there was no uncleanness in Mary. Therefore, purification was not fitting for her.

St. Thomas answers the objection by stating that if Mary willed to fulfill the precept of the Law, it is not because she needed to do so or because she could derive from it any utility or good for herself, but only because of the good which is in the precept itself. The sole goodness of her purification consists in the fact that purification is commanded. This value, so modest in appearance, is what specifies the virtue and the act of pure obedience. There is also a question here of a sort of purification of the virtue of obedience and its object. Mary's purification had no other *raison d'être* but fidelity to the Law. That is why St. Luke speaks about a purification "according to the Law" and St. Thomas emphasizes that "in herself" Mary needed no purification. If you no longer consider the Law, but only look at Mary, this rite is devoid of all significance. She was obligated in no way. Her obedience was wholly free and spontaneous. She was attracted, like the perfectly obedient, by the precept itself, as the perfectly humble are attracted by humiliation. We add that she was also attracted by her respect for the rites which, undoubtedly, could not purify from sin by themselves, but which prefigure ultimate purification by the grace of Christ. She submitted to the purification as Jesus submitted to the circumcision and shed for us the first drops of His blood whose last drop would flow with water under the Roman lance. If He willed to be circumcised, it was, St. Thomas tells us, to recommend to us by His example the virtue of obedience and that humility of heart which He wished us to learn from Him. Like Him, let us observe in all simplicity what is of precept in the time in which we live.

In order to clarify this important doctrine, it is good to return to St. Thomas' first objection to the circumcision of Christ.[3] The sole reason for the existence of figures is to symbolize the reality; these figures should disappear when the reality appears. We must therefore ask what precisely was the reality prefigured by the rite of circumcision which God had imposed on Abraham. It is evident, according to the text of Genesis, that it was nothing other than the covenant with the entire race. But this covenant was fulfilled in Christ, who was to be born of this race. Therefore, the significance of the rite of circumcision terminated at Christ's birth and there was no reason for this rite to be applied to Christ eight days after His birth.

St. Thomas responds by specifying the precise significance of the rite of circumcision imposed by God on Abraham. It is a question of a stripping of the generation of the old man for the regeneration of the new man. Now, this transformation can be effected completely only by Christ's passion and not by His birth, for the full accomplishment is reserved to His passion. Hence, circumcision and the other ancient rites retain their value and virtue until the passion of Christ.

While it is true that the figure or symbol should cease

[3] *Summa theol.*, IIIa, q. 37, a. 1.

to exist when the reality appears, Christ is a living reality, and that requires a gradual development, as is true of all living things. Time must allow the root and the stem of Jesse to develop into the bloody flower of Calvary and the fruits of redemption. Only then will be accomplished fully what was stated in the prophecy of David: *Regnavit a ligno Deus.* The declaration of Jesus Himself furnished us with the terms whose value we have already tried to weigh. *Non veni solvere legem, sed adimplere.* Let us carefully distinguish this *solutio* from the *adimpletio.* Persons other than Jesus, St. Paul for example, will proclaim the dissolution of the Old Law. The dissolution should not take place as soon as the new-born Jesus appears at Bethlehem, but as soon as He dies on the cross.

These principles of exegesis are in harmony with certain physical theories at the heart of the great Thomistic synthesis. The material predispositions which cause bodies to move toward their substantial change have only a preparatory role which, however, should endure until the coming of the final form, to the instant when it springs forth to confer a new reality and a new name on the composite. So also in the moral and supernatural order, in an instant and at the sound of a word, an unexpected creation springs forth, having been prepared by that which preceded. St. John places on the lips of the dying Jesus the supreme words: "It is consummated." It is the ultimate accomplishment which terminates everything, but which also supposes and summarizes all that had been said and done previously. The same St. John, who always had such a tender devotion for Mary, must not and cannot take her to himself until after the words: *Ecce Mater tua.* Again, it was necessary that Joseph's anguish should endure until the angels message liberated him. The same is true for the spouse as for the Beloved Disciple: *Ex illa hora accepit eam in sua.*

Simeon's Words

After considering the obedience and humility of Jesus and Mary, let us consider Mary's faith. This pertains to Mary alone, since Jesus cannot practice faith, just as Eve alone could be weak in faith in Eden. In Eve, as in us, grave disobedience follows from a weakness in faith.

Two victims came to offer themselves in the Temple: Jesus, who will be stricken later, Mary who will be stricken immediately. She is about to be struck first of all by the old man who represents and summarizes the entire Old Testament, and then, a little later, in this same Temple, by the Priest of the New Covenant, the Child-Priest twelve years old. Under these thrusts of the priest, Mary will die in order to live. This life comes entirely from faith and therefore from the only word which vivifies, the word of God. But this word also causes death. It is the sword of the spirit which wounds and cures, kills and revivifies. The rendings of the soul and heart by the sword of the spirit separate us from all else to unite us always more intimately to the One who said: "I am the resurrection and the life."

These effects of death and life are produced by the word, whether God puts it on the lips of His prophets or priests, whether it pleases Him to pronounce it Himself as a Child in the midst of the doctors of the Law who listen to Him with respect, or crucified and stretched to His full stature on the tree of the Cross in the midst of the doctors of the Law who blaspheme Him. In other words, the priest sacrifices not only by acts and gestures, but also, and sometimes even more so, by words. Words are mysteries of faith, as is said at the consecration of the Mass: *mysterium fidei*. Without faith, the words lose all their meaning and value. Whatever the words may be, crucifying or vivifying, pronounced by God or by His instruments, faith alone permits us to accept them and profit from them.

First of all, there are Simeon's great words. Let us comment on the first words: "This Child is destined." It is the same word which God used in Eden: "I Myself shall destine." The will of God, infinitely holy, "destines" and imposes the war between the serpent and the woman, between their two races. The serpent began the war, but God is the master of the war and of the woman who was a victim of the defeat and an instrument of the future victory. God renews this war which was begun by the serpent and gives it a new point of departure. This war is infinitely holy since God is the master of it. The perverse will of men, on the contrary, "destines" and transposes, if we may so speak, the angular rock of salvation into the rock of scandal and ruin for man.

Jesus is "destined." Each drop of His blood desires to make a saint of each man, but some men will say: "We do not want Him to reign over us." This is the signal for a conflict of will, a struggle without truce and without mercy between God and men, for God allows man his liberty. And here is the shocking result: Jesus is the ruin of many. Men have the immense misfortune of being able to triumph to such a point over the will of God that they have profited by His blood and His love to offend Him even more. The result is the rending of the Hearts of Jesus and Mary because the will of God is not done.

One drop of Christ's blood would suffice to redeem the entire world. His right is that His blood produce its effect and that all men become saints. That is what God has "destined," and that is why God became man.

Our Lord has a strict right to our becoming saints. But the human will can oppose God and God will respect its liberty. What does the human will answer to the sacred right of the Son of God regarding the sanctity of all His members? It says: "No, I will not," and it is the great contradiction which injures the sacred right of God and His Son.

There are few saints in the full meaning of the term and there is an immense mass of perdition. The problem of the number of the elect is hidden in an unfathomable mystery, but it is certain that Jesus was destined for the ruin of many. Simeon confirms it, completely filled as he is by the Spirit of God. It is not only "in spite of" Christ's blood that souls are lost; certain ones seem to want to profit from this blood in order to be more irrevocably lost. They abuse so many graces; they misuse what should sanctify them; they make use of it to plunge themselves into eternal disaster. This phrase seems hard to us who do not understand, but let us try to understand what it means to the Heart of Jesus and, by a necessary consequence, to the Heart of Mary. Let us not be astonished that the adorable Heart has been rent from the beginning. It bursts, so to speak, under the pressure of this mystery of horror.

This Heart loved too much and is loved too little, according to the words spoken to St. Margaret Mary. In humanity's answer to the advances of infinite love, there is a double excess: an excess of love, *propter nimiam caritatem,* and an excess of ingratitude. Caught between these two excesses, the Heart of Jesus is rent. The excess of love already sufficed to pierce it. The torrents of divine love emptying into a human heart would break it. But running against these violent torrents descending from the summits is a torrent of hate, of human ingratitude which rises from below and in this frightful whirlpool the Sacred Heart is almost pulverized and torn to shreds. It cannot be otherwise for the Heart of the Mother, who follows the destinies of the Heart of her Son, and this constitutes the mystery of her compassion.

We may be tempted to curse the wretched souls who are thus lost, but we must not look at what they do; we must listen to what Jesus says. Of what does He complain? He seems to complain especially of us, His friends. We are the ones who in a most cruel way say no to the incomparable Friend that He wishes to be, that He has been, and that He is for us. Blasphemers are too distant. Often they do not know what they are saying or what they do. From the point of view of their intentions, their injury is often only indirect. We, who know what we are doing, contradict directly. Our contradictions, our negations, our refusals cannot miss their mark, and they plunge themselves into the Heart of Jesus. This Heart wants to remain so near ours that everything taking place in us reverberates in Him either to console Him or to torment Him.

Undoubtedly, our Lord has not been "destined" for our ruin, for we were saved by Him. It is none the less true that we contradict Him all the time, that we are occupied all the time in saying no, in hindering His work and preventing Him from doing what He wants. We are not saints and we do not become saints because we say no to Him who is sanctity itself and who wants us to be saints. *Sancti estote quoniam Ego sanctus sum.*

Count how many times we say no to Him in a single day. We abuse, we do not use, grace. I am addressing myself at this moment especially to those among us whom grace has placed at the summit of all things, in the temple of the contemplative life. Count, if you can, the myriad benefits which rain on you during the course of a single day, the grains of mustard seed which contain the kingdom of heaven. Each of these benefits would be sufficient to produce sanctity in us. Can we say that we receive them? At any rate, we do not become saints! We say no! We refuse entrance to these marvelous invasions.

It would be completely otherwise if we were faithful, if we would always say yes to the divine Friend, according to the demands of every friendship. It is easy to strike the breast of others but we must strike our own: *mea maxima culpa*. With others, the fault is slight because they do not know. With me, the fault is very great because I do know or I should know. The "Father, forgive them" of the Crucified scarcely falls on me since, after all, I know what I am doing, or rather what I am not doing, what I neglect to do. I should love. I should be a saint.

We are trying to translate the sentiments by which the sorrow of Christ will pass from His heart to ours, and would save everything in and around us. The salutary sword would pierce us after it has pierced the Heart of Jesus and the Heart of Mary, whose mediation is more evident here than anywhere else. Thus the saints are initiated into the compassion of the mysteries of sorrow. They suffer with Jesus and Mary. The sword pierces them and they generously deliver themselves to it.

St. Teresa of Avila speaks of a wound so sweet that one would never want it to be cured. One suffers terribly, but receives as much delight as suffering. Sorrow and joy are ineffable when one is initiated into the redemptive mystery. It is the wound of love which kills, and yet only this wound can give life. It is this wound which makes saints.

Where can we find words lofty enough to express these things? The liturgy is filled with mysterious glimpses which are distant reflections of the lights of Eden, centered around the great promise of the Redemption. Anyone who is less than a Christian cannot touch this source, this center of the mystery.

Stabat Mater

Let us call to mind the *Stabat Mater*, which surpasses everything that modern piety can formulate. The chant is so simple, the words so profound!

Fac me plagis vulnerari. May I be touched by all your wounds, conquered and transformed by them in the depths and in each part of my being. May all of these wounds come into me, especially the wound of the Heart which is always bleeding in You, O Jesus! May I bear in myself this sweet wound of which one would never wish to be cured!

Fac me cruce inebriari. May I be drunk with the Cross, inebriated by the Cross and with the Blood of your Son, O Mary!

St. Thomas tells us that spiritual intoxication is an effect of the Eucharist when received by the saints. Christians eat, but the saints are inebriated by the Blood. The beloved of the Beloved knew this intoxication more than all the other saints together and can communicate it to her children. That she may do so is the object of our supplication, of our desires, of our tears.

Poenas mecum divide. Make me partake of these superabundant sufferings for your Son and for you. I cannot accept your being alone to support the crushing weight.

Passionis fac consortem. May I be the companion, the associate of the passion of the Son and of the compassion of the Mother! May I be the person who takes on himself a part of such heavy and such sweet weights! May I become a humble and blessed Cyrenean! The essential effect of every sanctifying grace—whether it be given to angels or to men—is to make us share in the divine nature. The essential effect of the redemptive grace of Christ is to make us share in the sorrows of His passion. Such a forceful word as *consors* specifies the doctrine on these two points. We shall be *consortes* of the nature of God only if we are *consortes* of the passion of His Christ. We shall participate in the divine nature by grace only if we are initiated into the suffering of the Man-God.

Let us meditate on each of these words. Like satellites, they revolve around Simeon's great prophecy. Under divine inspiration that old man came into the Temple and plunged the sword into the heart of Mary. Not yet in Jesus' heart; this would happen later. The iron of the lance would replace the sword; the soldier would replace the priest. But from this first hour, Mary was to be a victim. She was the dawn and she will be the setting sun of the mystery of the Redemption. She has sacrificed herself, offered herself to the Father until the Son offered Himself on Calvary. When Jesus died on the cross, Mary remained. She was the bloody purple of the setting sun when the sun disappeared in the shades of the night.

We must do all this with her so that we may be her companions and may be initiated into all the mysteries of her sorrow. It is impossible to enjoy the heart of Mary, the veritable depths of her heart, without consenting to suffer with her, to drink this chalice which is as truly hers as it is Jesus', and of which she intends that all her children drink.

You see the consequences: generosity, mortification, crucifixion, rending of the heart by the seven swords. They enter and re-enter with refinements of cruelty, but also with love and infinite tenderness. God knows how to diversify them according to His marvelous art. Everything must be accepted. This everything will always be a very little thing in comparison with the martyrdom of Jesus and Mary. Let us enter into these mysteries, let us try to live them, to make them the foundation of our life as they are the foundation of the life of the Church.

It is fitting that Simeon's annunciation at the beginning

of the New Testament summarize all the annunciations of the Old. The echo of the Temple, place of worship and sacrifice, should re-echo with all the distant voices. Simeon rises up as the supreme prophet before the Holy Family and before the immense family of souls who, until the end of time, will believe in the Man of Sorrows, the Man with a broken heart. Not only is the Heart of Jesus the Center and the King of all hearts, this mystery is the king and center of all others. It is the central mystery which radiates and reigns over all the others. It commands all human history, all human activity. All the repercussions, all the consequences will resound in Mary and through Mary in the hearts of all her children.

The prophecy of Simeon penetrates completely to the depths of everything. It explains the great torture of our Lord's heart, for which the stroke of the lance was the *coup de grâce*. His Heart has always been rent; it has always carried this wound of the Lamb who was immolated from the beginning.

What was this sorrow of the Heart of Jesus? Let us listen with much attention to the proclamation of the great charter of the King of all hearts. Let us contemplate through the rending of Mary's heart, the perspectives of the kingdom of heaven, which above is the kingdom of beatific love but here below is the kingdom of crucifying love. "This Child is set for the fall and for the resurrection of many in Israel and for a sign which shall be contradicted. And thy own soul a sword shall pierce, that out of many hearts thoughts may be revealed."

The Last Joyful Mystery

We arrive at the last joyful mystery but it is filled with sorrow for the divine Mother, perhaps more so than the preceding mystery. The Holy Family was returning from

Jerusalem to Nazareth. Evening came, and the Child Jesus was not to be found. This seems rather strange to us. With our occidental customs, we are tempted to say that Joseph and Mary could hardly watch over their dear Jesus. The fact is, however, easily explainable for one who knows certain oriental customs which have persisted almost to our time. Children traveled in a joyous group separated from the older people's less noisy group. It was therefore easy to lose sight of the Child Jesus. Evening came. Joseph and Mary see that He is no longer with the other children. They search for Him among the parents and friends. Not finding Him, they return to Jerusalem, overwhelmed with sorrow. Finally, after three days, they find Him in the Temple in the midst of the doctors.

How many lessons there are in this story, which is our own story! We, too, lose Jesus suddenly. In spite of all our cares, all our attention, He disappears. The Child Jesus? No one knows what has become of Him! We would then be tempted to search for Him where it is customary to find Him: among familiar things, friends, parents. But He is no longer there. The reason why He withdrew is precisely this: to make us climb higher. It is a way of growing in friendship. It seems very cruel to us, but fundamentally it is full of love.

It is useless to seek the Child Jesus where He was. Do not return to the sensible sweetness of the beginning of the spiritual life. Understand clearly that here the mystery of sorrow is redoubled. There is first of all the mystery of the search, crucifying in itself, but transitory and which, in the joy of the "recovery," results in the second mystery of a crucifixion of the heart. The first sorrow is to seek without finding, because one persists in seeking among the persons or things that one knows well, but Jesus is no longer there.

The second sorrow is in the act of finding, not the one being sought, but someone else, wholly new, incomprehensible, a stranger to the family. No one understands who He is nor what He says. For others than Joseph and Mary, the search is sometimes not only long, but interminable. They will never find Him. Always, they seek sorrowing, according to Pascal's great saying. For Joseph and Mary, and often for us too, there is joy because Jesus is found, but there is also sorrow because we do not find the same Jesus. It is no longer the Child Jesus whom our arms and hearts embraced so tenderly; it is the great Jesus whose unexpected attitudes and formidable majesty crush us. Whatever may be the cruelty of the first sword, it is surpassed by the cruelty of the second.

But where must we seek Jesus? Not in the direction of Nazareth, not too near the familiar home, but at Jerusalem, in the austere Temple, in the midst of the doctors. Let us note here the shades of meaning. In the Temple, that is, in the place of sacrifice, of prayer, of contemplation, the place of the study of holy things. In the Temple, but in what point precisely? Not near the altar, but apart, in the secluded shelter where the doctors are assembled around this twelve-year-old King whose wisdom and answers they admire and who has become the center of attraction and radiance for them all. It is not sufficient to be among the doctors as one was among parents and friends. Only to place oneself among them would never suffice, would even be dangerous sometimes. It is necessary to place oneself resolutely in the center. Only there can one open one's mouth with full confidence and security. There must be more than intimate contact, there must be immersion into the vital sphere of light and truth.

Even when you can no longer pray, you can always make yourself do so or be taught to do so, and again find the benevolent Master who inclines Himself toward you. Ask it for news of Him whom you have lost. Question the guardians of the city, as it is said in the Canticle of Canticles. These defenders of truth, these holders of the unalterable light know where He has departed and they search with her. The Spouse who seems absent is in reality there, waiting for you and calling you. Whatever the wretchedness of His representatives from other points of view, sacred science has always seen Him, has always continued to see Him. His glance is immutable because it is wholly spiritual. God is in the midst of the doctors.

We must have the courage to renounce familiar habits, which make us too dependent on our senses, so that we may go up to the temple and enter it. The temple is dark, empty, cold. We must not let our poor nature be discouraged at this emptiness, at these shadows. We must not remain on the threshold of the temple; we must go as far as we can, for it is within that we will find the doctors and their young King. Jesus is in the midst of the doctors. There the emptiness resolves into fullness, the darkness into the light of truth, the cold into flames of love.

Why Did You Seek Me?

Mary and Joseph have found Jesus. Mary rushes toward Him, her heart overflowing, her arms open: "Child, why have You done this to us?" She is only trying to express, with an infinitely touching simplicity, the sentiments of her maternal heart. It was indeed her right as Mother to speak thus. Everything was perfectly in order. Then, can the answer of Jesus be explained? Can it be said that at the sight of this sorrow and joy, Jesus shows Himself to be very different from what He had been with His Mother in the past and from what He is about to be with her again in the happiness of the long years at Nazareth?

Into His Mother's heart, pierced by Simeon's sword, where the joyful seed of a new *Magnificat* has just fallen, a new sword is plunged with a holy but terrible force by the sweet hand of the recovered Beloved. To pierce Mary's heart was proper to an old man, to a priest; but a child, her own Child! But let us not forget that this Child was a priest much more than Simeon could ever be, and in a sense the only priest; at any rate, the one who had always been a priest, by the consecration of the hypostatic union. Christ's priests will be priests for eternity, but they become priests in time, in the most holy moment of their ordination. Jesus has always been a priest, as He will always be. Since the priest's role is to immolate the victims in the temple, Jesus, when He immolates the purest of victims, is in His essential role. As Mary said what she had to say, Jesus did what He was supposed to do. Both together were perfectly in order, in the supreme order of the will of God and the profound nature of things. This is what constitutes the frightful grandeur of this scene.

Let us try to understand the lesson hidden in all this, perhaps the most fundamental lesson of all for the life of the Christian and for the life of a religious. Mary hastens toward Jesus. Never was there a maternal right comparable to this one. She listens only to her heart. She flies to satiate her tenderness at last and to drown all the anguish which has held her during the three terrible days. But she stops. She no longer recognizes her little Child. Even the look He turns toward her is changed. She does not know Him. He no longer expresses the joyful and confiding tenderness to which she was accustomed. The look by which Mary answers Him is changed also. Jesus' look is the one which has made our mothers weep when they understood that above the son of their flesh, there was the son of the spirit, the being who no longer belongs to them, the being of the divine vocation, the mysterious being which escapes all that is of the earth, enclosing himself exclusively in what is of the heavenly Father. There is something infinitely superior to all tenderness because there is a divine mission and by this mission we are sons of God before being sons of our mothers according to the flesh.

Jesus speaks very gently, very tenderly, but Mary feels the stroke of the sword. Listen to the terrible words: "How is it that you sought Me? Did you not know that I must be about My Father's business?" Let those who are mothers imagine, if they can, the cruelty of the sword which plunges at this moment into the heart of her who is a mother more than any other. Jesus' first and last word as related to us in the Gospel is "Why?" This is the word which begins and ends everything.

"Why did you seek Me?" He says to His Mother in the Temple. "Why have you abandoned Me?" He cries to His Father on the altar of the cross. This cry from Calvary is so frightful that the Evangelists have hesitated to translate it. They have given it to us in all the crudeness of the Semitic syllables: *Lamma sabactani*. The two "why's" correspond. Both contain something unfathomable, something incomprehensible. This Jesus who saw God, who enjoyed the beatific vision more than all the saints and all the angels together, is none other than the Man of Sorrows and of such a sorrow! However, I wonder if the Child's "why" is not as frightening, especially for us.

The two "why's" remain unanswered. They fall into the infinite void. The Mother does not answer the "why" of her little Jesus; the Father does not answer the "why" that His Son cries out from the cross. These are questions which cannot receive an answer. For the rest, the Gospel tells us: Mary and Joseph "understood not the word that He spoke to them." In any case, Mary understood one thing, that she must enter the school of Jesus, that she must become the disciple who accepts all so that she may know all, and she says her *fiat* with all her heart.

Mary here represents a unique right, the right of a mother over her child, and of such a Mother over such a Son! Never will this right be equaled. At the same time, Mary represents us all. The rights of creatures, whatever they be, must be sacrificed to the rights of the Creator. When God demands His share, nothingness demands its share. Then, what does this "why" of Jesus mean? What is the meaning of this reproach? What does this question of the Child to His Mother signify? It has occupied commentators a great deal. From the beginnings of the Church they have tried to explain it many times and in many different ways. At a time when the doctrine on the perfection of the Blessed Virgin was less clear, certain interpretations were brought to light which, since then, have been completely abandoned, St. John Chrysostom's among others. In a very gentle but very firm manner, St. Thomas declares that the expressions of St. John Chrysostom went too far in allowing an imperfection to be implied in Mary's words. Mary is completely perfect. In what she says to her Son when she finds Him in the midst of the doctors, she is as perfect as she is everywhere and always. Her words express her right and duty as a mother, and what rights and duties are more sacred than these?

From the point of view of human origins, Mary was everything for her Son. Everything which ordinarily takes place between the father and the mother is combined in her alone. She held all the rights over her Son. From the point of view of the resemblance of the features of the face, Jesus was Mary. I would perhaps be tempted to reproach Catholic artists for not having sufficiently indicated this resemblance. Jesus resembled Mary alone and could resemble her alone.

Therefore, let us repeat: In speaking to Jesus, Mary exercised the most sacred right which can be bestowed on a pure creature. How can we disengage the unfathomable lesson which is hidden in this scene? Am I going to say that Mary was wrong? Yes, Mary was wrong. It was not her fault and it did not prevent her from being immaculate and absolutely perfect, but she was going to find herself at this instant, along with her maternal rights, in conflict with the rights of God. Jesus was at the same time the Son of God and the Son of Mary. Mary had rights over her Child. She could satisfy them by pressing Him to her arms, by taking Him to herself forever. But there were also the rights of God over His Son, and these rights required that the Son be about His Father's business and that He be about His Father's business only. This is what makes the grandeur of this exceptional scene: the imminent conflict between the rights of God and the rights of Mary.

What is about to happen? As always happens when the finite meets the infinite, it is annihilated and evaporates before the great flame which devours everything. The rights of God must be first, and they take precedence while breaking the Mother's heart. The finite right is destroyed before the infinite right. This is essential justice. That is why Mary submits. She does not understand, because one cannot understand what is incomprehensible; but one can submit, and that is what Mary does.

Mary's Preparation by Jesus

Then begins the preparation which was necessary for Mary so that the *Stabat* might one day become possible. Mary was the holiest of all creatures, but destined to something so terrible that only a preparation by Jesus could make her ready for it and elevate her to the level of the Cross. Mary delivered herself, heart and soul, to this little Child who broke her heart. She followed Him everywhere, even into the most austere and hardest ways, and when the Cross was raised between heaven and earth, she was standing near it. The Cross was the supreme pulpit from which Jesus preached to the world. There Mary heard the last words, the last word of the lesson which had begun in the Temple in the midst of the doctors. Never were acts of faith more beautiful nor more deep-rooted than those by which Mary accepted this entire lesson from Jesus, from the Temple to the Cross.

Before reaching its object, the right of Mary meets the right of God and is absorbed in it like the dew is evaporated by the sun. Mary found it quite natural that there was no longer any right but God's, that before His infinite right neither her personal right nor she herself any longer counted for anything. She was now and had always been nothing more than a living *fiat*. The *fiat* was the innermost part of her being. She expressed it in answering Gabriel. She did not need to express it in answering Jesus. Do you know what she did? She took her little Child by the hand and led Him away to Nazareth where they knew long years of happiness together. The right of God had preceded all others; all the other rights could now be exercised. God was the first served, as Joan of Arc said, and things could follow their normal course.

If Mary had not accepted, if her maternal heart had not been able to suffer the cut of the sword, she would have closed off Nazareth, the only possible Eden since the fall. How many Eves will not return to any Eden simply because they do not know how to do what Mary did! It is the question of a very simple fact: to acknowledge the right of God in its integrity. It will perhaps bruise our hearts; there will be a moment of hard acceptance, but Nazareth will be opened before us. On this poor earth, ruined by sin, we have seen that Eden can no longer flower again except in the tiny "interior cell."

Our whole ambition should be to find Nazareth. The only path which leads there is the one I have just shown you. Nazareth is obedience, the struggle of obedience, let us dare to say, between Jesus and Mary, between the obedience of the Child to His Mother and the obedience of the saint to her Priest. In a few lines after the scene of the "recovery," St. Luke summarizes all Nazareth in the *subditus illis*, "He was subject to them"; He was nothing more than their little Child. All Mary's and Joseph's rights over him could be fully exercised because God's right had been fully satisfied.

Nazareth is the work of Joseph, so rough and yet so gentle! Ah, this labor of Joseph; how I wish it were mine! With what alacrity I would accept the wrinkles creasing my brow bathed with sweat, hands become calloused, hardened, and deformed from winning bread for Jesus and Mary.

My ambition should grow greater yet, become infinitely higher. Not only should I be Joseph, but I should be Jesus. Mary understood all that was contained in the word coming from the lips of the Crucified: "Behold thy son." I must also understand. Who is Mary's Son? It is Jesus! Therefore, if I am Mary's son, I must necessarily become Jesus. Saints are simply Christians who understood what had been said from the height of the Cross. The abnormal thing is for Christians not to understand, to go seeking everywhere else the joys which could be there and which would be perfect, which would so completely fill our poor hearts.

When the rights of God are respected, then and only then can all the others be exercised. If God's rights are violated, all the rest fall, the whole edifice rooted so deeply in Eden collapses into a single mass under the blow of Eve's disobedience. Eve disregards the rights of God, the keystone which sustains everything. Everything is broken and dispersed. Eve is sent out of the earthly paradise.

Mary allowed the divine rights to be exercised to the limit in Jesus and in her. Her maternal heart was broken from it and that is why she can again enter the only Eden which was still earthly and already heavenly: the Eden of Nazareth, the Eden of delightful intimacy with Jesus.

Not only was Mary's heart broken. She who destroys the serpent's head with her virginal foot knew, under the crushing weight of the terrible word, a kind of breaking of the intellect which reveals the mysterious saying from the Gospel: *Non intellexerunt verbum*. It expresses the blessedness of those "that have not seen and have believed." It is not only the broken heart that God does not despise; the sacrifice to God is also, perhaps especially, the sacrifice of the immolated spirit. The intellect, the most noble of our faculties, is like the first-born son of the substance of our souls, the Isaac from whom the Most High can at times exact the sacrifice on the mysterious mountains chosen by Him alone.

Mary has the right to re-enter Nazareth, her own Eden, only after the supreme proof of her faith, after the crushing of her heart at Jerusalem, the proper place for sacrifice. Mary believed in her Child, Son of the Most High, whereas Eve believed in the serpent, instrument of the most low. This is why Mary re-enters her Eden whereas Eve can only re-enter her Eden through the number of her sons who escape the influences of death which they inherit from her, thanks to the new Eve whom we salute as our life.

Only the Queen of Mercy, the Queen of the "repatriated," can cause justice to forget that these are the exiled sons of poor Eve as well as her own.

Here again, Eve's case and Mary's appear to us as two extremes between which all the others can find a place. We can more easily understand these cases and decide them in the light of the principles that we have just considered. Never can a creature sacrifice to God a right comparable to the right Mary had over Jesus. Never, in the mediocre and paltry conditions of our fallen state, will the struggle with the serpent assume the terrible and grandiose proportions of Eden's limits. We feel lost before the immensity of the perspectives. Let us ask the Star of the Sea to cause her gentle light to shine and to reveal to us, in the midst of tempests and possible shipwrecks, the humble and winding route which avoids reefs and leads to the port.

St. John and the Good Thief

The fifth joyful mystery is intimately related to the fifth sorrowful mystery. The swords in Mary's heart announce and prophesy the lance in Jesus' heart. The first words of the Child Jesus that we know—the words in the Temple—announce and prophesy the last words of Jesus dying on the altar of the Cross. This is especially true of two which are recorded for us by Mary's two Evangelists, St. Luke and St. John. We owe to St. Luke the words of Mary in the course of the first mysteries and to St. John the words of Mary at Cana and the last words on Mary: *Ecce Mater tua.* We would like to meditate here on the two last words which the dying Son addresses to the penitent thief and to the heart of the Beloved Disciple. These two words represent two plenitudes of grace, very different from one another. One is an outstanding triumph of mercy over justice; the other is a mixture and an incomparable harmony of justice and mercy. St. Paul dared to proclaim: "Where sin abounded, grace did more abound," and this is precisely the story of the Good Thief. St. John's story is full of purity and ardor. It attracts the effusions of supreme tenderness from this Heart which the lance is about to pierce.

Jesus Himself declares that He must be about His Father's business, the most profound business of contrasts and harmonies between justice and mercy. The Good Thief is one of the most wretched and most exiled of the sons of Eve. He has known criminal flights to the opposite direction from Eden, bloody vagrancies across the earth, as it is written of Eve's first-born, Cain, the first murderer who was cursed forever. St. Luke recounts the marvelous story of the thief's conversion, of his orientation toward the heavenly paradise where he will be with Jesus, and of his entrance into the only terrestrial paradise which is now possible for us: the paradise of perfect prayer. By perfect prayer everything here below can become Eden, or Nazareth—even the horrible cross, if we learn to accept its rigorous justice behind which will break the dawn of mercy. The Holy Spirit intervenes, by the most gentle and intimate of His motions, for this sinner nailed on the altar of his cross as for the old man impelled toward the Temple where the Holy Family is about to enter. To this thief who "stole" heaven, the Holy Spirit explains everything in the recesses of his heart and enlightens the only objects which can still strike his eyes, already half veiled by the approaching darkness. It is the divine Crucified whose lesson he finally understands; the other, the bad thief, continues to blaspheme: "If Thou be Christ, save Thyself and us."

Let us compare this despairing cry with the cry of terror, confident despite all, of the apostles in danger of perishing in the storm-lashed lake: *Salva nos, perimus.*

According to St. Ambrose, both St. Matthew and St. Mark refer to two crucified thieves who blasphemed. St. Luke states that one blasphemed and the other prayed. Perhaps the latter began by blaspheming but was suddenly converted. Blasphemy, in his heart and on his lips, gave way to prayer. In this thief, so utterly human, the pursuit of grace lasts but an instant. But in this sublime instant there is not only a place for contemplation of the divine Crucified, there is also a place for the superabundance of this contemplation in the apostolate. As soon as he is converted, he wishes to convert. Not only does he look at Jesus, but his look goes farther, to the other thief, who rebels against the attraction of this King. Following St. Luke's text very closely, we must even say that the apostolate precedes and prepares the redemptive contemplation as much as it is derived from it. In the same way Paul, the persecutor and blasphemer, on the road to Damascus, is transformed into an apostle. The Good Thief preaches to his companion of crime and of chastisement only to put him on the road to wisdom. He seeks to arouse fear in him, the sentiment of this justice which punishes them both and should spare Jesus. "Neither dost thou fear God, seeing thou art under the same condemnation? And we indeed justly, for we receive the due reward of our deeds. But this Man hath done no evil."

Before receiving the Good Thief into His paradise, Jesus receives him into Eden, the Nazareth of perfect prayer. In a little while, the same day, they will be in the closed garden of heaven. Let us adore the omnipotent mercy, as swift as a flash of lightning, which strips the night from this miserable soul and suddenly reveals to him the great secret. Grace, St. Ambrose cries out, is yet more fruitful than prayer. Here, according to custom, it superabounds, for the Lord bestows more than is asked. The thief asks only for a remembrance in His kingdom. The fulfillment is immediate and all paradise is opened.

Life consists in being with Christ. Where Christ is, says St. Ambrose, there is the kingdom.

Let us listen to St. Gregory: "In his crucified immobility which binds him completely, nothing remains free in this slave of death except his heart and his tongue. . . . With the heart, as St. Paul says, one can believe; with the tongue, one can confess the faith." The thief's tortured body has not moved, but everything has become changed around him. The cross is an altar, Calvary is the temple or place of sacrifice, Jesus on His cross is the priest.

Everything is revealed from the height of the Cross. The thief become an apostle preaches to the other thief the justice of their frightful condemnation. By the very fact that he sees the justice of his punishment, he sees the injustice of Jesus' punishment. He has done no wrong; He has done only good. "We have killed the living; He has brought the dead to life. We have stolen others' possessions; He has given to His neighbor all that He possesses" (St. John Chrysostom).

By the very fact that he recognizes and accepts justice, he is attracted and turns toward the merciful Heart of Jesus. Peace embraces justice in the depths of his will, which has become good. According to the divine precept, he has completely renounced himself and has taken to himself the cross which held him despite himself. This cross was indeed his own, since he was nailed there, but it was not yet truly his, since he had not accepted it. Only our will can truly bind us there. The cross held him, immobilized him on its arms of wood. His will seizes it, makes use of it as the instrument of his salvation. "You see only a crucified man," St. John Chrysostom exclaims, addressing himself to the thief, "but you confess the Lord. Under the appearance of the condemned you recognize and proclaim the majesty of a King." The thief appeals to this King, as soon as He will have come into His kingdom: *cum veneris in regnum.* We also appeal every day that this kingdom may come to us more quickly: *adveniat regnum tuum.*

Whatever may be the interior malice of our faults and their accursed wickedness in the eyes of men, God looks at the heart. As soon as this heart has returned to Him completely, there is the promise of a paradise. Prayer is not yet the final term of perfect blessedness of heaven, but it is a way that leads there, a way already blessed because it is intimately joined to the beatific end itself, according to one of St. Thomas' happy and frequent formulas: *via conjuncta termino.* Through prayer we are already in paradise because we are already with Jesus and also because we are with Mary. Prayer is a struggle, but it is also a triumph. It is not yet the complete presence, face to face, but it is a perfect heart to heart presence because one has entered into the heart of the King. The exile has found his homeland again.

According to Theophylactus, the Crucified, immolated and a conqueror, bears away in triumph the most beautiful and best of prizes. He leads with Him, into His kingdom of paradise, the penitent thief, the booty wrested from the claws of Satan. St. John Chrysostom connects this mystery with the mystery of Eden. Satan's violence had forced the first man from the terrestrial paradise; Christ's gentleness urges the last of the malefactors toward the celestial paradise. Who, even after the most terrible sins, could despair of entering there, since one act of faith opened it to this thief?

Not only the example of faith, St. Gregory remarks, but also the example of the other theological virtues is given us in this saint of the eleventh hour. "He indeed possesses faith who believes in the kingdom of this God whom he sees dying with him. . . . He possesses hope who begs so fervently for entrance into His kingdom. He possesses the most lively charity, even in death, who preaches to his brother and companion in crime, who is in agony on a neighboring cross." This convert seems heroic in his very conversion. We could almost call him a martyr, since he confesses in the midst of his punishment before those who blaspheme. There is a kind of transfiguration of the condemned man into a martyr.

.O Crux Ave

Like this thief who was finally repatriated, Eve also knew despair in the measure of the weakness of her faith. Despair is the fatal and necessary consequence of this weakness. One can lose hope without losing faith, but one cannot lose faith without losing hope. In the measure that Eve's faith was injured, it was inevitable that her hope would also be injured. Eve therefore knew something of the abyss of despair even to the moment when she could rely on the divine word announcing the victory of her race over the race of the serpent. Previously she had succumbed under the weight of her crime and her shame and had hidden herself before the face of God. But she lived again at the sound of His voice, as her children will continue to live by "every word that proceedeth from the mouth of God." She accepts the prediction of her sorrowful maternity, she "repudiates" the pride which was her sin. She seizes the Cross with all her heart, the Cross which is henceforth and forever hers, and begins to follow the Crucified whom she already knows is her Redeemer.

It is the same for her other crucified son, the Good Thief. There is no longer anything but the Cross, and that for a few moments only, but he suddenly perceives that it is his sole hope. For all, for Mary herself, for the Queen of the *Salve*, all terminates in this more than angelic salutation, *O crux ave*. We can never meditate enough on these two *Aves*: *Ave Maria* and *O crux ave*, which orientate all our hope toward Mary, *spes nostra*, and toward the Cross, *spes unica*.

This is what God accomplished with the new Eve when he raised her up, not before the tree of good and evil, but before the tree of the Cross, the tree of life. It is on her that the curse of Eden weighs. She is no longer the Mary of the Annunciation and the *Magnificat*, no longer the Mary of joy, but of sorrow. She is no longer the one who brought forth her only Son in joy, but the one who has just brought forth these numerous guilty sons who are the executioners of her Son. Mary felt the primitive malediction weigh on her: "In sorrow shalt thou bring forth children." This is why I say that this is no longer Mary; this is Eve. Mary must extend her arms and her heart to reach us all at the same time and with one embrace. Eve well knew that she bore in her all humanity, but for her it was a point of departure, she did not have to give birth to all humanity in one single act. Mary was obliged to do so. So it is that she is proclaimed our Mother by our Lord on the Cross: *Ecce Mater tua*.

Mary gave birth to all men, each and every one, each of us in particular. All her sons must be brought forth at the same time and in the same sorrow. She is the mysterious woman of the Apocalypse, with the crescent of the moon under her feet and the diadem of stars on her head, but full of sorrow. It is a question of bringing forth all men and all men are sinners to a greater or less degree. The more they are sinners, the more they are Eve's sons and the more, consequently, one would dare to say that their spiritual birth was sorrowful for Mary.

The thief had only a moment more to live. His past life had been shrouded in sin. At the foot of his cross, so near to Jesus', Mary must also give birth to him since she gives birth to us all. "The dragon stood before the woman who was ready to be delivered so that, when she should be delivered, he might devour" the agonizing man for whom despair lies in wait. Mary saves him by making him the son of her sorrow.

The revelations of the Father are made only to little ones. It is a universal law of divine revelations and, therefore, it applies to the revelations of Calvary: to the revelation to John and the revelation made to the thief. The question here is evidently of two different kinds of littleness: the first, full of purity and love; the other, moral annihilation in the depths of the abyss of misery. John's humility is due to the experience of grace; the thief's humility is due to the experience of sin.

Mary's maternity, like Eve's maternity, is universal and extended to all, and we are all sons of both. They are almost like two poles from which we withdraw or approach in a greater or less degree. John is very close to Mary and as far as possible from Eve. The thief is enclosed in the maternity of the first sinner. If justice alone were heeded, he would be annihilated, but a merciful revelation is addressed to him and he is touched by Mary's maternity and can be born to grace.

These sorrowful births at the foot of the Cross required of the new Eve such sanctity that the sanctity of Bethlehem and Nazareth was not sufficient. A complete preparation of Mary by Jesus was necessary. At the age of twelve, Jesus began to grieve His Mother. This incomparable grief followed her to Calvary so that when the hour came, the new Eve was capable of performing the actions which repaired the disaster of Eden.

We who are the sons of this maternal heroism, what can we do and what can we say in order not to be unworthy? Let us listen to the words of the *Stabat Mater:* "O Mary, make me weep devoutly with you. May my poor life be but a faithful compassion for Jesus and for you as long as I live. Mothers, they say, love their children in the measure that they have suffered to give them life. Remember that I have cost you infinite suffering since I have cost you Jesus. May the words of Scripture break and comfort my poor heart: 'Child, be mindful of the tears of your Mother.' O Virgin, terrible as an army set in array, terrible for your enemies, terrible also for your children, snatch me from my cowardice and fearful hesitation and plunge me into the blood of the Heart rent by the lance and the heart transpierced by the seven swords. O Mother, you are the source of love, the source opened by this sword so that I might drink long draughts and my thirst be quenched, even to the point of inebriation. Little does it matter whether the place is great or small in this army you prepare and lead to combat. It will always be a matter of accepting suffering and of being docile throughout life to the great example which was given by the Son and followed by the Mother."

The redeeming God calls us to the tree of life on which He is crucified. The redeeming God unites everything in Himself and attracts everything as soon as He finds a little humility, just as the avenging God dispersed the proud.

Come to Me and draw with joy at the sorrowful springs of the Savior. Draw the blood and water from the fountainhead of the Sacred Hearts. Thirst as I thirsted. If anyone thirsts, let him come to Me, let him come to Us, and drink!

Mary consents to give birth at the foot of the Cross to all who were banished from Eden, even to the last thief. Ransomed at the last moment, he is the first to enter the Eden which is reopened, the first to be borne there by the arms of the Cross. Jesus, the New Adam, after having accepted exile outside of the terrestrial paradise, after having lived the same life of labor and suffering and earned His bread by the sweat of His brow like all of Adam's sons, returns victorious into His divine kingdom. He leads in His wake all His brothers to cause them to participate in His eternal goodness.

"You shall be as gods." Satan's promise is realized through Christ. See what manner of love is ours from the Father, that we should be called and should be children of God. We know that one day we shall be like Him because we shall see Him as He is. We can dare to apply to ourselves the words which were blasphemy in Satan's mouth: "I shall be like the Most High." Our Lord promises this eternal life and similarity to God, not like the serpent arousing man against God by exciting his pride, but by giving the example of humility. "Learn of Me, for I am meek and humble of heart." It is by participating in this humility, and by this means alone, that we can deserve to become one day like the Most High and to be raised to the infinite glory of the Father.

Christ Speaks to His Mother

However holy Jesus' words to the thief may be, let us listen to the expression of a still fruitful piety. See with what tenderness the Mother is honored by her Son! From the height of the Cross, Christ gives testimony of it. His words to His Mother and His disciple are a proof of it, and John is the worthy witness of this testimony.

The sword of her Son's words pierced Mary's heart and

from there it passes to the hearts of her children. All are transpierced, from John, the sublime apostle and a pure contemplative, to this last of the thieves so stained with crimes. The thoughts of all must be revealed by the brilliance of this sword's passage. During the course of His bloody sacrifice Jesus, Priest and Prophet, no longer in the Temple but from the altar of the Cross, reveals to Mary her mission as Mother of the living.

The more each of us lives the supernatural life, the more is Mary each one's Mother. The brilliance of the life that comes to us from her is of such intensity that all the sorrows, hers as well as ours, evaporate in joy. She finds my sorrow in Jesus' sorrow, like a drop of water lost in the immensity of the ocean. She applies to each of these miserable drops of water the whole mystery of her maternal compassion. All these sorrows, hers and ours, are submerged in His and render her fruitful with a divine joy which is also our joy.

Thus, in all things, in sorrow and joy, she is for us the most efficacious helper. This help is the essential role of the spouse. Mary was Jesus' true companion, the *socia,* as St. Albert the Great says, and that is why we could dare to say that close to Jesus on His cross she stood not only as the Mother but also as the spouse. She stood before Jesus in the sorrowful darkness of Calvary as Eve had stood before Adam in the joyous splendor of Eden. In the ordinary course of things, man is formed by his mother and then, to fulfill his personal mission, he leaves his home and his mother and chooses another woman who will be the companion of his life. Jesus came to die. Mary is not only the Mother who formed the body of the Victim and could offer herself with Jesus, but she is also the companion who espouses the most intimate aspirations of the Heart of Him who desires to be for all, and especially for her, "the Man of Sorrows." It is not good for man to be alone in these sorrows any more than in the sacred intoxications of Eden.

How is Mary a spouse? What role can she play? Of herself, she can add nothing to the passion of Christ. Her role is in relation to us. In the designs of God, Mary is the Mother of Jesus, afterward the companion of His mission, and finally our Mother at the foot of the cross. But her divine maternity remains the most perfect reality and the final cause. The Scholastics would say: *finis cujus gratia.* She was predestined as Mother of God.

We are forced to make a choice from all the marvels offered here. Let us be guided in this choice by one of St. Thomas' indications in his *Commentary* on St. John.[4] The immense circle of Jesus' enemies surrounds His cross. Let us consider the limited circle of His friends, and first of all, the presence of women near His cross. Here it is the reverse of Eve. She was isolated, separated from Adam who was the tree of life for her. This was her loss and ours, although this isolation became culpable only when it reached the spiritual domain of her judgment.

Mary never isolates herself from Jesus. Only the executioners can physically separate her by violence from Him. Even then, as much as possible, she draws near the true Adam and the tree of life. Mary draws near, attaches herself to the Cross, and this is our salvation. Eve puts Satan between herself and God and hides herself with the serpent; Mary puts Jesus between herself and God.

Mary, says St. Ambrose, does not show herself to be less than what is proper to the Mother of Christ. The apostles flee, but Mary remains standing at the foot of the Cross and devoutly contemplates the wounds of her Son.

Let us admire with St. Thomas the constancy and devotion of the holy women. Let us recall the *devoto femineo*

[4] Chap. XIX, lesson IV.

sexu of the liturgy. In Eden Adam remained firm, right, and immovable in his faith, whereas Eve plunged herself into the labyrinths of doubt and deception. Here on Calvary, the men are the ones who flee, except one alone, the Beloved Disciple, who took his stand close to Jesus and Mary. The women are not far from the Cross, just as one of them will not be far from the sepulcher. "The weaker sex," says St. John Chrysostom, "stands erect at the foot of the Cross, more virile than the other." Here again we hear the echo of the liturgy, which speaks of "the strong woman with a manly heart."

Jesus' solicitude for His Mother is the model of the solicitude we should all have for our mothers and still more for Mary, the blessed among all mothers. "Of the holy women who surround the Cross," says St. John Chrysostom, "Jesus addresses only His Mother. By this He teaches us that we should give our mothers something more than others. If our parents are opposed to us in spiritual matters, we must no longer know them; but when they allow us full liberty in this regard, we should prefer them before all others." Regarding the first case, Scripture does not merely say not to know our parents, but it goes so far as to use the terrible word "to hate." But let us not forget that it adds that this hate must revert on ourselves if it is an obstacle to divine calls. What must be hated everywhere is what turns us away from God. Outside of these instances, we should in all things uphold our parents and love and respect them.

There is in St. John's Gospel another passage which is similar to this one. We refer to the presence of the Mother of Jesus at Cana and the attitude of Jesus toward her. However we translate the original expression for "what is it to Me and to thee?" there is always a striking contrast between these words and the words which come from the mouth of the Crucified. He had answered at Cana: "My hour is not yet come." Let us listen to St. Thomas, who says that Jesus meant that the hour of His passion had not yet come but that when that hour arrives, He will fully recognize her as His Mother. That is what Jesus does from the height of His cross.

At the joyful hour at Cana, Christ begins His miracles but repels, says St. Augustine, the Mother of His humanity but not the Mother of His divinity. At the hour of His punishment, the Man of sorrows, enduring all that humanity can endure, pours out His human tenderness, on her who is the very source of His humanity. In the brevity of his juridical style St. Ambrose completes these doctrines: Not only was it a completely new public duty, but also a completely new domestic duty that the Lord founded and proclaimed from the height of His cross.

The Disciple Took Her to His Own

After the constancy of the holy women, after the solicitude of Jesus for His Mother and for His disciple, it is the latter's obedience which is so prompt and perfect that St. Thomas points it out for our admiration. From this hour, or rather from this instant, everything is in common between John and Mary, for he accepts her and introduces her to all that is his own. It is not a question of goods of the temporal order, for it is said of all the apostles, and particularly of the sons of Zebedee, that they abandoned everything when they followed Jesus. Of these sons of Zebedee it is also written that they had left their father. John had to begin by abandoning his father in order to find such a Mother. What an abyss between Zebedee and Mary! Henceforth what belongs properly to John, as St. Augustine tells us, is the wonderful care he will lavish on the Mother that Jesus gave him.

Let us again glean from St. Thomas a few simple but

final words on this care which John devoted in filial devotion to the service of Mary. He served Mary as a son and she loved him as only a mother can love a son.

We shall add one more word, a word from Cana, one of Mary's words that we dare to place on Jesus' lips: "Do whatever she tells you." These words from Cana lead us back again to Nazareth, to the supreme example of the great virtues of humility and obedience.

After the flight into all the Egypts, the death of those "that sought the life of the Child," and after the threats of the dragon who desires to devour the child, the only possible return is the return to the Eden of Nazareth in the hands and in the heart of Mary. There, in the blessed solitude where He alone can lead us, God will finally speak to our own poor heart.

Obedience to Jesus, therefore, results in obedience to Mary. This path of a very special perfection is equivalent to the obedience of Simeon and Anna and the intimate movement of the Holy Spirit. It is an obedience superior to the obedience of the shepherds and the Magi, as St. Thomas proclaims. For those who know and practice this marvelous way, their intimacy with the Queen of the angels dispenses them from the annunciations which would pass through angels and through stars. In contact with the Spouse of the Holy Spirit, they are like the saints of the Temple, free from many exterior and even interior dependence. We should recall here all that that admirable St. Louis Grignon de Montfort says of our preparation through her. To cite once again the names of our two mothers in our last words: "The fervor and perfection of Mary's obedience effaces the last vestiges of the disobedience of Eve."